EDWARD A. FEIGENBAUM, Professor of Computer Science at Stanford University, is a founding father of artificial intelligence and one of the originators of the concept of knowledge-based systems—computers that use stored knowledge to make decisions that would normally be made by human experts. Feigenbaum is the author of scores of scientific papers and has edited and coauthored several books, most recently *The Handbook of Artificial Intelligence.* He helped found TeKnowledge, Inc., the first knowledge engineering company, and IntelliCorp, Inc., a consulting firm. Both firms are in Palo Alto, where Feigenbaum lives.

PAMELA McCORDUCK published two novels before she undertook a groundbreaking history of artificial intelligence, which has become a standard reference in the field. She recently wrote the script for the theme film of the United States Pavilion at the 1985 World's Fair in Japan, and has published nearly three dozen articles in specialized and popular magazines. She has been a lecturer at Columbia University since 1980, shop that aims to br intelligence to science brought to literature and art.

W9-CJT-576

Technology Today and Tomorrow from MENTOR and SIGNET

(0451)

THE
FIFTH GENERATION

Artificial Intelligence and Japan's Computer Challenge to the World

Edward A. Feigenbaum
and
Pamela McCorduck

Revised and Updated

A SIGNET BOOK

NEW AMERICAN LIBRARY

Published by arrangement with Addison-Wesley Publishing
Company, Inc.
The hardcover edition was published simultaneously in Canada.

Diagrams by Kenneth J. Wilson

First Signet Printing, September, 1984

1 2 3 4 5 6 7 8 9

PRINTED IN THE UNITED STATES OF AMERICA

To H.P.N. and J.F.T.

ACKNOWLEDGMENTS

We wish to acknowledge several people who were helpful in the writing of this book. First are all those at Japan's Institute for New Generation Computer Technology (ICOT) who were frank in their discussions and generous in their hospitality when we visited Japan. We would also like to thank our hosts at the industrial laboratories we visited: Fujitsu, Hitachi, Nippon Electric Corporation, and the Musashino Laboratories of Nippon Telegraph and Telephone Corporation. In exchange for their candor, we have honored their requests for anonymity. In the U.S. members of the Microelectronics and Computer Corporation (MCC) have been helpful, especially Gordon Bell and Bruce Delagi. Robert Kahn and Joseph Traub read early drafts of the manuscript and made useful suggestions.

Following the example of Henry Adams, we appear here as characters in our own book. Since one of us, Feigenbaum, has played an active role in the story we tell, and since both of us represent distinct though concordant points of view, to efface ourselves would not only have blurred those distinctions but might have hidden from the reader our special interests in the whole topic. We are decidedly not disinterested observers.

In the matter of Japanese names we have been inconsistent, but our inconsistency has a purpose. We have simply chosen the form that most Westerners are likely to be familiar with: thus the novelist Murasaki Shikibu appears with her surname first, whereas our contemporaries, like Kazuhiro Fuchi, appear with surnames last.

E.A.F. and P.M.
January 1983

CONTENTS

PART THREE

Experts in Silicon

PART FOUR

The Japanese Fifth Generation

PART SEVEN

**Epilog, or
It Is Hard to Predict,
Especially the Future**

Appendices

Preface to the Signet Edition

Readers familiar with the first edition of this book will find substantial revisions in this edition. The computer field is a rapidly changing one, and the ground shifts beneath us even as we write. Some of the new information came too late for us to include in the first edition; other revisions mend errors made in haste. But the major revisions are a result of the world's taking serious notice of the Japanese Fifth Generation Project. Optimists will be pleased with some of the news; pessimists will find news to confirm their gloomiest expectations.

To optimists we can report that an American response, having both industrial and governmental components, to the Japanese Fifth Generation is emerging. To pessimists we are compelled to report that while a response in the United States *is* emerging, it is in its nascent state, and appears in some aspects to be dangerously diffuse, responding not only to the challenge of the Fifth Generation, but also to the challenge from other Japanese national projects, such as the Superspeed Computing Project and the Robotics Project. By attempting to meet all challenges, we may end by meeting none.

Meanwhile, Japan makes steady progress toward its goals, not only on the Fifth Generation project, but also on related projects, such as supercomputers. Once upon a time—in the distant past of two years ago when we wrote the first edition of this book—supercomputers were an American exclusive. Today, Japanese firms are offering machines that challenge, and in some ways exceed, the performance of those American machines. There is every reason to believe that other Japanese goals in computing will be met, from microcomputers to artificial intelligence. Intermediate goals are being met precisely on schedule.

A good friend has scolded us for presenting this as a zero-sum game. When artificial intelligence becomes everyone's, he reminded us, quoting Alice, "all shall be winners, all shall have a prize." We agree and take great comfort in that. But if we may, in turn, quote Orwell, some prizes will be more equal than others.

In a recent talk to an American audience, Kazuhiro Fuchi, director of the Japanese Fifth Generation Project, likened this all to scaling Mount Everest: there are many paths to the summit and different routes should be investigated by climbers with differing skills. Implicit in Fuchi's metaphor is the undeniable prize of mountaineering, reaching the summit first. In the case of the Fifth Generation, it is not mere chauvinism that makes us persist in believing that whoever achieves this summit first will gain important economic, scientific, military and cultural advantages for their nation. It is the evidence of human history.

E.A.F. and P.M.

Prolog

Time magazine's "Man of the Year" for 1982 was not a man at all, but a machine—the computer. The computer revolution has barely begun, but already we see a startling penetration of computers in most forms of work people do, their gadgets and machinery, and their entertainment. The economists tell us that we have become a nation of knowledge workers: more than half of us are engaged in the various forms of knowledge and information processing. The computer is the knowledge worker's tool, as the planting and harvesting machines are to the farmer and the heavy industrial machines are to the manufacturing worker. The ascendancy of the knowledge worker is reflected in the ascendancy of the tool—the computer. It has been a long time since a child of technology has had such a profound effect upon our lives and our society.

Knowledge is power, and the computer is an amplifier of that power. We are now at the dawn of a new computer revolution. *Business Week* featured it as "the second computer age." We view it as the important computer revolution, the transition from information processing to knowledge processing, from computers that calculate and store data to computers that reason and inform. Artificial intelligence is emerging from the laboratory and is beginning to take its place in human affairs. Professor Allen Newell of Carnegie-Mellon University, a pioneer of artificial intelligence, once wrote that "computer technology offers the possibility of incorporating intelligent behavior in all the nooks and crannies of our world." The nooks and crannies are right now being filled with computers, and the intelligent behavior is following quickly along.

The American computer industry has been innovative, vital, and successful. It is, in a way, the ideal industry. It creates value by transforming the brainpower of the knowledge workers, with little consumption of energy and raw materials. Today we dominate the world's ideas and markets in this most important of all modern technologies. But what about tomorrow?

The Japanese have seen gold on distant hills and have begun to move out. Japanese planners view the computer industry as vital to their nation's economic future and have audaciously made it a national goal to become number one in this industry by the latter half of the 1990s. They aim not only to dominate the traditional forms of the computer industry but to establish a "knowledge industry" in which knowledge will be a salable commodity like food and oil. Knowledge itself is to become the new wealth of nations.

To implement this vision the Japanese have both strategy and tactics. Their strategy is simple and wise: to avoid a head-on confrontation in the marketplace with the currently dominant American firms; instead to look out into the 1990s to find an arena of great economic potential that is currently being overlooked by the more short-sighted and perhaps complacent American firms; to move rapidly now to build major strength in that arena. The tactics are set forth in a major and impressive national plan of the Ministry of International Trade and Industry (MITI) called Fifth Generation Computer Systems. The plan documents a carefully staged ten-year research and development program on Knowledge Information Processing Systems. The implementation began in April 1982 with the formation of the Institute for New Generation Computer Technology (ICOT) and coordinated laboratories of the major Japanese firms in the computer industry.

The Japanese plan is bold and dramatically forward-looking. It is unlikely to be completely successful in the ten-year period. But to view it therefore as "a lot of smoke," as some American industry leaders have done, is a serious mistake. Even partially realized concepts that are superbly engineered can have great economic value, preempt the market, and give the Japanese the dominant position they seek.

We now regret our complacency in other technologies. Who in the 1960s took seriously the Japanese initiative in small cars? Who in 1970 took seriously the Japanese national goal to become number one in consumer electronics in ten years? (Have you seen an American VCR that isn't Japanese on the inside?) In 1972, when the Japanese had yet to produce their first commercial microelectronic chip but announced their national plans in this vital "made in America" technology, who would have thought that in ten years they would have half of the world's market for the most advanced memory chips? Are we about to blow it again? The consequences of complacency, of our spirited attention to the near-in at the expense of the long view, will be devastating to the economic health of our most important industry. Even more important than its direct effect on the computing industry, present complacency will have serious economic effects on all industries. Since computing is the technology that drives all other technologies, a second-rate computing industry will also mean impaired industrial design and manufacturing, and enfeebled management and planning. The Japanese could thereby become the dominant industrial power in the world.

We are writing this book because we are worried. But we are also basically optimistic. Americans invented this technology! If only we could focus our efforts, we should have little trouble dominating the second computer age as we dominated the first. We have a two- or three-year lead; that's large in the world of high technology. But we are squandering our lead at the rate of one day per day.

America needs a national plan of action, a kind of space shuttle program for the knowledge systems of the future. In this book we have tried to explain this new knowledge technology, its roots in American and British research, and the Japanese Fifth Generation plan for extending and commercializing it. We have also outlined America's weak, almost nonexistent response to this remarkable Japanese challenge. The stakes are high. In the trade wars, this may be the crucial challenge. Will we rise to it? If not, we may consign our nation to the role of the first great postindustrial agrarian society.

I

THE NEW WEALTH OF NATIONS

1

Reason and Revolution

The reasoning animal has finally made the reasoning machine.

Who dares feign surprise at the inevitable? It's human to exhibit intelligence, and human to make machines. The combination, not to say the collision, of the two is the most human of stories.

The making of a reasoning machine requires a special ingredient, not secret exactly, but not something we're born with either: the getting of it is the begetting of intelligence. That special ingredient is knowledge. Knowledge is not the same as information. Knowledge is information that has been pared, shaped, interpreted, selected, and transformed; the artist in each of us daily picks up the raw material and makes of it a small artifact—and at the same time, a small human glory. Now we have invented machines to do that, just as we invented machines to extend our muscles and our other organs. In typical human fashion, we intend our new machines for all the usual purposes, from enhancing our lives to filling our purses. If they scourge our enemies, we wouldn't mind that either.

This version of the story is less about the reasoning machines themselves than the reasoning animals who've made the first (and admittedly primitive) examples, and

3

the reasoning animals who are bent on mass-producing them. The mass production is a clue to one of the themes that recur here, namely, the changes in quality wrought by changes in quantity, what scientists know as the "order of magnitude" effect.

In an otherwise unremarkable office building in Tokyo, a group of highly dedicated young researchers is engaged in designing a new computer generation that will transform the way the Japanese work, whether they are fishermen or powerful business executives, farmers or shopkeepers, scientists or schoolchildren. The vehicles of revolution are to be known as knowledge information processing systems, or KIPS. This new generation of computers will be more powerful than any other the world has seen—indeed, by orders of magnitude. But their real power will lie not in their processing speed, but in their capacity to reason. They will reason, moreover, with enormous amounts of information that will be constantly selected, interpreted, updated, and adapted as circumstances change those facts. KIPS are intended to bring knowledge—large amounts of it, tailored to any given user's needs—to any task a user might wish to do.

The Japanese expect these new computers, which users will be able to speak with in everyday conversational language, or show pictures to, or transmit messages to by keyboard or handwriting, to penetrate every level of society. They will assume no special expertise or knowledge of arcane programming languages. They will not even require the user to be very specific about his needs, because they will have reasoning power and will be able to tease out from the user, by questioning and by suggestions, just exactly what it is the user wants to do or know. Finally, these new machines will be inexpensive and reliable enough to be used everywhere, in offices, factories, restaurants, shops, farms, and fisheries, and of course, homes.

The Japanese expect these computers to be the core computers—that is, the computers most generally in use worldwide—by the 1990s. They expect such powerful reasoning and knowledge processing to transform their society. At the same time, they expect those same machines to save their society, too. Because they see no economic alternative for themselves in the long run, the Japanese will not only broker knowledge itself to the world, but they will also sell products and services whose design is so knowledge-intensive that their superiority must inevitably claim a large proportion of world markets.

How revolution, transformation, and salvation are all to be carried out is one of the topics of this book. How other countries will be affected by Japan's revolution, and how they are already beginning to respond to it, is another. That other countries must respond somehow, and what the penalties of an ill-considered response are, is still a third.

Throughout there are great themes. We have already spoken of one recurrent theme, how quantitative changes eventually bring about qualitative changes, the "order of magnitude" effect. Then there's the theme of courage and its rewards, and cowardice, or foolishness, and its costs. There's the hazard of new fortunes and the worse hazard of no fortune at all.

But the overarching theme is the centrality of knowledge in human life, now and in the future. As everybody knows, knowledge is power. Machines that can amplify human knowledge will amplify every dimension of power.

2

Knowledge Is Power

As early as the Chou dynasty, about the fourth century B.C., a certain Sun Tzu wrote a brief treatise called "The Art of War," which made much of knowledge for the successful conduct of war. Sun Tzu's wisdom would endure. Centuries later, his treatise was consulted by Chairman Mao and memorized in its entirety by officers of the Japanese Imperial Navy in World War II; a quote from it opens a U.S. Army field manual of the 1980s that marks the first significant change in army field tactics since the U.S. Civil War. Knowledge, says Sun Tzu, is power and permits the wise sovereign and the benevolent general to attack without risk, conquer without bloodshed, and accomplish deeds surpassing all others.[1]

The New York Stock Exchange recently published its own treatise which says, less poetically, the same thing: increased productivity derives from more capital, from better capital, but most important of all, from "working smarter" with the capital at hand.[2] American business leaders are as concerned with the art of war as Sun Tzu and his legion of international disciples have been, but in this century the battlefield has changed. Instead of the mountains and valleys of ancient China, the vital battlefield has become the international marketplace.

No nation understands all this better than the Japanese. And by the beginning of the next decade, the Japanese plan to be well on their way to utilizing the amassed knowledge of human civilization as their leverage to achieve a preeminent role in world trade. Other developed nations, in particular Great Britain and France, recognize the wisdom of the Japanese plan and are undertaking strategies of their own. Each such national program, including Japan's, revolves around the development of a new technology that embodies knowledge as its central feature—knowledge that will transform its holder's small advantage into a big, powerful, and eventually decisive advantage in any competition.

The United States, which pioneered the technology each of these national plans is based upon, and which has been preeminent in information technology for decades, has no such plan. A few industrialists and a handful of government officials are alert to these programs abroad and understand the consequences if the United States makes no rational plan of its own, but on the whole, Americans are remarkably indifferent to, even ignorant of, the challenges to our national predominance in everything from computing to finance, from industrial output to quality of life, that these other plans represent. We are, as usual, relying on matters to take care of themselves somehow or other. Because information technology moves so very much more quickly than other kinds of technology—halving in price and doubling in power every two years on the average—matters aren't likely just to take care of themselves in ways that Americans will be altogether happy with.

3

The Intelligent Machine as Automobile

To fashion machines that behave intelligently—that act in ways such that, were a human to act so, we would say, "Ah, that's intelligent behavior"—has been the explicit goal of a scientific field called artificial intelligence, which started more than twenty-five years ago with the introduction of the digital computer. Despite evergreen controversy and skepticism, the field has begun to create machines that, in some limited sense, reason. Often the reasoning power of these machines matches or exceeds the reasoning power of the humans who instructed them and, in some cases, the reasoning power of any human performing such tasks.

There's a fair parallel between intelligent machines and automobiles. In the world of artificial intelligence, it is, so to speak, 1890; the first automobiles have already appeared. They're hand-crafted horseless carriages, to be sure, but they're distinctly autos, different from wagons, carriages, and sleighs in good ways and bad.

The Japanese have studied this primitive horseless-carriage machine intelligence. They conclude that with certain major developments it can be a mass-market item. With the same kind of foresight Random Olds or Henry Ford once had as he examined the custom-built machines of Benz and Daimler, the Japanese have decided to improve upon greatly and mass-produce the intelligent machine. That means all the vigorous hand cranking, throttling, and wrenching a pioneer now accepts as the inevitable price of using the machine—the difficult programming languages, the struggles to make different programs compatible, the problems of putting human knowledge into machine form—are to disappear, eliminated in the new Japanese Fifth Generation of computers. This in itself would be remarkable enough, but the Japanese also intend to supply gas stations and roadways for the new machines, necessities for the users and sources of income for the supplier. Thus we recapitulate the story of personal transportation from the first hand-built Benz Patent Motor Wagon to the Honda Civic, for these new machines will also be "autos": self-propelled vehicles of the intellect.

The change from the speed of walking—about four miles an hour—to the speed of automobiles—about forty miles an hour—was an order-of-magnitude change that, while it didn't represent so very much in numbers, has transformed our lives utterly. (The next great order-of-magnitude change, from automobiles to jet planes that travel at 400 miles an hour, has made equivalent transformations in our lives.) This is central to what the Japanese plan for their new generation of computers: quantitative changes in computing speed, power, and reasoning that must make qualitative changes in our lives we can barely foresee. As for the computers that most of us are familiar with right now, they aren't horseless carriages. They're no more than bicycles.

4

What's the Big Idea?

The Japanese are planning the miracle product. It will come not from their mines, their wells, their fields, or even their seas. It comes instead from their brains. The miracle product is knowledge, and the Japanese are planning to package and sell it the way other nations package and sell energy, food, or manufactured goods. They're going to give the world the next generation—Fifth Generation[3]—of computers, and those machines are going to be intelligent.

"Japan, which has a shortage of land and a population density about 40 times that of the United States," say the Japanese, "cannot attain self-sufficiency in food, and her rate of self-sufficiency in energy is about 15 percent, and that of oil about 0.3 percent. On the other hand, we have one precious asset, that is, our human resources. Japan's plentiful labor force is characterized by a high degree of education, diligence, and high quality. It is desirable to utilize this advantage to cultivate information itself as a new resource comparable to food and energy, and to emphasize the development of information-related knowledge-intensive industries which will make possible the processing and managing of information at will."[4]

It was October 1981 when Japan first let the world at large know about its plans for the Fifth Generation of computers. The Japanese government announced that over the next decade it planned to spend seed money of about $450 million (participating industries are expected to match, and perhaps double, that amount) and would eventually involve several hundred top scientists in this project. Their goal is to develop computers for the 1990s and beyond— *intelligent* computers that will be able to converse with humans in natural language and understand speech and pictures. These will be computers that can learn, associate, make inferences, make decisions, and otherwise behave in ways we have always considered the exclusive province of human reason.

"Japan," the Japanese declare, "has come to be considered an 'economic power' by the other countries of the world. Thus, if we consider the direction in which our industries should proceed, it becomes clear that we no longer need chase the more developed countries, but instead should begin to set goals of leadership and creativity in research and development and to pioneer the promotion of such a project throughout the world." They add that by promoting this particular project, Japan is playing a leading role worldwide in the field of computer technology development.

Why have they chosen computing in particular? "Promoting a national project such as this in the computer industry, which has a strong effect on various leading technologies, will probably greatly influence the way in which research and development systems will be made in other industrial fields." Moreover, "our efforts will not only foster creative technology for our own computer industry, but will also provide our country with bargaining power. We also fulfill our duty as an economic power by investing in the development of such leading fields." In other words, the Japanese understand that if they succeed in this visionary computing project, they will acquire leverage over all kinds of industries, at home and abroad. The Fifth Generation is an exquisite piece of economic strategy.

About six months later, on April 14, 1982, an institute to guide the ten-year research and development program, called the Institute for New Generation Computer Technology (ICOT), was formally launched, its initial funding and new laboratories in Tokyo provided by the Japanese government. The first working papers to explore how such machines might be designed have been published,[5] the first scientists to work full-time on the project have been recruited. Elaborate plans have been drawn up which will allow the Japanese to move ahead step by step, evaluating their progress as they go, building on each success, and adjusting and revising for failure.

The Fifth Generation will be more than a technological breakthrough. The Japanese expect these machines to change their lives—and everyone else's. Intelligent machines are not only to make Japan's society a better, richer one by the 1990s, but they're explicitly planned to be influential in other areas, such as managing energy or helping deal with the problems of an aging society. Perhaps less grandiosely but equally important, the new machines will "serve as an active prime mover in all industrial fields by helping to increase the efficiency in those areas where increasing productivity has proven difficult," such as the primary industries (for example, agriculture and fishing) and the tertiary industries (for example, services, design, and general management).

But these are only the areas we can already see. There's a universe of possibilities essentially unknown to us that this research will open up.

"Development in unexplored fields can contribute actively to the progress of human society," the Japanese say.

"By promoting the study of artificial intelligence and realizing intelligent robots, a better understanding of the mechanisms of life will become possible. The approaching realization of automatic interpretation and translation will serve to help people of different tongues understand each other, to reduce problems due to misunderstanding and ignorance, and to lead to further growth based on mutual understanding of cultures. With the construction of a knowledge base made possible, the knowledge which mankind has accumulated can be stored and effectively utilized, so that the development of culture as a whole can be rapidly promoted. Mankind will more easily be able to acquire insights and perceptions with the aid of computers."

The Japanese have been sending scientific emissaries to the West for years to study the pioneering artificial intelligence research in the United States, Great Britain, and Europe. The Japanese have grasped the great scientific themes that run through artificial intelligence, and they feel ready to gather up a loosely knit group of ad hoc projects and to consolidate and develop them into what can only be called a momentous national project. Its success—even partial—will vault them into a position of distant leadership in conducting the world's information business.

Their Fifth Generation plans say unequivocally that the Japanese are the first nation to act consciously upon the realization that the new wealth of nations can be viewed as something besides financial capital, secured from manufactured goods or land rental, as it was in Adam Smith's time. In this they have acted on a truth that has been emerging and reiterated for nearly two decades. The world is entering a new period. *The wealth of nations, which depended upon land, labor, and capital during its agricultural and industrial phases—depended upon natural resources, the accumulation of money, and even upon weaponry—will come in the future to depend upon information, knowledge, and intelligence.*

This isn't to say that the traditional forms of wealth will be unimportant. Humans must eat, and they use up energy, and they like manufactured goods. But in the *control* of all these processes will reside a new form of power which will consist of facts, skills, codified experience, large amounts of easily obtained data, all accessible in fast, powerful ways to anybody who wants it—scholar, manager, policymaker, professional, or ordinary citizen. And it will be for sale.

5

An Engine for the New Wealth of Nations

In 1776, as auspicious a date for Americans as it was for capitalism, Adam Smith published his classic *Inquiry into the Nature and Causes of the Wealth of Nations*. Among its many other striking features, a modern reader cannot help noticing Smith's appreciation of—even infatuation with—the machine.

As students of economics will remember, Adam Smith presented a model of capitalism (and in his mind, society generally) that was a great, interacting whole—a machine— energized by the circular flow of goods and money throughout a closely interdependent set of sectors, a flow that could be described in a theory of distribution which Smith invented.

In his earlier *Essays*, which Smith considered of a piece with his *Wealth of Nations,* he had written: "Systems in many respects resemble machines. A machine is a little system, created to perform as well as connect together, in reality, those different movements and effects which the artist has occasion for. A system is an imaginary machine, invented to connect together in the fancy those different movements and effects which are already in reality performed."

In this, he was examining thinking, and its "natural preference" for connections and order, which Smith saw as the fundamental psychological law. But he was also justifying his own delight in connections, which is nowhere better expressed than in the grand vision of *The Wealth of Nations*.

Though Smith invented that theory of distribution, he

had drawn on many ideas of his time. His major intellectual debt was to Sir Isaac Newton. He adopted Newton's "experimental method," which blended the inductive reasoning of Bacon with the deductive reasoning of Descartes, as he examined the society he found himself in and the behavior of the humans around him. Smith's economic laws paralleled Newton's mechanical laws, and the Newtonian grasp of the whole is reflected in Smith's belief (which he shared with his friend David Hume) that humans exist in a social, not an isolated, state and that their interdependence must be observed and experienced in its entirety to be understood.

Thus Smith conceived of society as a giant machine, a system, for converting labor into capital, in somewhat the same way that physical machines convert energy into power according to Newtonian laws. The social machine produced wealth, which could grow, and brought its owners, the nations, political power. "The annual produce of the land and labour of any nation can be increased in its value by no other means," Smith wrote, "but by increasing either the number of its productive labourers, or the productive powers of those labourers who had before been employed."

With this we agree and take our leave from Adam Smith. For we shall argue that the new wealth of nations has its source not in land, or in labor, or in capital alone, but in *knowledge*. Knowledge will increase the productive powers of all laborers. The New York Stock Exchange study mentioned earlier estimates that better human capital, which is to say "working smarter," has accounted in the past for anywhere between one-fifth and one-half of total growth in productivity, depending on the decade being examined. The future promises even more startling increases.[6]

We also write inspired by a machine. It is different from the machines that surrounded and inspired Adam Smith, because its purpose is not to transduce energy, but to transduce information. We believe the kind of transformations it makes suggest a new model for explaining the human condition, a model more apt for the late twentieth century than Smith's now is.

Consider this: The Japanese have announced the development of a system of computers that will be, in their words, "a quantum leap over the technology of the last thirty years." Speaking of their own situation, they say:

"Our society is about to enter a transition period in various meanings of the term. It is an age of changes in internal and external environmental conditions such as the energy situation, and together with building a wealthy, liberal society, and overcoming the constraints of resources and energy, we must at the same time make international contributions as an economic power.

"In making our way through this new age, information-ization and the information industry which centers around computers are expected to play a big role. In the 1990s when Fifth Generation computers will be widely used, information processing systems will be a central tool in all areas of social activity to include economics, industry, science and art, administration, international relations, education, culture, daily life, and the like, and will be required to meet those new needs generated by environmental changes. Information processing systems will be expected to play an active role in the resolving of anticipated social bottlenecks and the advancing of society along a more desirable path through the effective utilization of their capabilities."

In short, the Japanese see information as the key to their continuing prosperity, information that pervades society "like the air" by means of widely distributed information processing systems. "In these systems," they say, "intelligence will be greatly improved to approach that of a human being, and, when compared with conventional systems, [the] man-machine interface will become closer to the human system." That means they aim to produce machines easy enough to use, and intelligent and fast enough in their responses, to come close to the kinds of transactions intelligent human beings are used to having with each other.

It's a distinct pleasure to report that while the Japanese have put a lot of planning and thought into their Fifth Generation project, they've spent no time at all in those arid little debates so beloved by Western intellectuals, debates centered on the questions whether a machine really can be said to think. They regard our obsession with that topic the same way we regard their eating raw fish—an odd, puzzling, but harmless cultural quirk. Instead, their debates are about the best way to design an intelligent machine, truly a new generation, the engine that will produce the new wealth of nations.

The Fifth Generation will achieve all this by departing significantly from the general, fundamental design that has characterized computers until now.

Most people label the first four generations of computers, each based on its central technology, this way: 1) electronic—vacuum tube computers, 2) transistorized computers, 3) integrated circuit computers, and 4) very large-scale integrated computers (VLSI). We are currently at the end of the third generation, and VLSI will dominate during the 1980s. The general design of all four is known as the von Neumann machine—after the computer pioneer and mathematician John von Neumann—and is composed of a central processor (a program controller) a memory, an arithmetic unit, and input-output devices. It operates in a largely serial fashion, step by step. It has served its purposes well. But the Fifth Generation will abandon it, or greatly modify it. Instead there will be new parallel architectures (collectively known as non–von Neumann architectures), new memory organizations, new programming languages, and new operations wired in for handling symbols and not just numbers.

The Fifth Generation will stand apart not only because of its technology, but also because it is conceptually and functionally different from the first four generations the world is familiar with. These new machines will be known as knowledge information processing systems, or KIPS.

That term is extremely important. It signals the shift from mere data processing, which is the way present-day computers function, to an *intelligent* processing of knowledge. These new machines are to be specifically designed for artificial intelligence functions. We shall explain that in more detail, but for now, let us summarize by saying that KIPS are specifically designed to do symbolic manipulation and symbolic reasoning.

Most of the world's work is nonmathematical in nature. Only a small segment of activity has as its kernel the kinds of formulas that we see in engineering and physics applications. Even in such "hard" sciences as chemistry, most thinking is done by inference, not calculation. The same is true of biology, most of medicine, and all of law. Most business management is done by symbolic inference, not calculation. In short, almost all the thinking that professionals do is done by reasoning, not calculating. As computing gets cheaper and the professions look to computer technologists to aid in relieving their ever-growing information processing burden, they will want to use methods that involve automated reasoning and use of symbolic knowledge.

Such methods are already in use. Modest pilot projects, with the name of *expert systems,* have demonstrated that a computer is capable of the same kinds of intelligent behavior as a physician making a diagnosis, or a geologist deciding where to seek minerals. And these expert systems do this in much the same way human experts do—by combining textbook knowledge with the rules of thumb that experience teaches, and then making informed guesses about the situation at hand, whether sick human being or range and basin. We call such expertise in humans intelligence, intuition, inspiration, and professionalism. When a machine demonstrates the same kind of behavior, there is no compelling reason not to call it intelligence then, too.

Our present computers can be programmed to do those tasks, and do them at a high level of expertise, often outperforming human experts (even the ones who've taught them). Moreover, computers can be made to exhibit expertise over a very wide range of fields, and new expert systems are being commissioned and designed all the time. But for the purposes of expert systems, our present computers are at a fairly primitive stage of design in terms of speed and power. The knowledge manipulation on a grand scale of humanlike intelligence planned for the Fifth Generation will require scaling up by several orders of magnitude in hardware and software.

Covering all the bets, the Japanese are not neglecting research and development to improve conventional computing. An effort called the National Super-Speed Computer Project is already under way to develop a computer *a thousand times* more powerful than any now available. It is a joint project of six major computer vendors (Fujitsu, Hitachi, Nippon Electric Corporation, Mitsubishi, Oki, and Toshiba) led by Japan's National Electrotechnical Laboratory. Seed money from the government and contributions from each of the six firms will eventually bring its funding to about $200 million, and it is scheduled for completion in 1989. Other projects, both government-supported and independent within the major firms, are also under way, addressing problems of picture processing and improved hardware in logic and processor technology. A group of visiting American scientists from the Los Alamos and Livermore National Laboratories observed after a visit to Japan in 1982: "The large-scale computing systems currently offered by Japanese manufacturers are approaching the best available." Later on they summarized their impressions: "Japan has launched, at the national level, an impressive effort to become the world leader in supercomputer technology. . . . Although it is not yet clear how many of the goals of these projects will be achieved, even partial success would be impressive and perhaps allow the Japanese computer industry to overtake the American computer industry in supercomputer technology."[7]

We believe the same assessment can be made about Japan's Fifth Generation project. Although some critics raise certain technical objections, we believe that by the very act of conceiving and beginning to develop this plan, the Japanese have put themselves in the world vanguard. Should they achieve only a fraction of their goals, they will still have attained an enviable primacy. As they say themselves, "that we have begun our Fifth Generation computer research and development project ahead of the rest of the world should be highly significant."[8] When we first reported this, few people, either Westerners or Japanese, believed it. A year later, it would be a commonplace. The turnabout was due to the facts themselves: the increasing evidence of significant development. Japan's Fifth Generation Project was by this time perceived as the epochal project that it truly is.

It is tempting to regard all this as just another skirmish in the trade wars, where engagements have already taken place in steel, automobiles, and consumer electronics. The thought of yet another confrontation, this time in the information processing industry, might well drive exasperated Americans to stuff cotton in their ears, figuratively speaking, to block out one more dreary tune of self-pity in what seems like our national dirge of declining industries.

However, our national self-interest, not to mention our economic security, does not allow us this luxury. Information processing is an $88-billion-per-year industry in the United States, and its loss would be disastrous. The default of this American industry, which has led the world for decades, would be a mortal economic wound.[9] But inextricably linked to that, yet different and perhaps more important, would be the social pain. Second-rate status has little to be said for it, except its advantage over being third-rate. Eventually, the pain might be political. The superior technology usually wins the war—whether that war is martial, entrepreneurial, or cultural. The superior intelligence, as Sun Tzu might have been the first to record, always does.

6

Japan Decides to be the First Postindustrial Society

In a piece of social forecasting that looks more prescient all the time, Daniel Bell, a Harvard sociologist, presented the outlines of what he called the postindustrial society. The Japanese, whom he hardly mentions in his 1976 book, have obliged him by beginning to shape a society with just the features Bell discerned would characterize postindustrialism.

What Bell calls the "axial principle" of this postindustrial society is the centrality and codification of theoretical knowledge. Along that axis are a new intellectual technology, the spread of a knowledge class, the switch from goods to services, a change in the character of work, and so on. In the Japanese case, the new intellectual technology is artificial intelligence, in this instance, machines that amplify human thought. This technology will take its place beside writing, printing, mathematics, and other technologies that have changed the way we think.

Bell also predicts that the primary institutions of the postindustrial society will be the university, academic institutes, and research corporations. Indeed, the three sectors combining to bring about the Fifth Generation are Japanese universities, independent institutes, and the research laboratories of eight of its major firms. The primary resource of the postindustrial society is human capital, says Bell. "Our one precious asset is our human resources," say the Japanese. The economic ground of the postindustrial society is science-based, says Bell. "The products of our country will be rendered unique and specialized in their respective fields due to their performance, design, and knowledge-intensive qualities," say the Japanese. "These achievements will further serve as a foundation for promoting the true knowledge intensiveness of our industries."[10]

Of course, the postindustrial society has its problems: What should science and education policy be? How shall the public and private sectors be balanced? How shall society cope with bureaucracies and an adversary culture?[11]

But these problems must seem an afternoon's work compared with the problems that have driven Japan to the Fifth Generation project. Japan is a nation of 110 million people (about half the population of the United States) who must live on an area just smaller than that of the state of Montana.[12] It has no natural resources and very little arable land. For most nations, this would be the occasion to pound on the doors of the World Bank. In the past, it has driven Japan unsuccessfully to war. Now, however, faced with these perennial problems, Japan has seized the initiative and shrewdly reckoned that its new Fifth Generation of KIPS could give Japan the lead in this race to become a postindustrial society.

The first and most obvious reason for this is the increase in productivity such machines will bring about. They are designed specifically to increase the productivity of knowledge workers—and here we mean professionals as surely as billing clerks—by orders of magnitude over what they can accomplish now. Knowledge workers, as we shall see, constitute the majority in the work force of developed nations, and their ranks will increase. Thus a significant improvement in their productivity will have profound economic effects.

The manufactured goods that Japan will sell will be so much better than the competition's, thanks to the degree of knowledge that will be brought to bear on their design and manufacture, that the Japanese expect to dominate markets in conventional products, too. But perhaps equally important to all the economic advantages the Fifth Generation promises is that intangible thing called quality of life. A society where knowledge is quickly and easily available to anybody who wants it will, we think, be an alluring place.

While many observers, especially Americans, have greeted the announcement of the Fifth Generation with some skepticism, the odds in this visionary national gamble are better than they might at first seem.

To begin with, the Japanese really do understand—and have formulated a national policy that anticipates—what the future will look like. In *Japan as Number One*, Ezra Vogel puts it bluntly: "If any single factor explains Japanese success, it is the group-directed quest for knowledge. . . . When Daniel Bell, Peter Drucker, and others hailed the coming of the postindustrial society in which knowledge replaced capital as society's most important resource, this new conception became a great rage in Japan's leading circles. But these leading circles were merely articulating the latest formulation of what had already become conventional Japanese wisdom, the supreme importance of the pursuit of knowledge."[13]

A review of the shifts in the American labor force may illuminate this. As late as 1900, it took nearly 40 percent of the labor force to feed Americans. Now only 3 percent are needed. In less than fifty years, labor economists expect the same sort of shift to take place in manufacturing so that industrial operatives will constitute 4 to 5 percent of the work force too, down from the 25 percent they represent now. Nobody (save, perhaps, the French) expects the fantasy of the 1950s to take place: we will not move into a society where work is optional and the disposal of leisure time is our biggest headache. Instead, the rest of us will be service and information workers. Bell says: "A post-industrial society is based on services. Hence it is a game between persons. What counts is not raw muscle power, or energy, but information. The central person is the professional, for he is equipped, by his education and training, to provide the kinds of skills which are increasingly demanded in the post-industrial society."[14]

Knowledge is a Japanese passion. In the circulation figures of their newspapers (comparable to those of the United States, with a population half the size), in the scope of their educational TV programs, in the performance of their schoolchildren in subjects such as mathematics and natural science, in the numbers of Japanese who complete high school and postsecondary schools, in community groups that band together to study possible solutions to problems that confront them—in all these the Japanese reverence for information is obvious. The numbers in the Japanese labor force again tell the story: the Japanese are moving rapidly and eagerly into a well-educated, information-rich postindustrial society.

As for natural resources, those countries that depend on their resources alone have been dramatically disillusioned. In a phrase that can only evoke a sigh from oil-poor nations, oil wealth has been characterized as "a very mixed blessing" by none other than the former executive director of the International Monetary Fund. Yet he makes his point. The oil-exporting countries are extremely diverse, ranging from Algeria to Norway, from Kuwait to Mexico, but they have had surprisingly similar economic problems: the squandering of revenues, hyperinflation, stalled industrial development, an actual drop in agricultural production, and deeply painful social clashes among their various sectors—laborers, consumers, religious leaders who feel cheated, and government officials who feel accursed. Ali A. Attiga, an OPEC statesman, says that history may show that the oil-exporting countries "have gained the least, or lost the most, from the discovery and development of their resources." Although the oil-importing nations will probably not get out their handkerchiefs, a comparison between the standard of living in Japan and that of nearly any OPEC country says a great deal.[15]

For the Japanese, without land or natural resources, do have the vital component of the new wealth of nations. They have that national passion for knowledge and the vision and will to parlay the passion into developing a technology that will reshape the world.

Having specified the number of disciplines, areas, and skills where the Fifth Generation will have a great impact, the Japanese announcement adds in strained syntax but justified optimism: "It is felt certain that Fifth Generation computers will trigger the realization of developments and phenomena heretofore undreamed of."

It all seems to smack of science fiction, but it is real and deeply important to the Japanese. In this book we shall argue that it is deeply important to all of us.

Simply put, Japan's survival as a nation is at stake. The Japanese are acutely aware that to remain competitive in world markets, they must increase productivity in those areas that so far have been neglected. The primary industries, such as fishing and agriculture, must become knowledge-intensive in order to become more productive. The tertiary industries, meaning services, management, and design, for example, must also become knowledge-intensive for the same purpose. As for secondary, or manufacturing, industries, their products will be superior because of their much higher quality, based on all the knowledge that will be poured into their design and manufacture.

The Japanese are a proud people, with a history of cultivated civilization stretching back even before the unification of their nation under the Yamato court in the second century A.D. Thus, more important than it may at first seem, the Japanese intend to show by this project that they are capable of originality and not merely the copycat development of technologies originating elsewhere. Japan's national self-esteem is deeply bound up in the Fifth Generation project, and it is that pride that fires the national will to accomplish it.

7

Today I Am a Man

The October 1981 International Conference on Fifth Generation Computer Systems seemed to Edward Feigenbaum like a coming-out party. Or, he fancied as he sat in the huge auditorium of the National Chamber of Commerce in Tokyo, like a bar mitzvah. To think about an event in Tokyo as a bar mitzvah amused him by its incongruity, and yet the more he thought of it, the more it seemed to have the right flavor. It was the coming-of-age party of a promising and diligent boy—Japanese research in information processing—who was about to be a man. It was an auspicious event.

In the fall of 1980, a slender report had arrived at his Stanford University office entitled "Preliminary Report on a Fifth Generation of Computers." Feigenbaum had glanced at it briefly, made copies for some friends, and then put it in his "to read sometime" pile. But in November, when he was in Europe, Donald Michie, a pioneer in artificial intelligence research at Edinburgh University, had reminded him about that report. Michie had been very exercised about it, thought it represented a definite threat to Western computer technology, and was telling that to anybody who would listen. Feigenbaum acknowledged that he may have overlooked something here.

In the summer of 1981, a much more complete version of "Preliminary Report on the Fifth Generation of Computers" arrived, and this time Feigenbaum paid close attention. Parts of the initial report that had seemed superficial were developed with detailed plans of action. He was impressed.

The Japanese intended to base their designs on a scientific viewpoint that had been introduced into American artificial intelligence research fifteen years earlier, the concept called knowledge-based systems. This view had proven its validity over the years and had long since taken its place as a fundamental method in the work of American scientists. The Japanese called their proposed new computers knowledge information processing systems, or KIPS. The term itself acknowledged that the most important step in making computer programs that behave intelligently was to provide these programs with large bodies of knowledge on given topics. The Japanese were showing that they, too, accepted knowledge and facts, rather than grand principles alone, as the critical difference between an intelligent system and an unintelligent one, human or computer.

Feigenbaum shared the Japanese planning report with his wife, H. Penny Nii, a computer scientist, and, moreover, Japanese by birth and rearing until she left Japan at age sixteen to study in the United States. Upon finishing the report, she wasn't sure which surprised her more: the technical proposals the report contained or the un-Japanese tone of it: its explicit statements about Japan's taking its rightful place as a world leader, shedding its outdated copycat image, and claiming a role as a revolutionary innovator in high technology. She knew the Japanese culture, and within that culture, statements like this were very unusual.

Thus, when an invitation came from the Japan Information Processing Development Center—organizers of the International Fifth Generation Computer Conference—for him to address the meeting, Feigenbaum accepted. His curiosity was thoroughly aroused. Feigenbaum is a computer scientist who had learned programming in the mid-1950s on the Johnniac (named, incidentally, for John von Neumann), when the building of each computer was a hand-crafted team project, and he'd been lucky enough to be in a programming project for that machine at Carnegie Tech in Pittsburgh.

Since then, he had seen computers change from such singular objects into a major world industry. He had seen computer science transformed from a small body of lore borrowed partially from mathematics, partially from electrical engineering, and partially from the experience of building a machine, into a major academic discipline. His own department at Stanford (he had arrived on the day of its formal beginning as a department in 1965 and had served two three-year terms as its chairman) was acknowledged as a world leader. Scholars came from all over to visit, cross-fertilize, and carry away ideas. In twenty-five years, the computer as artifact had pervaded his society, yet he knew it was still only the beginning.

Now he sat in an auditorium in Tokyo listening to simultaneous translations of the Japanese presentations, and he felt great admiration for them. By sheer hard work and brains, the Japanese might pull off an intellectual coup that would probably turn out to be an economic coup as well. He looked at the other Westerners in the audience, perhaps seventy or eighty of them altogether— half to two-thirds Americans—and wondered if they shared his admiration.

The majority of the audience, of course, was Japanese. Feigenbaum assumed that many of them already knew about the Fifth Generation project, given the consensual nature of Japanese society. Indeed, this conference struck him as a very essential, almost final piece of the consensus-building process, enlisting the support of a broad managerial and engineering community in Japan for this epochal project. (That was their word, *epochal*. He thought they were right.) Thus the meeting was as much ceremony as science conference.

Another American at the conference was Mitchel Resnick, a *Business Week* correspondent. Resnick had come to the Fifth Generation conference almost by accident. *Business Week* was doing a major issue on Japanese technology in general, and the research team's visit to Japan just happened to coincide with the Fifth Generation conference. Resnick had been puzzled on opening day. He had listened to the simultaneous translations of the opening talks and sensed that the interpreters, with their monotone translations, were leaving out a lot of the excitement. But Feigenbaum's talk on the second day had put things into context.

The first thing Feigenbaum said was that no constraint evident in the hardware would limit the success of the Fifth Generation project—the hardware engineers would be able to deliver whatever was needed. The 1970s were the years of great hardware ideas. The 1980s would be transitional years. The 1990s would be years of great software ideas, and most important, those great software ideas would completely transform the concept of "computing."

Acknowledging the need for innovations in science and technology, Feigenbaum also cautioned the conservative, risk-aversive Japanese managers that innovations in management would be necessary too. And not only would risks be necessary, but those who took such risks, even if they failed, must be rewarded.

Did Feigenbaum believe the Japanese could develop the Fifth Generation? Resnick asked him the question directly. Solutions to the very difficult problems of software, Feigenbaum replied, could be found, but would require significant levels of innovation.

Yes, Resnick persisted, but could the Japanese *do* it? Some Japanese managers Resnick had been able to interview in the halls were unenthusiastic about the venture. Though the Japanese would never attack each other openly the way Westerners so joyfully do, beneath the polite accord Resnick sensed an undercurrent of doubt. There were intimations that this project was much too revolutionary, too futuristic. If industrialists were going along with the project it was partly because they were getting a free ride, so to speak; the government's Ministry of International Trade and Industry (MITI) was providing the funds exclusively for the first few years. The first phase might be well along before cautious managers would have to make a decision whether to commit their own corporate funds. All they had to agree to commit now were people. But that wasn't an inconsiderable commitment: if a Hitachi engineer was working on the Fifth Generation, then he wasn't working on the normal progression of Hitachi processors.

As the conference went on, Resnick got the impression that in part, it was an elaborate lobbying effort. It was easy, from across the Pacific, to believe that mighty MITI had a mint in its basement to print any money it needed, but in fact, as Resnick learned, MITI had to lobby for its funds just like everybody else, and there were plenty of other claims on the public purse of Japan. But if MITI could show this conference was making a big impression on foreigners, it had good arguments for going ahead with the project.

And Resnick in fact thought Japan was making a very big impression on the foreigners. The Japanese running the project and giving the talks had been immersed in the project for so long that they had lost some of their excitement. The conference announced a new project, but for the broad group of Japanese scientists, engineers, and government officials who had participated in its development, it was merely the summary of some three years spent in careful planning. But for those non-Japanese scientists hearing about the Fifth Generation for the first time, there was an infectious wave of excitement that grew as the conference went on. The Japanese seemed cautious and tentative compared to the enthusiasm of the foreign visitors.

In that sense, the lobbying effort would prove successful. Professor Tohru Moto-oka of Tokyo University, chairman of the organizing committee for the Fifth Generation conference, had said to Resnick in an interview that he was concerned that the seed money for the Fifth Generation might be delayed a year—many people in the Japanese government were concerned about deficit spending, and it was much easier to postpone funding for a long-term, ambitious project than to cut budgets elsewhere. But a few months after the conference ended, the first seed money would indeed be allocated and the project would be under way.

An instant institute was formed in April 1982. Forty of the brightest young computer researchers in the country gathered under one roof to build hardware, software, and applications programs for the prototype of the new generation of knowledge information processors. The researchers were under intense pressure to produce the prototype system within two years. Their director would be Dr. Kazuhiro Fuchi, former head of the Information Sciences Division of MITI's Electrotechnical Laboratory and clearly the main architect of the Fifth Generation project.

Could the Japanese do it? Resnick had asked again and again. Most foreign visitors replied the same: the project was ambitious, its goals would be very difficult to achieve, and it might not succeed. But the very fact that the Japanese had launched themselves so conspicuously on this undertaking put them into the major leagues in computing; even partial success would be something to be reckoned with.

Could the Japanese do it? Resnick asked Feigenbaum again.

Feigenbaum chose his words carefully. "They have two hundred people with a unified vision. That's very powerful. We know more than the Japanese, but no one has developed a plan like they have." (The 200 would include not only the forty researchers at ICOT, but all the researchers in the firms that would contract to do work under ICOT's direction.) Resnick would quote that and identify the speaker as "one U.S. researcher." Later in the same article he would quote Feigenbaum by name as saying, "The Fifth Generation artificial intelligence machine is the machine we've all been waiting for." And that was what Feigenbaum believed.

Still, Feigenbaum felt obliged to remind the Japanese that they'd had virtually no experience in building the applications programs called expert systems—or knowledge-based systems—the programs for which the new Fifth Generation computer hardware was being planned. During his talk, when he had cited examples of expert systems, not one had been Japanese. "Now that's not bad; it's indicative of early effort," he said. But then he added: "If I were a MITI planner, it would make me nervous to base a project costing countless millions of dollars, or yen, on that very small experience base. It makes me nervous to hear these grand designers talk about these grand designs without telling the audience exactly why some element was chosen, what piece of experience gave rise to the insight that a certain type of architecture was needed, or a certain type of software. Remember, this is not a project in grand art; this is a project in science, engineering, and technology. There have to be reasons for things. It's not only elegance and beauty [that counts], but also functionality."

Fuchi of the Electrotechnical Laboratory (later to be named director of the new Institute) answered him with elaborate courtesy. "As of now, accomplishments in Japan [in knowledge engineering] worth mentioning as first-class performances may be rare, but though small in volume, there is a certain level of accumulation and history in Japan also. I wish to take this opportunity to say that few as these may be, plans are being made based on them as well as on the consensus of the various people concerned.

"Metaphorically speaking, if your countries are like adults, then Japan may be likened to a baby, but in my own mind, Japan is actually closer to boyhood.

"It may seem funny for me to talk about how a boy should behave, but boys must learn from adults, and listen to them and respect their opinions."

But Fuchi concluded, "Adults may sometimes have too much experience."

II

IT'S NOT JUST THE SECOND COMPUTER REVOLUTION, IT'S THE IMPORTANT ONE

1

Can a Machine Think?

Pamela McCorduck was introduced to the idea of artificial intelligence—making a computer behave in ways that mimic intelligent human behavior—in 1959, by Feigenbaum, as it happened. It was a time when computing, its natural child called artificial intelligence, and certainly they themselves were all much younger. That youthfulness might explain why she couldn't then take seriously the question of whether a machine could really be said to think, though many people she met spent a great deal of time debating the question feverishly. She had no opinion one way or the other; she just didn't find it an interesting question.

Some fifteen years later, when she came to write a history of artificial intelligence, that question had still not gone away, despite the performance of chess-playing programs, puzzle-solving programs, and even an expert system that working chemists were using as an intelligent assistant. In its most common form, it was less a question than an assertion: machines cannot think. The assertion had been made confidently in the mid-nineteenth century, when the first digital computer was conceived, and was reasserted scornfully with the appearance of the electronic computer; it became the occasion for bluster when researchers in artificial intelligence announced their goals in the mid-1950s. But despite the performance of programs that kept demonstrating behavior that, in humans, would be considered intelligent, the assertion wouldn't go away. McCorduck forced herself to take an interest.

Critics over AI's quarter-century of existence have ranged from computer specialists who were struggling with the difficulties of making a primitive new technology do the simplest operations of addition and subtraction, merge and sort; to philosophers, who might not know much about computing but knew thinking took place only inside human heads (and also sensed that one more piece of their turf was being claimed by the pesky empiricists, even as natural philosophy had been carted away to be physics, chemistry, and biology); to ordinary citizens, who simply could not accept the idea that "thinking" and "machine" had any right to appear on the same platform.

The arguments against machine intelligence fall into four broad categories:

First are arguments of emotion. Machines can never think because everybody knows machines can't think. Thinking is, by definition, a human property. Tacked onto this set of arguments are some ad hominem attacks on the practitioners of artificial intelligence. "Charlatans" has been a favorite epithet, as if AI people knew that what they were up to couldn't possibly work, but were willfully defrauding their supporting agencies of money and the public of its peace of mind.

Second are arguments of insuperable differences. Thinking requires creativity and originality, and no machine can be creative or original. Anyway, intelligence requires a special kind of experience, acquired only through interaction in the real world and with others of like mind. Intelligence requires autonomy, and no machine can ever be autonomous. Even if the machine does a few tasks well—it plays chess, or it makes a correct medical diagnosis—it won't be able to do anything else, to transfer its expertise in medicine to writing a beautiful poem, for example. Intelligence means being able to cope with a variety of tasks. If a machine could do all these things, it still wouldn't be conscious of having done them, and consciousness is a significant part of intelligence. And aren't there mathematical theorems that prove that machines are incapable of intelligence?

Third are arguments of no existing examples. Even if

computers are capable of intelligent behavior, nobody has yet succeeded in making them behave that way. Whether they ever will remains to be seen.

Finally, there are arguments from ethics. Even if machines were capable of intelligence, should we really embark on such an awesome, perhaps sacrilegious, project? Just because it could be done doesn't mean that it ought to be done.

Each of these arguments has been addressed elsewhere. For example, the observation that silicon processors and neurons are different from each other is apt, but their functions can be very fruitfully compared. Computers are learning to cope with a variety of tasks. Human civilization moved along briskly and "intelligently" long before the notion of consciousness—largely a nineteenth-century European invention—arrived. In any event, if the essence of consciousness is to hold an internal model of yourself in relation to the external world, then computers can be imbued with consciousness, too. As for the ethical arguments, each advance in knowledge has the possibility of bringing misfortune to the human species; we must always ask ourselves whether, on balance, new knowledge will bring us good or evil, knowing very well that such a thing is almost impossible to predict. On the whole, we humans have chosen knowledge over ignorance and been the happier for it.

But the arguments from emotion were the ones that caught McCorduck's attention in the beginning, and they have been the ones to persist. They fascinated her for two reasons. First, she wondered what deeply sensitive nerve was being jangled by the idea of machine intelligence—for so she had to assume from the shrillness of the voices raised against AI. And second, she had to decide why she herself was undisturbed by the idea of an intelligent machine.

The arguments from emotion usually came in disguise. They materialized in learned papers just as often as they appeared in scoffing letters to the editor. They were cogently argued just as often as they collapsed under the weight of their own sarcasm. The anti-AI philosophers, for instance, were by turns amusing, impenetrable, and disputatious. But they were not open to counterargument as a rational person might be, or to any proof that things they asserted "could not be done" had indeed been done.

That only upped the ante. If a philosopher argued that a machine could never play good chess, and then somebody devised a machine that demonstrably could, and what's worse beat the philosopher in a match, he revised his claim to say that a machine could never play *championship* chess, and so it went.

One common assumption in these arguments was a virtually unexamined belief that everybody knew what intelligence was. Or creativity, or originality, or autonomy, or consciousness, for that matter. Yet if artificial intelligence research had done nothing else, it had shown how empty most theories of intelligent behavior were (likewise theories of creativity, originality, autonomy, and consciousness). When you wanted to make a computer behave intelligently, you had to have a very precise idea of intelligent behavior in order to specify it to the computer in detail. In neither psychology nor philosophy did such precise models of intelligence exist.

So there were really two problems to deal with in asking whether a machine could think. One was the whole area of human intelligence and what that meant. The second was whether any machine was capable of the same sort of behavior. Human intelligence is still surprisingly elusive for scientists, but some things can be said about machine intelligence.

2

Mind as Mechanism

The word *intelligence* derives originally from the Latin *legere*, meaning literally to gather (especially fruit), to collect, to assemble, and hence to choose and form an impression. *Intellegere* means to choose among, hence to understand, perceive, and know. If we can imagine an artifact that can collect, assemble, choose among, understand, perceive, and know, then we have an artificial intelligence. In broad terms, that is what the coming knowledge-processing artifacts will do, be they Japanese or American.

If we can imagine? Of course we can. We always have. Thinking machines, artificial intelligences, have intrigued us for as long as we have had written records. The *Iliad* describes some splendid robots, inventions of the god Hephaestus, that were ordered up by various gods and goddesses who wanted things done. The Greeks considered such devices to be no more than wonderfully handy tools; their counterparts are today's industrialists standing in mesmerized delight before a robotic assembly line.

But elsewhere in the Mediterranean sunshine, there were voices raised against the idea of graven images. Motives were complex, but briefly put, to aspire to creating a thinking machine seemed to veer dangerously near divine territory, a trespass humans might essay at greatest peril.

This fundamental division between attitudes toward intelligent machines has persisted throughout Western civilization, appearing in guises appropriate to the times. The Middle Ages, for instance, had legends about brazen— that is, brass—heads invented by alchemists that solved knotty mathematical problems, and there was a manlike clay creature called the Golem that was created by the chief rabbi of Prague and used by him as a spy among the Gentiles.

By the beginning of the machine age, an obsession with artifacts that embodied "intelligence" had developed, culminating in Mary Shelley's novel *Frankenstein*. Dr. Frankenstein's nameless monster has come to stand for science run amok, and hardly anybody remembers that Victor Frankenstein brought it on himself (and his unlucky friends and acquaintances) by treating his own creature so callously.

At about the same time *Frankenstein* was being read, dramatized, and debated, the whimsical and eccentric mathematician Charles Babbage was conceiving a machine that is generally agreed to be the ancestor of our modern digital computer. Babbage's machine would never be built in its entirety—the machining skills needed to make the millions of precision parts required by the Analytical Engine existed nowhere on the face of the earth.

Even so, Babbage was pestered by people who asked

whether his machine could be said to think. His colleague, the brilliant young mathematician Ada, Countess Lovelace, wrote an engaging essay describing the Analytical Engine and said no, it could not really be said to think. That assertion has been quoted many times since, but without the Countess's prudent qualification that experience with the machine itself would have to answer that question with finality.

These days we can argue that Babbage and Lady Lovelace did indeed entertain ideas that their machine would think. Babbage, after all, had conceived of it to do away with what he called the "drudgery of thinking." No matter. That argument would go on long after the bones of Babbage and the Countess were dust.

It took enormous foresight, even a century after Babbage, to imagine that large, crude vacuum-tube wonders of the early 1950s, the first generation of computers, might do anything more interesting than calculate bomb trajectories. It took not only foresight; it took insight. What made artificial intelligence come alive as a science was the perception that the computer was badly misnamed. "Computer" implies only counting and calculating, whereas this unpromising hunk of wires, tubes, switches, and lights was, in principle, *capable of manipulating any sort of symbol.*

Though younger men eagerly pointed it out to them, that insight was simply unacceptable to many computing pioneers. John von Neumann, for example, who is widely acknowledged as a giant in computing, left as his last piece of published writing a long argument that computers would never exhibit intelligence.

Undeterred, the younger men went to work on the problem anyway. The earliest examples of artificial intelligence in the late 1950s and early 1960s reflected their personal interests. For example, there were programs that played chess and checkers and proved theorems in plane geometry and logic. Though the examples seem far removed from real-world applications, the research was earnest. These young scientists were explicit in their faith that if you could penetrate to the essence of great chess playing, you would have penetrated to the core of human intellectual behavior. No use to say from here that somebody should have paid attention to all the brilliant chess players who are otherwise not exceptional, or all the brilliant people who play mediocre chess. This first group of artificial intelligence researchers (and they called themselves that, the term "artificial intelligence" having been coined around 1956) was persuaded that certain great, underlying principles characterized all intelligent behavior and could be isolated in chess as easily as anyplace else, and then applied to other endeavors that required intelligence.

In part, they were correct. Certain strategies of intelligent behavior would eventually be uncovered. Those strategies are probably familiar to any reader. They include searching for a solution (and using "rules of good guessing" to cut down the search space); generating and testing ('does this work? no; try something else); reasoning backward from a desired goal; and the like. But AI researchers have had to uncover and make them specific, because computers respond not to exhortations but to programming. The seminars in creativity and problem solving that abound in our schools and firms these days owe much of their content to early AI research.

These strategies are necessary, but not sufficient, for intelligent behavior. The other ingredient is knowledge—specialized knowledge, and lots of it. Again, in retrospect, this is easy to see. No matter how natively bright you are, you cannot be a credible medical diagnostician without a great deal of specific knowledge about diseases, their manifestations, and the human body.

This thoroughly unwelcome addition to the grand principles, this messy bunch of details, facts, rules of good guessing, rules of good judgment, and experiential knowledge offended those who thought that intelligence, like physics, ought to be clean, lean, and neat. Intelligence isn't (and, incidentally, neither is physics). A certain amount of intramural war took place in the artificial intelligence field, deploying graduate students, until the new hybrid view prevailed—the expert system—that integrated general, humanlike strategies of problem solving with a large base of factual and experiential knowledge specific to the problem. Fortunately, controversy and changing views are what make science different from dogma, so everybody is still speaking to everybody else. Moreover, it's important to remember that artificial intelligence is moving ahead on many fronts: robotics, natural language understanding, image and speech understanding, cognitive modeling, and theorem proving, to name a few. The work in expert systems is a major part of, but not the only, work going on.

The advocates of expert systems—or knowledge-based systems—had one great thing going for them. The combination of task-specific knowledge and techniques for manipulating it in their programs actually worked in the real world. Theories are powerful, useful abstractions, but if they are to have worth beyond the contemplation of their elegant form, they must be tested against reality.

Paradoxically, at the same time artificial intelligence research was infused with new vitality, thanks to expert systems driving research ahead, people outside the field—who up to then had been able to tell for themselves whether a chess program was winning or losing, or whether a robot skirted an obstacle or crashed into it stupidly—were suddenly at a loss to know if artificial intelligence was "working" or not. The only people who could really appreciate what was being done were the experts whose domains AI had entered and enhanced, such as chemists and physicians.

There were charges from outsiders that AI had reached a plateau, that AI had not delivered on its promises, that AI was an embarrassment to serious scientists, that everyone with common sense knew a machine couldn't think. With the exception of those whose funding was affected (as happened in Great Britain about this time), AI researchers didn't take these charges very seriously because, first, they were too busy working on projects, and second, they were blessed with a sense of history. As a scientific field, AI has existed for about twenty-five years. A quarter-century is a short time in science. In biology it was more than two thousand years after Aristotle that Mendel made his observations about genes, and nearly another century followed before Crick and Watson discovered the double helix explaining Mendel's observations. AI researchers allowed as how human intelligence might be as complex as human biology.

But typical of computing, and typical of things to come in the postindustrial society, the time between significant advances in AI has shortened dramatically. The Japanese have just begun another dazzling speed-up, when we are hardly coping with the considerable scientific, economic, and psychological impacts that AI has already had upon us all.

3

A Machine as Smart as a Person

The difficulty most of us have in thinking about intelligent machines is that our concept of "machine" is conditioned by the machines that have surrounded us all our lives. Almost without exception their function is to process energy—that is, to amplify, to distribute, to transform, or otherwise to modify energy. Thus the automobile transforms fossil-fuel energy (itself already transformed by refining) into kinetic energy, and that transformation amplifies human kinetic energy and serves human purposes. We can drive farther than we can walk. Furthermore, all such energy transformations can be clearly described by the classical scientific disciplines.

The computer, however, is a different kind of machine. It processes not energy, but information. Of course, there is some energy involved, just as information transformation is involved in telephones and broadcast media, but except to certain kinds of engineers, the energy transformations of the computer are its least interesting features.

To understand the essential function of computers as machines we have to shake the old metaphors from our heads and begin thinking in a new way. The computer is the main artifact of the age of information. Its purpose is certainly to process information—to transform, amplify, distribute, and otherwise modify it. But more important, the computer *produces* information. The essence of the computer revolution is that the burden of producing the future knowledge of the world will be transferred from human heads to machine artifacts. Ecclesiastes to the contrary, there may be something new under the sun.

The artifacts have been misnamed, however, and this is misleading us. The word *computer*, with its overtones of counting and calculation, tells us only what the machine's historical uses have been, not its potential. Recognizing this, as we have mentioned, the Japanese are renaming the Fifth Generation of computers "knowledge information processors," or KIPS, a term that also suggests that knowledge and information are separate entities.

We've come through a transitional time when telephones and televisions straddled both the information and the energy worlds. With the very first computer generation we were thrust firmly into the new age. And now we are embarking on the next stage—the Age of Intelligent Machines.

The hot breath of cranks is on one's neck: "What do you *mean*, intelligent? These so-called intelligent machines won't be as smart as humans, will they? They can't possibly be; humans are teaching them everything they know."

"You know," Feigenbaum says to McCorduck one day, "there's no such thing as a machine that's as smart as a human."

She looks at him with surprise. Have all these programs that outperformed the experts been a fraud? Has she not heard him correctly? She makes him repeat himself, but still doesn't get it.

"Could you explain further?"

"It's easy. You start out with a task you want a machine to do. You specify it very precisely, drawing on human expertise. You use all the expertise your team of experts has, but the machine still isn't as smart as they are. But of course the moment you have the program and the knowledge all laid out in detail in front of you, you can immediately see how to make improvements. And suddenly the program has surpassed human performance. There was no moment you could put your finger on when the machine was just *as* smart *as* the human. For a while it isn't as smart, and then suddenly it is smarter."

With their methodical attention to detail, their tirelessness, their immunity to boredom, and their very high speed, all coupled now with reasoning power and information, machines are beginning to produce knowledge, often faster and better—"smarter"—than the humans who taught them.

And in all humility, we really must ask: How smart are the humans who've taught these machines? On the evolutionary time scale, thinking animals are relatively recent arrivals. Evolution hasn't had a great deal of time to work on the perfection of human cognition. The right answers to the questions "What complex of diseases is my patient suffering from?" and "What's a good experimental plan for cloning a particular gene?" and "How do I synthesize a new drug I recently discovered?" are surely just under our nose, but we can't see them. Yet at this moment, admittedly primitive expert system programs can answer those questions. In the future, harder questions will routinely be answered by smarter machines.

We humans are very good at converting sensory signals to cognitive symbols and at solving problems that require common sense. But in the face of large amounts of data we quail: we are unsystematic and forgetful, grow bored, get distracted. Writing and book technology helped us overcome some of those problems; interactive smart computers will help some more. We should give ourselves credit for having the intelligence to recognize our limitations and for inventing a technology to compensate for them.

4

Believing in AI

One participant at the Fifth Generation conference rose to make some objections to what he'd heard. They weren't serious objections, but he concluded with this: "I think that just to summarize my view, we're interested in the next generation of computers, at the moment we are thinking in terms of those computers as AI machines, and by and large I agree with you. But I didn't want to lose sight of the fact that a number of people in the audience don't believe in AI and therefore might wish to envisage the Fifth Generation computers as something different."

It was a curious turn of phrase, "don't believe in AI," as if AI were a matter of mystical faith, not susceptible to empirical proof. In fact, it alluded to a controversy that loomed very much larger than the choice of the best programming language to use, or whether the knowledge-based approach was the most fruitful way to get computers to behave intelligently, or any of the other scientific disputes that have enlivened artificial intelligence research in its quarter-century of existence. Whether the Fifth Generation would eventually be a newly designed symbolic reasoning machine or, instead, a bigger, better version of the first four generations of computers would all be resolved in the fullness of time.

What would not be resolved, at least in the minds of those who presently entertained doubts, was whether to believe in artificial intelligence. To say you don't believe in artificial intelligence—and there are a great many people who make that statement, with all manner of emphases, reasons, and choler—is to say that you don't believe a machine can be said to think, no matter what it does.

From the moment somebody first proposed that a computer might be made to behave intelligently, there had been a loud chorus of opposition. No amount of intelligent behavior on the part of computers was going to persuade the disbelievers. The very phrase "believe in" suggested dogma, doctrine, one might or might not, according to catechisms. *Moi, je suis socialiste,* says one of Stephen Daedalus's friends to him. *Je ne crois pas en l'existence de Dieu.* Myself, I'm in hardware. I don't believe in the existence of artificial intelligence.

Feigenbaum had heard this argument so often that he now had a little story he liked to tell. It concerned the great physicist Niels Bohr, who was visited by one of the young physicists of Europe. The young scientist was shocked to see nailed up over the great man's front door a horseshoe. "Professor Bohr," he said, "surely you don't believe in that old superstition!" The physicist thought for a moment, then responded cheerfully, "They say it works whether you believe in it or not."

5

Scuba Gear for the Mind

One of the objections the scientific neighbors raise to artificial intelligence is what they call the wild, perhaps even irresponsible, prophecies made by the people in the field. To be sure, prophecies were made which have not yet come true. For example, one set of predictions in 1958 said that within ten years a computer would be the world's chess champion. The ten years passed, and so, by then, had most scientists' interest in computer chess. But when twenty years had elapsed, computers were playing chess well enough to win tournaments. Nearly all the research that pushed them beyond the duffer stage had been done by the AI equivalent of garage and basement tinkerers. Chess machines, which now perform at championship levels and thus play chess better than 99 percent of us, continue to be a labor of love among a small group of workers and are not, as they were when the prediction was first made, a central test bed for discovering rules of intelligent behavior. Intellectually speaking, a good chess player is nothing more and nothing less than a good chess player. As we shall see later, this result led to an important insight about intelligence as the specialization of knowledge.

Experts in every field love to make predictions about the future. Predictions undoubtedly serve important psychological, social, and planning functions whatever their correspondence to the eventual future. And, by comparison, artificial intelligence has come a lot closer to realizing its prophecies than many other branches of science. Why, then, do so many people get upset when it comes to predictions about artificial intelligence?

The answer to that question seems clear. What's offensive about the predictions made by artificial intelligence researchers is the same thing that offends some people about the idea of artificial intelligence in the first place: the fact that it exists. Undeniably, scientists are beginning to create machines the purpose of which is to amplify human intelligence, a sort of scuba gear that will permit the human mind to go where it hasn't been able to go before—perhaps, in the opinion of some, where it should not go. The offended obviously don't see artificial intelligence as anything so liberating as scuba gear. Artificial intelligence threatens, in a deep and none too subtle way, their view of themselves. As humans we've taken our very identity from our intelligence. The notion that something else (what's worse, a creation of our own hands) might also be intelligent requires a considerable realignment of our self-image.

In a very real and immediate sense, intellectuals are experiencing what many other workers before them have undergone, the replacement of their special skills by machine. Professor Edward Fredkin of M.I.T. once provided some perspective on this issue: "Humans are okay. I'm glad to be one. I like them in general, but they're only human. It's nothing to complain about. Humans aren't the best ditch-diggers in the world, machines are. And humans can't lift as much as a crane. They can't fly at all without an airplane. And they can't carry as much as a truck. It doesn't make me feel bad. There were people whose thing in life was completely physical—John Henry and the steam hammer. Now we're up against the intellectual steam hammer. The intellectual doesn't like the idea of this machine doing it better than he does, but it's no different from the guy who was surpassed physically."[1]

There are others like Fredkin whose identities aren't the least bit threatened by the possibilities of an intelligent machine. The momentousness of such an event thrills them. That it is coming in steps, and not overnight, doesn't particularly disturb them, except for those who not only welcome it but wish it would hurry up because there is so much to know and do, and an intelligent machine would help them know and do it faster. There are also among them those who think the term *intelligence* is overburdened with pseudoscientific malarkey and could use a little empirical rigor. For them, assigning the word *intelligence* to a computer's behavior doesn't seem like any great apostasy.

And there, perhaps, lies one key to McCorduck's own tranquillity in the face of artificial intelligence. That insight didn't come at once. It began to dawn as she was comparing the arguments against thinking machines with the reasons given in the nineteenth century to explain why women could never be the intellectual equals of men. She found hilarious parallels between them. Initially, it only seemed like amusing lecture material to cite why women could never truly think—reasons of emotion, insuperable differences between women and men, no existing examples, and, yes, even ethical considerations—but by and by she began to sense that there was a larger truth waiting there. *Intelligence* was a political term, defined by whoever was in charge. This accounted for its astonishing elasticity. And for her the question—can a machine think?—became once more a nonquestion, a nonissue of no consequence.

6

About Scribes and Power

Yet a more basic question arises, which is: Does the computer really matter? The answer is yes, in both a personal and a global sense. The computer has significance for us all, but it also has significance for each of us.

For most people today, computers are like an appendix: nothing to think about until it gives us trouble. Few recite the clichés of the computerized society—how it was supposed to turn us all into ciphers (or machines or robots) —mainly because that just isn't how matters turned out. Instead, a recent Harris poll reports that 60 percent of Americans feel that the computer has improved the quality of our lives on the whole. But if computing is useful to most people, it's not necessarily lovable.

Moreover, computers are for the most part remote, abstract, intangible. It's hard to be persuaded that a computer blight of some kind would really affect our lives the way the great oil crunch of 1974 did, or the way local droughts have made us change our water use.

Actually, the removal of computing from our lives would have severe consequences. We don't readily see that, because our computer-typeset newspapers still arrive in the same shape as always on our doorsteps; our weekly newsmagazines—marvels of computer-controlled satellite technology—are still delivered by the mail carrier; we still write out personal checks; we still issue fancy engraved stock certificates to represent investments that are mere blips in a data base. In short, a scrim of commonplaces hides the revolution from our notice.[2]

And reservations of various forms continue to be expressed. There is concern about depersonalization, or about privacy, or whatever the current complaint happens to be. How much of this comes from the awkwardness of an emerging and novel technology? Are the reservations people express in truth a reflection of their puzzlement with this most untransparent of machines? Computers aren't as easy to use as they could be, even today, when the human interaction with them has improved greatly over what it once was. Computer behavior is structured in ways that seem to be different from, even alien to, human thinking patterns and human language.

As a consequence, most of us rely on intermediaries between us and the computer, called programmers. In this we are like medieval nobles or Egyptian pharaohs, who were illiterate and had to rely on scribes to send messages back and forth. The personage had no way of knowing whether his scribe was representing his thoughts authentically, catching nuances he meant to make, or even that nuances might be possible. He gave the orders and hoped they were transmitted accurately; the reverse process took place at the other end, where his cousin personage listened to the message. The opportunities for mischief were great, because the real power lay in the hands of the scribes, the select few with the knowledge of writing. To the illiterate, now and in the past, the technology of writing surely seemed weird and discomforting; perhaps they resisted it on that account alone. Yet what power, what real intellectual power, they could have had if they could have framed their own messages.

In Charles Dickens's *Bleak House*, a monument to the value of information if ever there was one, we meet Jo, an illiterate sweep, who shuffles through the streets of London utterly ignorant "as to the meaning of those mysterious symbols, so abundant over the shops and the corner of streets, and on the doors, and in the windows! To see people read, and to see people write, and to see the postman deliver letters, and not to have the least idea of all that language—to be, to every scrap of it, stone blind and dumb! It must be very puzzling . . . to think (for perhaps Jo does think, at odd times) what does it all mean, and if it means anything to anybody, how comes it that it means nothing to me?"

So it is to many in their relationship with computers. We use the word *literacy* in its widest sense, recognizing, of course, that the term has many degrees: some people can manage to read a classified ad but not a popular thriller; some people can read a business letter but not compose one; some writers of poetry and prose use language as an instrument, plucking from it compositions that stir and satisfy the human imagination at its deepest level.

So the problem of reconciling "natural" thinking patterns with the prevailing technology is hardly new. We forget how difficult it is to learn to read, and that many humans don't manage it well to this day. Perhaps if children learned even primitive present-day computing at the same time they were learning to read—and these days, a few of them do—computing wouldn't seem any stranger than reading.

Word literacy has given us power, access to an opulent, soaring world of mind—an alteration of thought processes—that is denied the illiterate. Computing literacy, even in its present form, opens still another world, one that all eventually may enter as routinely as they enter the world of letters, and it will confer perhaps even more power than the mighty pen and press have already given us. This is not idle promotion. As human muscle-power has been amplified by many special-purpose machines, so human mind-power will be amplified. The computer will change not only what we think, but how. The network adventure that follows is a modest, early example of this.

7

Redesigning Design

The intelligent computers of the Fifth Generation will not be stand-alone devices, as the industry phrase puts it. Each machine an ordinary user sees in the office or home will have substantial reasoning power, orders of magnitude over what is now possible with symbolic inference programs—the Japanese, we're reminded, expect to improve today's machine speed of ten to a hundred thousand syllogistic, or logical, inferences per second (LIPS) to 100 million to a billion LIPS.

But such awesome powers of reasoning are only a fancy form of solipsism if they have nothing to reason about. Thus the KIPS in homes and offices will be connected to central machines that contain (or have access to) rich and highly flexible knowledge bases that, in turn, connect and communicate with many other users.

We can get an inkling of how intellectually powerful that kind of rapid knowledge exchange is by considering an "escapade," as its leader calls it, in computer networking that took place in the United States in the 1970s. The leader of the escapade was Lynn Conway, an expert in the design of VLSI chips at Xerox's Palo Alto Research Center (PARC) in California. The problems she and her group faced in VLSI design were problems that anyone can understand, because in principle they arise in nearly every human endeavor. The difference lies in how Conway and her colleagues were able to solve those problems, thanks to the rapid exchange of information the computer network called the ARPANET permitted.

The goal of Conway's adventure was the custom design

of microcircuit VLSI chips. The design of these chips is a vital part of the trade wars right now, and nearly everybody grasps the general idea that the more components— wires and transistors—that can be miniaturized and integrated onto a single chip, the faster, cheaper, and more effective computing becomes. But the design of these densely integrated chips has been as much art as science.

Two approaches to their design have predominated. Those two approaches are comparable to the difference between commissioning an architect to build your dream house and hiring a contractor to build you a prefab model. The architect, of course, can give you exactly what you want, from oversize kitchen to conical-shaped bathroom, but such customization is going to cost you a great deal of money. A prefabricated house, on the other hand, costs less because it has been mass-produced and economies of scale have been introduced, but its purchaser has to make do with whatever the mass design offers and not much more.

IBM has mainly taken the mass prefabrication approach. It "wastes real estate"—space on the chip—in order to achieve simplification. For complex computing applications, however, a number of chips must be used to achieve what one custom chip could achieve, and the interconnections among chips are notorious computing trouble spots.

The Intel Corporation, on the other hand, produces custom chips. No real estate is wasted, but the cost is very high: the possibilities of chip design produce a deafening combinatorial explosion. How to cope? The individual chip manufacturers coped by developing design rules and methodologies that were specific to each manufacturer's technology and that were closely guarded as company-proprietary secrets. Most of the best minds in the nation in computer science were thereby excluded from the challenging activity of inventing generic and teachable design methodologies for VLSI, specifically design rules, and by exploration discovering new dimensions to the expertise needed for VLSI. To bring these minds into the work was an important national need.

What was the solution to this problem of the fusion of human intellectual endeavor? Traditionally, when such problems have come up we have exercised several strategies. We have, for example, adopted new and untested methods piecemeal, hoping for the best: a small group does an ad hoc thing here, a small group does another ad hoc thing there. Over many years, methods are refined. Some methods are widely accepted by the community, are standardized in building and safety codes, handbooks, tests that apprentices must pass in order to become journeymen, and finally in textbooks, where they are taught to a new generation of students. This has normally taken many years, often generations, until the textbook stage was reached.

In the case of VLSI design, however, there wasn't enough known to put into a handbook, and what knowledge there was scattered itself in a variety of human heads in many different places, different firms, different disciplines. The pressures of the trade wars wouldn't allow the usual leisurely congregation of knowledge to take place.

Lynn Conway pondered the problem, not only for VLSI design but for design in general. She observed that whenever new design methods are introduced to a design community, a large-scale effort is necessary to test and validate those new methods. An immense amount of exploration is necessary: the more explorers involved in the process, and the better thay can communicate, the faster the process runs. The problem, then, was to take new, unsound methods and turn them into sound ones.

But a second problem remained. How could you get designers to accept new methods, to change the level of abstraction at which they designed, to feel comfortable with the new methods instead? This kind of change in human attitudes was as difficult to bring about as technological change, but once again, the more designers involved, and the better they could communicate, the faster the process would go.

Was there an alternative to the traditional long and undirected process of evolving design methodologies, an alternative that would not only produce better methods but get those methods into use in the design community? Carver Mead at California Institute of Technology believed that there was, and so did his charismatic colleague Lynn Conway. Together they set out to find The Way, with Conway taking the role of Chief Missionary.

8

A Network of Minds

At Cal Tech, Carver Mead had been teaching experimental courses on microcircuit design since the early 1970s. The Mead-Conway collaboration began yielding important results during late 1976 and early 1977: they were able to formulate some simple rules for composing switches to do logic and formulate other simple concepts for estimating system performance. To these they added some examples that applied and illustrated the methods, and they put this material into the first draft (in fact, three brief chapters) of a textbook.

This preliminary draft was used by a handful of universities in the fall of 1977, revised as a result of suggestions there, and used in a larger number in the spring of 1978. With immediate feedback from each of these courses, Mead and Conway could further refine their text.

For feedback they depended heavily on the ARPANET, the great merging of computers and communications technologies that established the paradigm for modern digital network systems. The ARPANET was originally set up by the Advanced Research Projects Agency of the Department of Defense and, by now, had been embraced by the U.S. computer science research community as a major part of the social foundation of the field.[3] The network can transfer messages among many users; it can also transmit designs and other large-scale computing information. Thus Mead and Conway received messages not only from instructors who were using their proto-textbook, but also from graduate students who were its primary target. They received designs—drawings—as well as words. Moreover, in the next few months, other collaborators joined them, adding bits of expertise. By the summer of 1978, less than a year after they'd begun, they had a full text to work from.

In the fall, Lynn Conway took the material to M.I.T., where she taught an experimental course built around the text she and her collaborators had put together. "It soon became clear that things were working out very well and that some amazing projects would result from the course." Fortunately, she was able to turn those designs into real chips—their designs rapidly transmitted over the ARPANET again, so commercial manufacturers on the West Coast could fabricate the chips. "We were able to get the chips back to the students about six weeks after the end of the course. A number of the M.I.T. '78 projects worked, and we were able to uncover what had gone wrong in the design of several of those that didn't."

She was also able to uncover a few more bugs in the design process she and Mead had described in their text, find topics that needed amplification, and make other necessary changes. "You can see that the project implementation did far more than test student projects. It also tested the design methods, the draft textbook, and the course."

The textbook, along with a fully developed instructor's guide, was quickly published in 1980. Mead and Conway's *Introduction to VLSI Systems* is widely acknowledged as a classic in the field, currently in use on more than one hundred campuses.[4]

"I remember thinking: Well, okay, we've developed a text, and also a course curriculum that seems transportable. The question now is, can the course be transported to many new environments? Can it be transported without one of the principals running the course?" Conway and her colleagues conducted intensive "instructors' courses" at Xerox and videotaped them for distribution to university faculty members, and by early fall 1979 courses were ready to roll.

"We at Xerox gathered up our nerve and then announced to this group of universities: if you run courses, we will figure out some way so that at the end of your course on a specified date, we will take in any designs that you transmit to us over the ARPANET; we will implement those projects and send back wire-bonded, packaged chips for all of your projects within a month of the end of your course!"

It took nerve bordering on folly to make such an offer. The cost of designing and fabricating a prototype chip is in the $15,000 to $20,000 range, and the time involved, with luck, is three to four months. But Conway had seen the enormous value to her M.I.T. students of having their designs become realities; and pooling designs on a single chip could lower costs. With this capability for fabricating VLSI designs, it was as if a student architect would see a house he'd designed suddenly leap from the drafting board to a hillside. It taught the young designers in weeks what would have taken months, even years, to learn under ordinary circumstances.

About a dozen universities participated, and it all took on the characteristics of a great "network adventure," coordinated by Conway and her colleagues at Xerox with the support of ARPA. Students, researchers, and instructors all contributed continuously across the electronic network.

There were several small miracles as a result of the fall 1979 adventures, not the least of which were the cost and time saved in the prototyping process. By using new design methods, and the multiproject chip approach, and by using what Conway calls a fast-turnaround silicon foundry, the projects cost a few hundred dollars instead of the many thousands they normally cost, and the time involved was twenty-nine days instead of the customary three to four months.[5]

"You'll notice a common idea running through all these events," Conway says. "Fast-turnaround implementation provides a means for testing concepts and systems at many levels. It isn't just used for testing the project chips. It also tests the design environments, the courses and instructional methods, the text materials, and the design methods."

Key to it all was the network and the computers that hung off it. "It isn't like the phone, where the more people you try to contact, the more time-overhead is added so that you start spending all of your time trying to get your messages around instead of going on and doing something new." Instead, the networks get knowledge rapidly out to a large community, not only because of their technical advantages, but also because of their social advantages: any participant can broadcast a message to a large number of other people very quickly. Thus easy, quick, and radical modification is possible before things are irreversible.

Another advantage of the network is that it's relatively easy to get people to agree upon certain standardizations when they're persuaded that those standards will move information more quickly and give them access to interesting servers and services. "Such networks enable large, geographically dispersed groups of people to function as a tightly knit research and development community. New forms of competitive-collaborative practices are enabled by the networks. The network provides the opportunity for rapid accumulation of sharable knowledge."

Lynn Conway had begun by asking the question, How do *unsound methods* become *sound methods*? In this adventure she had her answer. "You'll note the experimental methods described here aren't limited to application in the exploration of microelectronic system design. I find it fascinating to think about applying these methods to the rapid exploration of other domains of engineering design that may be operating under new constraints and thus be full of new opportunities."

She stresses the human dimension of this effort: "So when you see someone interacting with a personal computer connected to a network, rather than jumping to the conclusion that you are observing a reclusive hacker running an obscure program, you might ask yourself, 'I wonder what adventures this person is involved in?' Remember, you may be observing a creatively behaving individual who is participating in, or perhaps even leading, some great adventure out in the network!"

She adds reflectively: "These events are reminiscent of the pervasive effects of the telegraph and the railroads, as they spread out everywhere during the nineteenth century, providing an infrastructure people could use to go on adventures, to go exploring, and to send back news of what they had found. I think of personal computers and the computer communication networks as a similar sort of infrastructure, but here and now, as we explore the modern frontier—the frontier of what we can create."[6]

9

"Knowledge Is an Artifact, Worthy of Design"

Lynn Conway's adventures on the ARPANET have a number of implications. One was soon seen by a colleague of hers at Xerox PARC, Mark Stefik, a Stanford-bred AI scientist who was interested in the kinds of knowledge necessary to produce expert systems. He saw that Conway and her widely dispersed fellow adventurers had *shaped* knowledge from a barely related group of ad hoc practices into systematic principles of design, universally agreed upon and adopted, which ended up producing better designs, faster and more cheaply. Now, all this might have eventually happened in the course of time, but that time would have been years, perhaps decades, under old ways of diffusing knowledge. With the computer network, it happened in two years.

Thus, Stefik reasoned, bodies of knowledge can be *engineered*—planned, produced, and put in place—for a variety of purposes, such as learnability or efficient use on the job. There is an undeniable give-and-take between what model we humans hold in our heads about some segment of the world's knowledge and the new information we can acquire about it. If we have a sufficiently powerful mental model, we can easily acquire new knowledge and reshape the model accordingly. But if our model is weak, then learning and applying new knowledge become tasks of frustration, rage, or simply confusion.

Suppose, then, that from the beginning of our encounter with a new topic we are presented with a well-engineered mental model. It's a sturdy, capacious structure, which we can grasp pretty easily to begin with and to which we can add those details that make the difference between understanding and not understanding. This kind of engineering, this planning of knowledge for the best shape, depending on the specific use humans wish to put it to, already has some prototypes. The VLSI project is only one dramatic example.

This kind of engineering is also an answer to the very legitimate complaint that most of us are overwhelmed by information; our built-in, natural capacity for about four different items we can consciously and simultaneously attend to is at the breaking point. Well-engineered knowledge will subsume the confusion of details, data points, and ever-changing information under orderly, general, and plausible interpretations that allow us to note and forget, or subcontract out to the machine, while we humans use our remaining processing power to attend to more important matters. When we learned how to tie our shoes, we had to think very hard about the steps involved. It was difficult, and at first our laces came undone with depressing frequency. Now that we've tied many shoes over our lifetime, that knowledge is "compiled," to use the computing term for it; it no longer needs our conscious attention. Managers, professionals. and nearly everyone else will find in the future that a great deal of the knowledge they now have to attend to carefully and consciously will, in the future, be "compiled" in the intelligent machine, because it has been designed to do that.

Stefik also points out that although knowledge can be engineered to meet various objectives, some of those objectives might be in conflict with each other. For example, propagation of new knowledge to a group of experts in a field, say the details of the side effects of a new drug to physicians, might be different from the same information organized so that another expert, an epidemiologist, finds it useful. Stefik and Conway put it this way: "To the knowledge engineering slogan 'Knowledge is power,' we add 'Knowledge is an artifact, worthy of design.' "[7]

Intelligence in the network adventure is human, not artificial. But we offer it to illustrate the difference that the computer can make, speeding up by orders of magnitude the exchange and evaluation of information over ordinary means. The network proved, once more, that enough quantitative difference makes a qualitative difference: decades are reduced to months; hundreds of people can contribute creatively and effectively from all over the country instead of a limited team under one roof; the results of that collaboration can be propagated quickly and usefully to everybody.

Conway's experiment also shows that even in delicate enterprises requiring the utmost creativity, the old adage that too many cooks spoil the broth simply doesn't hold. Two major obstacles have traditionally prevented a collection of cooks from making one good soup. The first is that the broth will be ruinously salted or peppered by some zealot while the others aren't looking. The second is that the broth will be too bland, the result of the committee compromise.

What prevented the first problem, the ruinous seasoning, was the technology itself. Nobody can irrevocably throw in too much salt. To put it another way, if somebody has an idea that seems worth trying, it can be tried, examined, tested, and adopted quickly and effortlessly if it's good—and abandoned quickly and effortlessly if it isn't.

What prevented the second problem, at least in this case, was a set of well-understood goals that were acceptable to all participants. But those goals had themselves been refined by the same process of massive, speedy trial-and-error.

Using only the technology of the 1970s, the network adventure demonstrates the computer's ability to change not only *what* we think, but *how*, even as traditional literacy once did. Despite the grave warnings about how the computer would inevitably dehumanize us, it has not. We are just as obstreperously human as ever, seizing this new medium to do better one of the things we've always liked to do best, which is to create, pursue, and exchange knowledge with our fellow creatures. Now we are allowed to do it with greater ease—faster, better, more engagingly, and without the prejudices that often attend face-to-face interaction.

In the kind of intelligent system envisioned by the designers of the Fifth Generation, speed and processing power will be increased dramatically; but more important, the machines will have reasoning power: they will automatically engineer vast amounts of knowledge to serve whatever purpose humans propose, from medical diagnosis to product design, from management decisions to education.

10

The Manifest Destiny of Computing

While we weren't looking, the burning question of a decade or so ago—"Can a machine think?"—turned from white heat to white ash. Part of the reason for the burnout is that artificial intelligence and the debates surrounding it showed us above all what a shaky grasp we had on the nature of thinking. We were revealed to be as sure of our convictions about intelligence as our ancestors had been about the flat earth, and in the embrace of equally specious assumptions. It began to emerge that human vanity, not human science, was the real issue.

Another part of the reason for the burnout was the performance of the programs themselves. As we shall see in the next section, when a machine is performing at the level of a well-trained and intelligent human expert, even in fairly narrow domains of expertise such as medical diagnosis, it's hard to keep denying intelligence to it. Thus, by the beginning of the 1980s, it is safe to generalize about machine intelligence this way: machines can perform very well, sometimes exceeding their human mentors, in tasks that require large amounts of specialized training, along with large amounts of symbol manipulation. They don't do well at all in situations that require rapid sensing, such as hearing or seeing, to understand the situation. And they don't do well in reasoning with what we eloquently and correctly call "common sense." Some researchers are beginning work on programs that understand naive physics ("If I step down too hard on that, it will break") and naive psychology ("If I keep getting mad at her, she's going to get mad at me"), but the work of providing common sense to computers has a long way to go because so much everyday knowledge is involved. This is one reason programs to understand natural language are so difficult to devise: language moves in a commonsense world.

AI has presented us with a paradox: all the elegantly structured symbolic artifacts that we think make us most human, such as mathematics and logic and the ability to splice genes or infer the underground geological facts from instruments, are what computers handle best, because the more highly structured knowledge is, the easier it is for us to codify it for computer use. On the other hand, getting around in the real world is not a highly structured task—the average house pet can manage it easily, but machines cannot. This is not to say that they won't ever be able to; it's a statement about affairs at the moment.

In the computer we have made for ourselves an instrument of great power. We can imbue it with intelligence. Why not? Our own history presses on us: we have ached to make such an artifact as long as we have records of human ambition. A survey of the precomputing literature on artificial intelligence, which is to say all the tales of magical creatures that take on expected (and unexpected) characteristics of their creators—the sorcerer's apprentices, Faustian homunculi, Chou dynasty robots, and Shinto *ningyo karakuri* (doll mechanisms)—compel the inescapable suspicion that something big is afoot, lurching uncertainly through human history, East and West. It persists so obstinately that McCorduck likes to think of it as a project, in the Chardinesque sense of something one unfolds toward, not in unbending lines but languidly, pausing in the byways, the grand plan apparent only in retrospect. But inevitable, for all of that. The twentieth century is the first time we have been able to realize our dream in any concrete way. The computer, even in its early, awkward, exasperating childhood, is changing our lives as we hoped, we knew, it would.

Here come the Japanese, aiming to give us computers that anyone can use, even, in principle, the illiterate, because these machines can show and tell and understand in voice and pictures. They'll be computers that do a lot more than count: they'll reason, guess, understand, and behave intelligently. It happens to be the Japanese who have announced something called the Fifth Generation. But the central idea of the Fifth Generation is not specifically Japanese; on the contrary, it's specifically human. It might have come from any number of sources. Who first brings it to us is, in the long run, beside the point. (In the short run, who has it first is a matter of significant economic consequence.) For our children's children, intelligent machines will be a fact of life as books and television are facts of ours.

Feigenbaum likes to see all this as a sort of manifest destiny of computing. The manifest destiny of the American nation was perceived early. Though they represented only thirteen states on the eastern seaboard, the framers of the U.S. Constitution debated what role the western states would eventually play and how the constitution they were then drafting could be drawn up to accommodate them properly in the future. Just so, the manifest destiny of computing was also perceived early. Even when *how* to do it was beyond the technology, the farsighted believed it would be done and hacked away at it, giving computer science some of its most potent tools in the process.

The Japanese have their own way of phrasing the same idea. In the words of Kazuhiro Fuchi, director of ICOT and visionary behind the Fifth Generation effort, "The route to knowledge information processing represents a practical philosophy and an inevitable direction for development of information processing technology. The question is . . . whether to stand still or proceed, as there are no other paths to choose from."[8]

III

EXPERTS IN SILICON

1

Expert Systems and Knowledge Engineering

To answer in some detail the question of just what the Japanese plan to do, it is important to understand something at the heart of the Fifth Generation, the applied side of artificial intelligence called knowledge-based systems. What knowledge-based systems are, how they came about, and how they are still under development are the themes of the next few sections.

In some sense, all artificial intelligence is applied, because unless experimental results confirm theory, unless a program exhibits the intelligent behavior it is meant to exhibit, the theory loses credibility. But knowledge-based systems have a particularly strong flavor of the applied, because they are characterized by large amounts of specific knowledge. A speech-understanding system, for example, not only will know what the subject matter under discussion is (and various facts about it), but will also have semantic, syntactic, lexical, phonemic, phonetic, and pragmatic knowledge about the language the speech is being spoken in and the discourse, will know things about the vocal habits of the specific speaker it is listening to, and so on.

We have already remarked that a shift took place in AI research over the past two decades. It was a shift from a search for broad, general laws of thinking toward an appreciation of specific knowledge—facts, experiential knowledge, and how to use knowledge—as the central issue in intelligent behavior. This shift came not as a consequence of irrefutable arguments that immediately persuaded all researchers by their cogency and correctness. Rather, the shift came about because demonstration projects that used large amounts of specific knowledge simply worked.

The project that began AI's shift to the knowledge-based viewpoint was DENDRAL, an expert system that was able to infer chemical structure from data available to physical chemists. The effort began in 1965, shortly after Feigenbaum's move to Stanford University. There he met a kindred scientific soul, Joshua Lederberg, professor of genetics and Nobel laureate, who had long been fascinated by the possible uses of computers to model and to assist scientific thinking. Together they began to write the reasoning programs that could infer molecular hypotheses from chemical data.

They saw immediately that the programs could not perform in an effective, practical, expert manner without considerable knowledge of physical chemistry. So Lederberg recruited the talents and expertise of another scientific visionary, Carl Djerassi—well known as a physical chemist, but even better known as "father of the birth control pill"—from the Stanford chemistry department. The interdisciplinary team from computer science, genetics, and chemistry labored for years to produce an expert system so knowledgeable and effective that its ability to explicate the details of molecular structure from chemical data now exceeds human capability, including that of its designers. DENDRAL has been in use for many years at university and industrial chemical labs around the world.

Despite its obvious power and utility, DENDRAL did not meet with immediate universal acclaim. McCorduck remembers hearing Feigenbaum lecture in the early 1970s at Carnegie-Mellon, where he was talking about DENDRAL and, more important, talking about the usefulness of the knowledge-based approach to artificial intelligence.

Feigenbaum's lecture was an interesting occasion for many reasons. He had done his graduate work at Carnegie, and his thesis advisor and spiritual father, Herbert Simon, whom he deeply admired, was in the audience. (In the mid-1960s, he'd once written a warm letter to Simon saying that if there were such a thing as a Nobel Prize in computer science, Herb Simon should be the first to receive it. As it happened, Simon had to make do with a Nobel Prize in economics in 1978.) Beside Simon was Allen Newell, another artificial intelligence great, and scattered about the room were some of the best and brightest in computer science in general and artificial intelligence in particular. But the Carnegie mood was skeptical, if not atheistic, when it came to the idea of knowledge-based expert systems. If artificial intelligence were to become a science, it ought to have discoverable grand and universal laws, like physics and chemistry.

Feigenbaum talked about DENDRAL and then threw out a challenge. "You people are working on toy problems," he said. "Chess and logic are toy problems. If you solve them, you'll have solved a toy problem. And that's all you'll have done. Get out into the real world and solve real-world problems."

Now, AI workers had not chosen simplified—or "toy"— problems just to be perverse. It is sound science strategy to choose a simplified problem and explore it in depth to grasp principles and mechanisms that are otherwise obscured by details that don't really matter. But Feigenbaum was arguing to the contrary, that here *the details not only mattered; they made all the difference.*

There were murmurings among the graduate students. Maybe Feigenbaum was right. Maybe if you built a smart chess machine, all you had in the end was . . . well, a smart chess machine. And not immediately, but later, Carnegie-Mellon came around, and a group of Carnegie researchers built remarkable knowledge-based systems, HEARSAY and HARPY, to understand continuous human speech. The vocabulary was limited, and the systems moved less than gracefully between one speaker and another, but in their limited way they worked. Much more important, they provided some useful ideas about how knowledge might be arranged and used and improved upon. There would be more such systems to come from Carnegie-Mellon scientists.

The modeling of mind by mechanism—artificial intelligence and its sibling, cognitive science—has traveled many paths and a great distance in its first quarter-century. The paths have converged on the central thesis that understanding, problem solving, all the other functions of intelligence, even learning, are all crucially dependent upon knowledge. One must know first to be able to understand later. One must even know first to be able to know more later.

2

The Domains of the Experts

Knowledge-based systems, to labor the obvious, contain large amounts of varied knowledge which they bring to bear on a given task. Expert systems are a species of knowledge-based systems, though the two terms are often used interchangeably.

Just what is an expert system? It is a computer program that has built into it the knowledge and capability that will allow it to operate at the expert's level. Expert performance means, for example, the level of performance of M.D.s doing diagnosis and therapeutics, or Ph.D.s or very experienced people doing engineering, scientific, or managerial tasks. The expert system is a high-level intellectual support for the human expert, which explains its other name, *intelligent assistant*.

Expert systems are usually built to be able to explain the lines of reasoning that led to their decisions. Some of them can even explain why they rejected certain paths of reasoning and chose others. This transparency is a major feature of expert systems. Designers work hard to achieve it because they understand that the ultimate use of an expert system will depend upon its credibility to its users, and the credibility will arise because the behavior is transparent, explainable.

The dual usage, "knowledge-based systems" and "expert systems," violates the precision some scientists favor. In brief, a system that can understand images, or understand speech, may rely on a large knowledge base to achieve its perceptions, but it doesn't call on any special human expertise to do it. Normal human beings are born with eyes, ears, and the equipment behind them to process the signals those organs receive, and they quickly acquire the knowledge needed to understand the signals. But normal humans are not born knowing, and do not quickly learn how to manage a large construction project or diagnose a disease; that takes expertise, learned over a long period. Other scientists find this distinction pedantic, and a little linguistic chauvinism has even emerged. The term "knowledge engineering" finds great favor with the Japanese, because engineers have high status in Japan, but engineers don't enjoy any such glory in the United Kingdom, which favors "expert systems" instead. So it goes.

Expert systems operate particularly well where the thinking is mostly reasoning, not calculating—and that means most of the world's work. Even though a lot of professional work seems to be expressed in mathematical formulas, the fact is that, except in mathematically based sciences, the difficult choices, the matters that set experts apart from beginners, are symbolic, inferential, and rooted in experiential knowledge. Human experts have acquired their expertise not only from explicit knowledge found in textbooks and lectures, but also from experience: by doing things again and again, failing, succeeding, wasting time and effort, then learning to save them, getting a feel for a problem, learning when to go by the book and when to break the rules. They therefore build up a repertory of working rules of thumb, or "heuristics," that, combined with book knowledge, make them expert practitioners.

We shall describe in more detail what expert systems look like and how they are designed—or engineered. But first, to demonstrate the usefulness of expert systems, we'll survey the range of fields where they have been applied already.

Perhaps the largest single group of expert systems is centered in medicine. The most knowledge-intensive expert system in existence is the INTERNIST/CADUCEUS system at the University of Pittsburgh, the creation of a physician, Jack Meyers, and a computer scientist, Harry Pople. INTERNIST/CADUCEUS (known informally as "Jack in the box") does diagnoses in internal medicine at a level of expertise that allows it to solve most of the CPCs, or clinical pathological conferences, that appear in the *New England Journal of Medicine* and constitute a kind of test-your-wits quiz for doctors. By now, INTERNIST/-CADUCEUS covers more than 80 percent of all internal medicine; its knowledge base encompasses about 500 diseases and more than 3,500 manifestations of disease. It will soon undergo formal clinical trials.

Although INTERNIST/CADUCEUS was designed to aid skilled internists in complicated medical problems, the program will probably have a future life as a diagnostic aid to physicians' assistants and in rural health clinics, in military medicine, and in space travel.

At Stanford University, several medical expert systems have been designed. MYCIN diagnoses blood and meningitis infections, then advises the physician on antibiotic therapies for treating the infections. Like every other expert system, MYCIN acts as a consultant, having a conversation with its user, the physician. The physician supplies the patient history and laboratory results—external data the computer couldn't possibly infer—and then the program begins to reason about possible diagnoses. If the physician is uncertain why the program has arrived at a given diagnosis, or why certain drugs have been suggested as therapy, he can ask the program for its line of reasoning. For example, the physician might ask: "Why are you asking me this?" or "How did you reach this conclusion?" MYCIN can even tell the physician why it rejected certain lines of reasoning. In evaluations of MYCIN's skills at diagnosis and therapy, MYCIN was judged to perform at the level of human specialists in infectious diseases and above (sometimes far above) the level of other nonspecialist physicians. Another medical diagnosis program has been constructed by using the inference procedure of MYCIN and substituting a different knowledge base, this time for pulmonary diseases. It is used routinely at Pacific Medical Center in San Francisco.

A ventilator is a piece of medical equipment that assists a critically ill patient with breathing. Another expert system developed at the Pacific Medical Center called the Ventilator Management Assistant (VM) provides real-time advice to clinicians about patients undergoing mechanical ventilation. VM provides a summary of the patient's status, easily understood by the clinician; recognizes unusual events

in the patient/machine system and provides suggestions
for corrective action; gives advice on adjustment of the
mechanical ventilator based on an assessment of the patient's
status and therapeutic goals; and maintains a set of expectations and goals for each patient. VM works with multiple
streams of data that are sent by the monitoring system
over a period of time. Before VM, the integration of data
from monitoring devices was done by human caretakers.
Interpreting the data was time-consuming and error-prone,
and it only provided limited information on the patient's
condition over time. VM maintains an ongoing, moment-
to-moment perspective so that it can make analyses based
on both past and current circumstances.

Still other expert systems in medicine exist for digitalis
dosing, glaucoma diagnosis and treatment, renal disease,
arthritis and rheumatism, fetal illnesses, and even the development of new drugs.

In biology, an expert system called MOLGEN, for
Molecular Genetics, gives advice on gene cloning in genetic engineering and helps molecular biologists analyze
DNA sequence data. MOLGEN will take a statement of
the goal of a gene cloning experiment from a genetic
engineer and produce one or more plausible experiment
plans for achieving that particular cloning—advising on
the details of the necessary but intricate steps that must be
performed in the lab to achieve the cloning. MOLGEN's
extensive knowledge base can also be queried as an
"intelligent encyclopedia" of modern molecular biology.
MOLGEN, too, like DENDRAL, has a big community of
users in university and industrial molecular biology and
genetic engineering laboratories.

Knowledge-based approaches to speech and image understanding by computer have been under way for some
time. Understanding of continuous speech (as opposed to
mere recognition of individual words) started at Carnegie-
Mellon and other places in the 1970s and began to be
successful when designers were able to add context—
knowledge of the topic in addition to knowledge of speech
and linguistic acts—to the process of understanding. Speech
understanding is a special case of a more general problem
called signal understanding. Signals can come from any
instrument, not just a microphone or a TV camera.

A defense-related application of expert systems in signal
interpretation, whose essentials are no longer classified, is

HASP/SIAP, a passive sonar surveillance system designed to interpret ocean sounds in very noisy circumstances. To do this by conventional computing methods using statistical techniques would require expensive supercomputers, and even then it is questionable whether the problem is tractable. It made no sense to spend the computing time of a supercomputer, doing cross-correlations and autocorrelations of signals in a massive amount of sonar data, when, in fact, most of the information needed for the correct interpretation wasn't present in that signal, but was to be found in the knowledge surrounding the situation. What knowledge? The hefty intelligence manuals on a shelf, information from spies, what the neighboring station saw yesterday, what's normal, the fact that it's winter and not summer, what the newspapers said about merchant shipping traffic, and so forth. Reasoning with all that knowledge is much more important than trying to dig a little bit of signal out of a lot of noise.

In tests performed by defense scientists, the HASP/SIAP program performed at levels equal to and sometimes exceeding human performance. The designers estimated that "doing it smart," reasoning from knowledge, required a hundred to a thousand times less computing. That translates into a big saving in defense dollars. Similar savings by "doing it smart" were evident in the DENDRAL project. Because the DENDRAL program knew so much about chemistry and the methods of mass spectrometry, and because it was so systematic in its reasoning, it could solve chemical structure problems using low-resolution spectral data that chemists could solve handily at that time only by using high-resolution instruments. Inexpensive low-resolution instrumentation plus knowledge-based reasoning equaled the performance of expensive high-resolution instruments.

3

Expert Systems in the Marketplace

As might now be obvious, expert systems lend themselves especially well to the two generic kinds of problems. First are the combinatorial problems, where straightforward ("unintelligent") methods of enumeration lead to explosive (and unmanageable) numbers of possibilities. One illustration of this is in chess, where it was a long-held popular fallacy that computers played chess by exploring every possible move. But a chess game has 10^{120} possible moves; the fastest computer operating today could not explore them all in the time that remains before the burnout of our sun!

Combinatorial explosions appear ubiquitously, but the human mind deals with them efficiently by at once eliminating from attention most of the possibilities that are unlikely to prove fruitful. Humans focus on likely possibilities by using knowledge that describes in various ways what's being searched for. Moreover, we use handy rules of thumb (called heuristics) that usually bring us close to a solution but don't guarantee it. For instance, if your pet dog is lost, chances are you'll first comb the immediate neighborhood, then eventually call the local pound, and finally place a classified ad in the newspaper. But if you live in San Francisco, you won't also call the Los Angeles County Animal Shelter, or the Reno one, or even the London R.S.P.C.A., though there is an ever-so-slight statistical probability that your dog has wandered far across the globe (shipped by mistake, let's say).

The second kind of problem expert systems handle well is the interpreting of large amounts of signal data, as in the cases of HASP, VM, DENDRAL, and several other knowl-edge-based systems now operational.

As it happens, both kinds of problems come up in many business applications, and thus it is that expert systems are finding ready acceptance by people whose eye is on the bottom line. One of the first lessons in college economics is the esoteric platitude called the Law of Comparative Economic Advantage. A simple form of the law is that machines will replace people where machines can do the work more cheaply. To find the points of penetration, then, look for relatively cheap "machine power" and rela-tively expensive people. Cheap computer power has ar-rived (the microelectronics firms literally print computer programs on chips, like pages of a book). And the most expensive people in our society are the experts. They are expensive because the "value added" by their work is high, and because they are scarce (it takes years of education, training, and experience to make one). The Law of Com-parative Economic Advantage alerts us to the potential economic impact of expert systems, reminds us to look carefully at the value added to human endeavor by the use of the system, and guides our thinking to those places of high economic leverage where the addition of cheap intellectual assistance offers large economic advantage.

Firms that have been early adopters of the expert sys-tems technology have scanned their work for such points of penetration. They seem to share the view expressed by one company president: "It's like walking into a field of gold nuggets just lying on the ground. You can reach down and just pick them up. You don't even have to dig for them. The only problem you face is making sure that you pick up a big one!" Shortly, we will look at the shape and size of some of these nuggets.

Knowledge technology is kin to software technology and in many ways is software's most highly evolved form. Soft-ware has excited venture capitalists as few emerging indus-tries have ever done. The reason is simple: the ratio of earnings to invested capital for the typical viable firm in the industry. Earnings, the numerator, have been good, often excellent, rarely huge. But the denominator, in-vested capital to generate those earnings, is remarkably small. Software is not produced in a factory with platoons of workers and major capital expenditures for the manu-facturing. Software is produced in small, modestly fur-

nished offices by bright individuals working usually in
small teams at the terminals of a medium-size computer or
at computer work stations of modest cost. "Production" of
the developed product amounts to copying (at computer
speeds!) tapes or diskettes. Because the investment needed
is small, the ratio can be attractively large—in the extreme,
approaching infinite for the fabled garage-shop software
houses that sell their products through computer magazines and Computerland stores. Computers can do nothing without their software, and good software is difficult
to write. Value added to a customer installation is therefore
high, guaranteeing reasonable earnings for products whose
sales are well managed.

Expert systems have economic value in several different
ways that have been identified, some obvious and some
subtle. Let's look at a few typical business problems and
how expert systems can have made a difference on the
bottom line of millions of dollars.

Case Study 1
Capturing, Replicating, and Distributing Expertise

The problem: "We see a major new business opportunity.
We have expertise to exploit it, but not nearly enough. If
we use our experts to train others, we will be too late. It
takes years of training and experience to make one of our
experts because the knowledge that makes our experts
good is not so well understood and codified that it can be
taught directly."

Schlumberger Ltd. is the world leader in the lucrative
business of making physical measurements of the rocks,
oil, and gas in newly drilled oil wells. They have announced that they see a major business opportunity in
making additional interpretations for their oil company
customers of the measurements and tests that they currently perform. They now operate dozens of field interpretation centers that offer this service, each of which
most be staffed by interpretation specialists. Their knowledge engineering groups in the United States and France
have produced expert systems for the analysis of geologic
dip and the analysis of lithology, and more are planned.
Schlumberger chairman Jean Riboud has said that their
entry into artificial intelligence work is as important to
their business as the surge in oil exploration and will

"change the order of magnitude" of their business. That change represents a great deal of economic value, since Schlumberger's wire-line service business has gross revenues of $2 billion per year.

One of Schlumberger's competitors sees a quality assurance problem. Oil well measurements are expensive, and customers demand that they be top quality. Making those measurements is a tricky technological affair. Making them right demands engineering expertise at the oil well site and sustained vigilance and diligence, day and night. Customer refunds for incorrect measurements are a constant and big financial headache—in this case a $40-million-per-year headache. The cure is not a "heightened awareness" program to improve vigilance and diligence, but an expert system to take over the difficult and tedious work of the (not so expert) people currently doing the job.

The French national oil company, Elf Aquitaine, contracts its oil well drilling to drilling firms. But if the drilling firm encounters drilling problems deep in a new hole, Elf likes to have its own drilling experts at the well site because errors made in coping with problems can be extremely costly in both money and time. Occasionally holes that have cost $1 or $2 million to drill must be abandoned or redirected because of serious mistakes made in recovery from drilling problems. Elf's experts are constantly on airplanes, flying to remote drilling sites; the rigs and crews sitting idle as they wait for the experts' arrival, are themselves costing $100,000 a day or more. An expert system called the Drilling Advisor, done for Elf under contract by Teknowledge, Inc., with the help of an Elf drilling specialist, diagnoses a variety of drilling problems and offers recommendations for corrective action as well as recommendations for preventing further problems of the type encountered. The economic leverage in this domain is high. Elf speculates that it may be able to "pay back" the research and development costs of the expert system in its first successful field use!

Our world is one that is increasingly more populated by machines of every variety and description. As we all know, machines break. We are often more than discomfited when they do; we are paralyzed. Our population of machines is increasing faster than the population of repair specialists. And the repair specialists cannot keep up with the changes in technology that are being incorporated into the machines.

One of the most important business applications of expert systems is helping the people who repair machines. IBM's Field Engineering Division has supported the development of expert systems for diagnosing and repairing computer systems; General Electric is doing the same for locomotives. The need rises above the concerns of economic benefit to concerns of national security, in the view of the U.S. armed services. They have high turnover in specialties such as equipment repair, hence little time for personnel to gain the experience required; and an alarming gap is developing between the "low-tech" education their recruits have received and the "high-tech" nature of the modern military equipment they will have to repair. Thus the armed services are looking at expert systems to assist very inexpert recruits.

Case Study 2
Fusing the Knowledge of Many Experts

The problem: "There is no one specialist whose expertise spans the whole problem. It can only be solved by the interaction of several specialists and the intelligent fusion of their separate expertise."

Hitachi is developing two systems for knowledge fusion. In one, the problem is the diagnosis of manufacturing problems in the fabrication of integrated circuit chips. The manufacturing of microelectronic chips involves the smallest tolerances ever achieved by mankind in routine manufacturing. Because of the near perfection needed, many of the chips produced are faulty. The percentage yield of good chips is critical to profitability. Defects in chips must be routinely analyzed. If yield begins to drop in a systematic pattern, the various scientific, engineering, and manufacturing experts must pool their analyses as quickly as possible to diagnose the source of the problem and take remedial action. This may sometimes take days or weeks, often while expensive equipment lies idle. The rapid fusion of expert analysis and judgments available with an expert system is seen to have high economic leverage. Even modest improvements would be worth millions of dollars per year.

Hitachi also does major construction jobs, the planning and management of which require many different engineering, design, and construction specialists to interact and fuse their plans, as well as judgments of potential problems and possible risks. For this task, Hitachi is developing an expert system called a Project Risk Assessment System. The system does a job similar to a "PERT chart" analysis but allows the use of symbolic knowledge and qualitative judgments of performance and risk.

Case Study 3
Managing Complex Problems and Amplifying Expertise

The problem: "Our problems involve so many combinations and possibilities to construct and explore, and therefore our people miss things, or get them wrong. Our experts are good, but not good enough. Computers should be able to solve the problems better."

Not always, but sometimes, expert systems can manage the intrinsic complexity of problems better than human experts. This is especially true of problems that are combinatorial, involving a great deal of trial-and-error, "trying out" combinations of problem elements systematically. Problems of design and configuration are examples, as are problems of data analysis, hypothesis formation, and diagnosis.

Digital Equipment Corporation manufactures computers that are almost always customized to some degree to conform to specific customer needs. Configuring each machine to be manufactured is therefore a somewhat new problem. Large numbers of computer modules need to be put together subject to large numbers of constraints and conditions. DEC engineers use a configuration expert system to plan the manufacture of their VAX computers. The system is reported to plan correctly in more than 99 percent of the cases, achieving a record better than the manufacturing specialists (to their delight). Savings accrue not only because the solutions are fast and inexpensive, but also because costly mistakes are avoided more frequently. Often a mistake is introduced at the time of customer order. It is important to catch the mistake at order time rather than at the time of manufacture, since the company may have to bear the expense of "making good" on an order once it is accepted, regardless of errors. So DEC is extending the expert system for use by the sales force. The aggregate savings to DEC from the configuration expert systems will be millions of dollars per year.

The genetic information carried by DNA is symbolized as a sequence of the letters A, C, G, and T. Modern molecular genetics has powerful methods for determining the sequences of animal and plant DNA, and the sequences are piling up by the thousands in big data banks. But to determine what is "interesting" in various ways about the sequences (within one sequence or across several) is a tedious, difficult, error-prone process that even the best human experts cannot do easily or particularly well. Intelli-Corp, a small firm, saw this need and filled it with a variety of programs that assist biologists and genetic engineers in sequence analysis and interpreting experimental results. The programs add value not only because they save time of the scarce expertise in the new and exploding field of genetic engineering, but also because they outperform human experts in doing the work thoroughly and correctly. The reward to IntelliGenetics is early gross revenues of $1 million per year, with much more in the offing as its "customer industry," genetic engineering, matures.

An American industrial giant whose name is a household word in the United States recently began its first expert systems project. The task was to diagnose failures in steam-driven electric power generating plants based on chemical measurements taken in the steam effluent of the plant. Tests of an early version of the expert system (a version far from complete) were done using data from an actual plant failure and closure in 1981. The expert system reasoned its way to a correct diagnosis of the difficulty (that is, the actual problem that had caused the plant closure) in seconds. That in itself was not remarkable because the diagnosis was not extraordinarily complex. What was remarkable, though, was the fact that human experts operating the plant had failed to discover the correct diagnostic line of reasoning for a few days. The plant had actually been shut down for four days, at a cost to the company of $1.2 million, almost all of which could have been saved if the expert system had been in place.

Case Study 4
Managing Knowledge

The problem: "The problem we face is that excellent performance in our field requires *knowing so much*. The knowledge we use seems to change so often—it's hard to keep current. And there are so many aspects, exceptions, and subspecialties to be aware of. Solving any one problem is not so hard if we only had the requisite knowledge and could use it systematically."

Let's look again at the kind of industrial firm that has engineers designing complex systems, manufacturing operations building them, and salespeople selling them. Another one of those American industrial giants whose name is a household word manufactures business equipment. It specializes in systems of linked components of many different types, automating the information flow within the plants and offices of its customers which are other large firms. Because the pace of technological development in the office and factory automation field is swift, available components are constantly changing, along with the intercommunication technology, the software, and other aspects of modern business systems. New types of components become available. Prices change often as new technology drives down costs. The sales force cannot cope as the ground keeps shifting beneath them. They make errors of commission and errors of omission. For example, they write orders for systems that cannot be built; or, out of ignorance, they bid a system with a lower capability or a higher price than was necessary and lose the bid to a smarter firm.

The "business as usual" sales information and periodic sales meetings do not provide enough detailed information for the sales force to cope. If this problem were somehow magically fixed, they might not be able to cope because of the inundation. Since "business as usual" isn't working, the company is experimenting with expert systems for assistance to the sales force and order entry checking. They estimate that 25 percent of orders currently taken are in error (a European firm with a similar problem states that 100 percent of its orders are written with error). The company did a quick and approximate estimate of the value of a well-developed expert system for their task. They estimated a possible cost saving of up to $100 million per year. The period for "paying back" the R&D costs could be as short as a few weeks.

Knowledge engineers at SRI International, working with scientists of the U.S. Geological Survey, built an expert system PROSPECTOR for advising during the process of field exploration for minerals—a field geologist's intelligent assistant. The program was knowledgeable about geology and mineralogy in general, but also was given specific knowledge about particular regions, such as the Mississippi River basin and the major mountain ranges of the United States. In 1982 the expert system was used by a company exploring for and mining molybdenum in the Cascades (State of Washington), and a find was made, the value of which has been variously estimated at several million to $100 million. The find was not one that the company experts had themselves conjectured; the company is reported to have been dumping tailings from a nearby dig on the site of the deposit!

Case Study 5
Gaining a Competitive Edge

The problem: "The techniques we use are well known throughout our industry and used by all. Our market share is small and stable. To bump it up, we need some new idea that will improve performance. Even a small improvement will be significant since it will help to distinguish us from the pack."

A major instrument manufacturer makes electrocardiographic (ECG) instruments. The ECG machine not only records the ECG but analyzes it for the physician. Computer analysis of ECG was developed in the 1960s. By the late 1970s the techniques had been widely diffused in the medical instruments industry, and performance had reached a stable rate of correct analysis judgments of about 75 percent. University and industrial research has failed to change this percentage. Something more than the well-known statistical and pattern recognition methods is needed. The company's market share has been steady at 5 percent. Based on marketing studies, the company believes that if it can increase the percentage of correct analysis judgments from 75 percent to 85 percent, it can increase its market share to 30 percent. The increased sales of these instruments will, they believe, be worth a few million dollars per year in earnings. With this in mind, they have decided to bet on the expert systems approach and have started such a project. If successful, the payback period for the R&D will be much less than a year.

*   *   *

But there are more offbeat problems that lend themselves to the expert systems approach. When Feigenbaum and some other Stanford colleagues founded Teknowledge, Inc., a knowledge engineering firm in Palo Alto, and the word got out that they would custom-design expert systems, fascinating industrial problems poured through the door.

For example, a specialty metal alloys company in the Midwest presented the problem of loss of human resources—all their experts were fifty to sixty years of age and were getting ready to retire; was there a way of capturing their expertise in a knowledge base before they disappeared? The same problem, a "corporate memory," came up in another firm, which has a successful business in manufacturing custom-designed instruments. Over the years, an enormous amount of expertise has been built up, but it's almost all in human heads, not in documents. Unfortunately, people die, retire, and forget. Why not a knowledge base that stores the collective corporate expertise, and an expert system that watches over the shoulders of designers and reminds them about what their predecessors already know?

The power of the expert systems comes from the knowledge they contain. That knowledge is, at present, stored in the heads of human experts, and getting it out—what AI researchers call the knowledge acquisition problem—is the biggest bottleneck that the knowledge engineers currently face. Expert systems are now proven performers. But knowledge acquisition is the great research problem that AI laboratories must face and solve in the coming decade.

4

Anatomy of an Expert System

Here we explore expert systems in a bit of technical detail. Readers who wish may skip to the next section on p. 86.

Are there generalizations we can make about the nature and structure of expert systems? Indeed there are. By the late 1970s, expert systems, and the knowledge engineering necessary to construct them, had developed some broad common characteristics.

Basic Structure of an Expert System

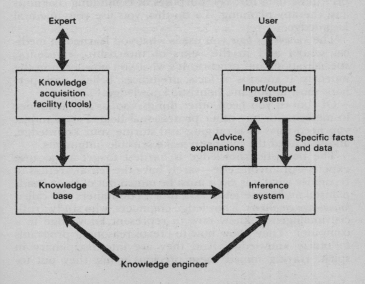

Knowledge is the key factor in the performance of an expert system. That knowledge is of two types. The first type is the *facts* of the domain—the widely shared knowledge, commonly agreed among practitioners, that is written in textbooks and journals of the field, or that forms the basis of a professor's lectures in a classroom. Equally important to the practice of a field is the second type of knowledge called *heuristic knowledge,* which is the knowledge of good practice and good judgment in a field. It is experiential knowledge, the "art of good guessing" that a human expert acquires over years of work.

For an expert system to solve a problem at a high level of expertise—comparable to an M.D., a Ph.D., or a longtime practitioner in a given field—the program must have both kinds of knowledge in its knowledge base. *Knowledge bases* are not the same as the data base we often hear about. The difference between the two can best be illustrated by analogy.

Suppose you are a physician approaching the bed of your patient. You pick up the patient's chart.

Your *data base* is that patient's record, including patient history, measurements of vital signs, drugs given, response to drugs, and so on. It's today's problem. You must interpret these data for, say, purposes of continuing diagnosis and therapy planning. To do this, you use your medical knowledge.

The *knowledge base* you use is what you learned in medical school and in the years of internship, residency, specialization, and practice. It's what you now learn in the journals. It consists of facts, prejudices, beliefs, and, perhaps most important, heuristic knowledge.

Of course, you need other things, too, as a practitioner in medicine or any other professional field. For example, you need ways of arranging and storing your knowledge, and you need the means to make sensible judgments.

The heuristic knowledge is hardest to get at because experts—or anyone else—rarely have the self-awareness to recognize what it is. So it must be mined out of their heads painstakingly, one jewel at a time. The miners are called *knowledge engineers.* Knowledge engineers, who study artificial intelligence, know how to represent knowledge in a computer. They know how to create reasoning programs to utilize knowledge. And they are interdisciplinary in spirit. Having mined these precious gems, they put together knowledge bases that form the most important part of expert systems.

In addition to knowledge, an expert system needs an *inference procedure*, a method of reasoning used to understand and act upon the combination of knowledge and problem data. The inference procedures, or problem-solving methods, used by knowledge engineers do not need to be arcane or complex. Even simple methods, used in commonsense reasoning or taught in first courses in logic, are adequate. In fact, there is a virtue in employing simple inference procedures since they are easily understood by end-users, the people being assisted by the expert systems, when these users are reviewing the system's line of reasoning. End-users will not come to trust the reasoning of an expert system, and therefore will not use it, unless they can easily understand what it is doing.

For example, one simple form of reasoning that is commonly used is *goal-directed backward chaining*, the common mental strategy of "working backward" from a desired goal to what you know about achieving it at your starting point. Suppose the goal is, for example, to drive from San Francisco to New York City. Goal-directed backward chaining would look something like this: first you would picture yourself at your destination, parking your car on Riverside Drive in Manhattan. Your picture would suggest whether it's daytime or evening, and from that cue you would consider the time of day you want to arrive. As an experienced New York City driver, you know you want to arrive toward evening, because parking is easier then. Thus you calculate backward, knowing about how much time you want to drive the last day (not too much; there'll be a big party the first night you're in New York and you want to be bright for it). So you decide you should spend your last night on the road in Harrisburg or Pittsburgh. Pittsburgh is more attractive because you have so many friends there; but on the other hand, you'll have to leave time for visiting with them, so you don't want to drive too far the next-to-last day either. Thus *that* previous night, you should stay outside Indianapolis. And so it goes, all the way back to your starting point in San Francisco. You have data and goals, and you use inference procedures to make that knowledge work toward your goals.

AI researchers have identified, dissected, and then replicated many such procedures that human beings use all the time, and knowledge engineers, who build expert systems, are skilled at choosing the right set of inference procedures for the type of program they are writing.

An expert system also requires methods of representing the *knowledge* it is to contain. This is a technical issue and a matter of some professional dispute, but essentially it means that both a logical structure and a set of appropriate data structures are necessary, through which the special knowledge in the knowledge base (arriving on Riverside Drive in the early evening, friendly places to stay in Pittsburgh) can find its way into the memory of a computer.

There is also a formidable problem of knowledge-base management, analogous to data-base management. How shall knowledge be organized, controlled, propagated, as well as updated in terms of its features and properties and their relationships with each other in a knowledge base? These and other tasks need to be done automatically within the system; the end-user can't be burdened with any of that.

Knowledge-base management systems and systems for inference have been accumulated into software packages, frameworks that allow researchers to move into other areas of expertise and build entirely new expert systems in much less time than it would take to do from scratch. By "much less," we mean that time can be reduced by an order of magnitude: what took fifty man-years can now be built in five. Thus the MYCIN system was dismantled, so to speak, its knowledge base replaced with a new knowledge base, and it became PUFF, the pulmonary disease expert, and SACON, the structural analysis expert in engineering. The kernel of them all is the software package EMYCIN (for Essential MYCIN), which contains the knowledge-base management system and inference procedures necessary for these types of problem solving.

In sum, scientific issues central to artificial intelligence underlie knowledge engineering and can be enumerated as the parts of an expert system. First is the problem of *knowledge representation*. How shall the knowledge of a domain of work be represented as data structures in the memory of the computer in a manner in which they can be conveniently accessed for problem solving?

Second is the problem of *knowledge utilization*. How can this knowledge be used in problem solving? In other words, how should the inference engine be designed?

Third, and most important, is the question of *knowledge acquisition*. How is it possible to acquire the knowledge so important for problem solving automatically, or at least semiautomatically, in a way in which the computer eases the transfer of expertise from humans (practitioners or their texts or their data) to the symbolic data structures that constitute the knowledge representation in the machine? Knowledge acquisition is a long-standing problem of AI. Like "intelligence," learning has proven to be a catchall term that's too vague to be useful in creating intelligent computer programs. It served no better purpose to ask whether a machine really could be said to "learn" than to ask whether a machine really could be said to "think," even when it improved its behavior by experience (as one of the earliest programs in artificial intelligence had done, a program that eventually played championship checkers).

Now we are able to be more precise about the problem of machine learning, and with this increased precision has come a new term, *knowledge acquisition research*.

This is the most important of the central problems of artificial intelligence research. The reason is simple: the power to enhance or amplify the performance of AI programs resides in the specific knowledge of the problem domain that can be brought to bear. Thus, efficient knowledge bases must be large and of high quality.

This knowledge is currently acquired in a very painstaking way; individual computer scientists work with individual experts to explicate the experts' heuristics—to mine those jewels of knowledge out of their heads one by one. If applied AI is to be important in the decades to come— and we believe it is—we must develop more automatic means for what is currently a very tedious, time-consuming, and expensive procedure. Right now (and it cannot be repeated often enough) the problem of knowledge acquisition is the critical bottleneck in artificial intelligence.

5

The Knowledge Engineer at Work

H. Penny Nii is at once a pioneer, a connoisseur, and a purist in the field of knowledge engineering. Nii was trained as a conventional programmer, putting together systems for ordinary computers, with all the finicky plodding that requires. After a few years of that, she understandably grew bored and decided to return to school for graduate study.

She chose Stanford, and there she encountered heuristic programming, a method of making a computer function that offered considerably more scope for her wide-ranging interests than systems programming could. The term *heuristic* derives from the same Greek root as *eureka* ("to discover"), and it refers to a rule of thumb or a rule of good guessing. Heuristics do not guarantee results as absolutely as conventional algorithms do (or claim to), but heuristics offer results efficiently that are specific enough most of the time to be useful.

Heuristic programming provides a variety of ways of capturing human knowledge and ultimately giving it to others—or even back to the expert himself, who, being human, is vulnerable to such mistakes as overlooking, forgetting, misinterpreting, or just getting tired.

By now, with some ten years' experience overseeing the construction of a number of precedent-setting expert systems, Nii has a fairly standard way of approaching a new expert and his domain. Her way isn't the way all knowledge engineers work—for example, she doesn't use a tape recorder during interviews—but it's typical enough to be illustrative.

First, of course, she must persuade a human expert to agree to devote the considerable time it will take to have his mind mined. Experts, by their nature, are busy people, constantly being called upon to do just one more thing. But for a variety of reasons, experts can be persuaded to participate, and so the project begins. Once Nii has secured the expert's cooperation, she immerses herself in his field, reading college textbooks, articles, and other background material, in part to understand what the field is about, and in part to pick up the jargon that pervades every field. Now she is ready for the first interview.

At the beginning, she asks the expert to describe what he thinks he does, and she also asks him to think about how he solves problems. She urges him to choose a fairly difficult problem to examine. Nothing makes everybody lose interest faster than an easy problem, and furthermore, an easy problem reveals little that's significant about someone's expertise. Nii's guideline is that although the problem under consideration should be nontrivial, it shouldn't be too hard, either. She generally prefers problems that will take humans a few hours to solve, because if a problem takes days to be solved by a human, it's probably too difficult or ill-defined to be engineered into an expert program using current AI techniques.

Having collected this initial information, she brings it back to the other members of the team, the programmers. Though the programmers do the actual coding, it's up to the knowledge engineer to choose which of several available problem-solving frameworks—inference procedures—best suits the new domain. The programmers must get a first version up and running in a few days. Strangely enough, those first few days (as opposed to weeks) are critical psychologically for hooking the expert into the project. Experts, even as the rest of us, like their gratification sooner rather than later and are much likelier to continue to commit that precious resource, time, to a project they can see is making progress.

Of course, there are likely to be major flaws in the first version of the expert system. Perhaps the expert hasn't really articulated very well what he does. Perhaps he's been misunderstood. Perhaps—and this is often the case—the method he has claimed to use is a textbook fiction and has very little to do with his practice in the real world. He groans as he sees the program on display before him: "Not that way," he says.

"Then how?" Nii asks. "Where did we go wrong?"

But if he couldn't articulate it at first, perhaps he's no better at it now. Thus Nii asks him to talk his way through the model problem, verbalizing each step as he goes. This time, she observes, is usually very different from the textbook version he first gave of his problem-solving techniques.

She watches him carefully. Sometimes he says he relies on data that in fact his eyes never come to rest on, or maybe she sees he uses them at a different stage from the one he says he does. All this must be integrated into a new, amended version of the expert system and brought back to the expert to validate or correct before his interest strays elsewhere.

Nii says that during the interviews she is not necessarily listening to the facts the expert gives her so much as how he manipulates his knowledge. As he talks, she is systematically evaluating mentally the various AI knowledge representation and inference methods—object-oriented techniques, blackboard techniques, production rules, to name a few—seeing how well one or any of them matches the expert's behavior. She asks questions: "Would this make sense?" "Can you do it that way?" These are not only to extract more knowledge from the expert, but also to test the model of his work she's building up in her own mind. Moreover, she has to determine whether this expert is special in his interpretations and assumptions, or whether there's uniform agreement in his field. When she compares his knowledge to textbook knowledge, she usually discovers that the textbook is so general it's nearly useless. Typically, an expert confronted with a textbook assertion will say: "That's true, but if you see enough patients/rocks/chip designs/instrument readings, you see that it isn't true after all." At this point, knowledge threatens to become ten thousand special cases.

There is, in addition, the problem of keeping the expert focused during the interview—even the minds of experts will wander. One of Nii's tricks is to concentrate on the specific problem she has asked the expert to provide, the model problem that will not only keep everybody's interest lively, but will also serve as a good test for her own model of how thinking in the field is shaped. All these processes are repeated day after day, the expert being continuously presented with an updated version of the computer program that is intended to mimic his behavior.

Despite these good intentions and careful preparations, sometimes everything goes off on the wrong track—the expert chooses an inappropriate problem, or the knowledge engineer chooses the wrong tools with which to express the process. Nii has written, "One of the difficulties of writing knowledge-based programs is that at least two parties are constantly shifting their points of view: the domain expert and the knowledge engineer. As the knowledge in the program accumulates and the problem becomes clearer, the knowledge engineer may find better ways to represent and process the knowledge. The resulting behavior of the program may inspire the expert to shift his view of the problem, creating for the knowledge engineer further problems to be solved. Development of expert programs involves a process of finding a workable relationship between experts and programmers and slowly evolving a program structure that will work."[1] It's an elaborate and tricky pas de deux.

Nii has organized a set of heuristics that pertain to knowledge engineering:

You can't be your own expert. By examining the processes of your own expertise you risk becoming like the centipede who got tangled up in her own legs and stopped dead when she tried to figure out how she moved a hundred legs in harmony.

•

From the beginning, the knowledge engineer must count on throwing efforts away. Writers make drafts, painters make preliminary sketches; knowledge engineers are no different

•

The problem must be well chosen. AI is a young field and isn't ready to take on every problem the world has to offer. Expert systems work best when the problem is well bounded, which is computer talk to describe a problem for which large amounts of specialized knowledge may be needed, but not a general knowledge of the world.

•

If you want to do any serious application you need to meet the expert more than halfway; if he's had no exposure to computing, your job will be that much harder.

•

If none of the tools you normally use works, build a new one.

Dealing with anything but facts implies uncertainty. Heuristic knowledge is not hard and fast and cannot be treated as factual. A weighting procedure has to be built into the expert system to allow for expressions such as "I strongly believe that . . ." or "The evidence suggests that . . ."

•

A high-performance program, or a program that will eventually be taken over by the expert for his own use, must have very easy ways of allowing the knowledge to be modified so that new information can be added and out-of-date information deleted.

•

The problem needs to be a useful, interesting one. There are knowledge-based programs to solve arcane puzzles, but who cares? More important, the user has to understand the system's real value to his work.

Nii insists that her expert systems explain their line of reasoning for arriving at any conclusion. The explanation allows the human expert to understand the program without delving into the details of the code. Explanations also reveal bugs, not only in the coding, but in the knowledge base itself, which can arise from clerical errors, incomplete knowledge, inappropriate use of knowledge, or inconsistencies, which may arise from disagreement among experts. In programs that contain *uncertain knowledge,* a term that covers all the "maybes" of a situation, a user cannot blindly accept results without considering the line of reasoning that led to them. That the expert system must explain its reasoning is a requirement that Nii worries neither the Japanese nor the Europeans involved in knowledge engineering understand or appreciate.

The knowledge engineer is both a generalist and a specialist. She must be able to put herself so carefully and accurately into the mind of the expert with whom she is dealing that eventually she can mimic his thought patterns with great precision. There lies her generality. But she must also be able to frame his knowledge in ways that allow her team of programmers to convert that knowledge into working computer codes. She is the chief surgeon, the master builder, the master of the nets. Yet the knowledge engineer's role in expert systems is a transitory one. Her job is so sensitive, critical, and painstaking that nearly everybody agrees it must soon be automated unless AI is to be throttled by its own success.

6

Other Unsolved Problems in Expert Systems

Though the first efforts to build expert systems have yielded an important intellectual foundation and a useful set of tools for certain kinds of work, they are, at the moment, limited. A human expert solves problems, all right, but he also explains the results, he learns, he restructures his own knowledge, he knows when to break the rules, he understands what is relevant to his task and what isn't, and when he does make a mistake, it isn't catastrophic. Moreover, he knows when he's in over his head—when to call in outside help. Apprentices in any craft or profession soon learn that there are almost as many exceptions as rules; part of learning to be an expert is to understand not merely the letter of the rule but its spirit; to understand what can be done and what cannot. Expert systems do not yet understand these things.

Work in expert systems has explored only problem solving, explanations, and learning in any depth. Of these, performance is still the best understood—we can see whether something works or not—whereas explanations and learning (or knowledge acquisition) have barely begun.

Thus work on expert systems is currently in the stage of examining case studies that suggest architectural principles. If there is a principle so far—and most AI experts would prefer to call it a fundamental piece of wisdom rather than a principle—it is that in knowledge lies the power. But the knowledge is inexact and incomplete because, almost by definition, the kinds of problems attacked by AI rarely have complete laws or theories. And as we have seen with the knowledge engineer at work, an expert's knowledge is often ill-specified or incomplete because the expert himself doesn't always know exactly what it is he knows about his domain.

There are other problems: expert systems aren't always flexible enough to be updated as quickly and easily as they must be, and they deal in relatively narrow domains of expertise. The problem of natural language exchange between humans and computers is difficult, and so dialogues between users and programs must be limited.

Designers of expert systems have learned, to their sorrow, that research environments, where such systems are constructed, are different from user environments. For example, the expert system R1, which configures VAX computers for the Digital Equipment Corporation, displayed a 90 percent accuracy in problem solving in the laboratory. When it was first used in the field, the accuracy dropped to 60 percent. Users didn't understand how the program worked, they used incorrect data, the problem mix was different in the field from what it had been in the laboratory, and so on. The evaluations made of expert systems in the research environment can only be rough approximations of the results when the program is placed before users. Thus expert systems must be refined and restructured continuously.[2]

Finally, there are the human problems which, in microcosm, reflect problems many workers will have to face. This is a revolution, and all revolutions have their casualties. One expert who gladly gave himself and his specialized knowledge over to a knowledge engineer suffered a severe blow to his ego on discovering that the expertise he'd gleaned over the years, and was very well paid and honored for, could be expressed in a few hundred heuristics. At first he was disbelieving; then he was depressed. Eventually he departed his field, a chastened and moving figure in his bereavement.

What persuades an expert to give over—first to a knowledge engineer and ultimately to a machine—the very expertise that has made him unique? After all, this was grounds for riots at the start of the industrial revolution, and in the early 1980s laborers were eyeing robots with nervousness, if not malevolence.

In part, it's the same impulse that makes people write books: we hope perhaps not for immortality, but at least for a wider propagation of our special knowledge, and that hope springs from motives both grand and petty. This can be seen most graphically at the moment the expert system takes hold of the expert's own imagination. For weeks, perhaps longer, he has watched what is most charitably described as a burlesque of his thinking processes dancing across a display. All of a sudden (or so it seems) the burlesque sharpens into adroit imitation: there before him are the very reasoning processes he has originated, nourished, and cherished over a professional lifetime. His excitement mounts, and he becomes an enthusiastic partner in the last few steps of perfecting the electronic image of his mind. He becomes infected by the "immortality syndrome" as one researcher calls it—elation at the thought that what he knows, has so painstakingly acquired over a lifetime of experience, will live on beyond him.

Humans need expert systems, but the problem is they don't often believe it. Psychologists over the last fifty years have shown that the number of pieces of data the conscious human mind can most comfortably handle at any given moment is about four. That isn't very many. A program that attends to multiple pieces of data the human mind once had to embrace, and that compiles it into a single plausible interpretation, sets the human free to turn his attention to other, less easily engineered pieces of knowledge and bring them to bear on the problem. If the process is recursive—if new knowledge can also eventually be engineered—the user moves gladly on to new problems. When it really becomes apparent to experts that a "thinking" task can actually be turned over to a machine to do quickly and accurately, and indeed, better than through human effort, most are exhilarated and delighted with the prospect. But until that very point, these same people maintain their staunch skepticism that it can actually be done.

Despite these problems, expert systems have had some considerable success. They have changed AI researchers' ideas about what might constitute intelligence, and they have succeeded in attracting a fair amount of attention outside the field, especially from entrepreneurs. The time necessary to construct the average expert system has dropped from about fifty man-years to five, thanks to experience and the development of new tools.

But the problems remain, and they are hard. It's tempting, perhaps, for the nonspecialist to scoff and ask why scientists didn't anticipate all this before they plunged ahead with expert systems. Science is done as it can be. Some problems do not emerge until other problems are first solved. This has been the history of artificial intelligence, and all other science, too. One might just as well ask why it took Beethoven more than two years of countless compositional experiments and revisions to write the great choral movement of his Ninth Symphony. Couldn't he get it right the first time?

7

Speculations in Knowledge Futures

If the creation of artificial intelligence is among the most challenging and controversial tasks the human mind has ever put itself to, if the difficulties often seem overwhelming, that has never prevented the field from being surrounded by fantastic predictions for the future. But the truth is that no one knows exactly what surprises are in store for us all. We can only speculate.

The "Mechanical" Doctor

Many kinds of expertise are unevenly distributed in the world. Medicine is a perfect example. That is one reason the U.S. National Institutes of Health have been at the forefront of supporting expert systems research. It isn't just that the natives of Ulan Bator don't have the same access to medical care as the natives of Los Angeles; it's that the natives of Fresno don't have it either, and poor people in Los Angeles aren't as fortunate in their medical attention as well-off people.

If the idea of a machine doctor repels you, consider that not everyone feels that way. Studies in England showed that many humans were much more comfortable (and candid) with an examination by a computer terminal than with a human physician, whom they perceived as somehow disapproving of them. "Mechanical" doctors are in fact systems that move methodically through possibilities, making inferences and drawing conclusions. They often outperform the very experts who have programmed them because of their methodical ways; they don't skip or forget things, get tired or rushed, or fall subject to some of our other human failings. They will be on call at the patient's convenience, not just the physician's. And they can bring medicine to places where none now exists.

The Intelligent Library

One application anybody interested in knowledge will welcome is the intelligent library. Nowadays, a library has information, even knowledge, but you must supply the intelligence. You pick among topics in the card catalog; you browse in the stacks, sorting and choosing; you go to the reference librarian in despair.

The intelligent library, based on knowledge information processing systems, will supply intelligence along with knowledge and information. It will be active, not passive. It will conduct a dialogue with you, inferring from what you tell it what it is you really want. You can ask a question, state a goal, and by asking you questions in turn, it will infer your desires and try to meet them. It will even prompt you with connected topics you hadn't, at that moment, thought of. It will test your hypotheses, verify your hunches, and explain until you really understand.

All this is done by inference: sometimes the library doesn't have the direct answer, but it can reason its way through the information glut and present you with plausible scenarios, explaining at your request its reasons for arriving at those scenarios.

Does the end of libraries as we know them mean the

end of books? Probably not for a long time, if ever. We still write (some) letters, even though we have telephones, Telexes, and other forms of sending messages to each other. Books may very well become pieces of art in the distant future; meanwhile, their great advantages of high resolution, portability, and random access (you can riffle through the pages so easily) will have to be met by any system that wants to replace them. One can imagine such solutions: a personal book-size "reading machine" that allows you to slip chips in and go with them where you will, spring hillside or pleasure cruise; that even allows you to flip from written word to spoken word if you'd rather hear than see.

The Intelligent Tutor

A leading Western intellectual, realizing that he knew nothing about science, recently cried out that the universe had gone silent on him. That reaction seemed a bit perfervid, but if he can hold out, help is on the way.

There are many topics we know nothing about, but would like to know something about, if it weren't so painful to learn. As it happens, the pain is inflicted in two ways: first, it is difficult to make your mind grasp concepts that are quite alien from those you're used to dealing with; and second, it is a terrible embarrassment for a grownup to keep on admitting that he just doesn't understand. Thus most of us simply close off whole areas of human intellectual achievement because the difficulties overwhelm us. If, however, we had an infinitely patient, intelligent, and nonjudgmental tutor, we might feel different.

"What can you tell me about physics?" you ask your intelligent tutor in a discreet aside. SHALL WE BEGIN WITH THE UNIFIED THEORY? it asks. "Sure," you say, "why not?" Your intelligent tutor may be talking to you; words may be appearing in print on some sort of receiver, but soon pictures will start to appear. Even today, with the help of computer graphics, phenomena that could not be pictured any other way can be realized pictorially: theorems become breathtakingly beautiful visual designs, their regularity and elegance presented in a visual—and visceral—way that rewrites the old Chinese adage to say that a picture is worth ten thousand terms.

With the intelligent tutor, the experience of knowledge will be available at any level you want, from general, undetailed introduction for the novice to detailed instruction in specialties only an expert might want. When the first explanation of a concept fails to penetrate, the intelligent tutor (either because you have told it so explicitly, or because it has determined that fact for itself by testing you slyly) will try rephrasing the concept, using analogies, pictures, mathematical terms—whatever is necessary to make you understand. If you don't understand even then, it will tactfully tell you what you can indeed absorb, and neither of you need worry about what you cannot.

Knowledge Simulators: "Games" for Teaching

If such tutors are available for adults—and the Japanese count on them to continue the process of lifelong learning for their ever more elderly population—what might education for children look like?

One answer came from a recent symposium devoted to video games. That might seem like an odd forum in which to ponder the educational possibilities of the intelligent computer, but learning was the main theme of nearly all of the speakers.

Several speakers who are working on the frontiers, well beyond the relatively simple shoot-'em-ups in present-day arcades, reminded their scholarly audience that video games are in their infancy in every sense of the term. But even at this primitive stage, it is easy to imagine the kinds of games that are possible in the future, once much higher degrees of computer speed and memory are available, coupled with highly sophisticated graphics capabilities and reasoning power. Perhaps the most important property these future games will have is that although they'll be fun, for that's in the nature of games, they'll teach—painlessly and naturally.

Already certain special groups have such "games" specially designed for them. Pilots learning to fly the latest commercial jet do not take one out for a spin the first time at the controls. Instead, they have $10 million toys called simulators that give them as precisely as possible the feeling of flying the craft they will eventually fly for real.

We have peculiar and mainly pejorative associations with

the idea of games—surely they can't be serious, and they have little to do with the business of functioning in an adult world. But of course games have everything to do with that. Scientists often describe what they do as a glorious game, and so do securities analysts (the phrase is "to play the stock market," after all). Some games designers argue persuasively that even today, at the admittedly primitive level where video games have arrived, they can stimulate the intellect and teach various skills and facts as well as anything yet devised. A current game called "Time Zone" pushes the player backward into history, allowing him to participate in the assassination of Julius Caesar (but not to prevent it), to persuade Benjamin Franklin face to face to sign the Declaration of Independence (but not to succeed at that), and so forth. Present-day games even have time constraints—in "Detective," evidence will disappear if the player doesn't reason his way to it quickly enough, and once gone, it's gone for the duration of the game. The player must use his wits to compensate. Does such a game teach reasoning skills, or is it simply fun?

If all this is how children might someday learn, what is to become of classrooms? In the very long run, they may meet the same fate as other precomputing organizations, which is to say, having outlived their usefulness, they will simply wither away and die. But for the foreseeable future, classrooms of some sort will surely exist, if only because the most exuberant games, or simulations, or fantasies, or whatever name we have for those activities by then, will require installations of a size and expense that most families won't want to undertake for themselves. Moreover, children need the company of other children, and the new classrooms will be one place where they'll get it.

Will human teachers disappear? Probably not. But children will learn in a much more independent fashion than they do now, having control over what they learn and when they learn it. Will children be equipped to make those decisions wisely? Only if the learning games they are presented with are designed to impart wisdom. AI researchers have long hoped that by discovering how to design an intelligent computer program, they will shed some light on the human learning process—at the moment, after all, we do nothing but spray words at our pupils and hope some of them stick. One of the great challenges educators and cognitive psychologists face in the next few years is to design games that teach the skills necessary for participation in a new world. Perhaps their first task is to identify those skills.

The Intelligent Newspaper

Some people think current events are fascinating. Some people think they are so ephemeral that any time spent on them is time squandered. Your intelligent newspaper will know the way you feel and behave accordingly.

It will know because you will have trained it yourself. In a none-too-arduous process, you will have informed your intelligent newsgathering system about the topics that are of special interest to you. Editorial decisions will be made by you, and your system will be able to act upon them thereafter. It will have hundreds, perhaps thousands, of competing news sources to choose from, and it will understand (because you have told it) which news sources you trust most, which dissenting opinions you wish to be exposed to, and when not to bother you at all.

You could let your intelligent system infer your interests indirectly by watching you as you browse. What makes you laugh? It will remember and gather bits of fantasia to amuse you. What makes you steam? It may gather information about that, too, and then give you names of groups that are organized for or against that particular outrage. What's going on in the neighborhood? You'll be happy to know the crime rate is down over this time last year (or unhappy to know it's up); that Mr. and Mrs. Morton in the next block have just had a baby girl named Joanna and thank everybody for their interest. You can even program in some randomness: surprise me every now and then, you can say to your intelligent newsgatherer, and your trivia file will grow apace.

KIPS at Home

Although expert systems will probably be developed for businesses first, home applications will probably not be far behind. Home video games and computers are simply precursors of much more sophisticated systems that might offer advice on everything from nutrition and tax computation to exercise and legal questions. An electronic, interactive Dr. Spock might assist parents even more effectively than the printed Dr. Spock has for decades.

Expert systems might advise on any number of other tasks: talking you through the job of a fixing a leaky toilet—not the model toilet that appears in the fix-it books but is always just different enough from yours to be almost useless, but your toilet—step by step. Or your automobile, or your home computer. How about the gardening coach you can carry through the vegetable patch, discussing proper fertilizers, weather patterns, pest control, and the pleasures of dirt under your fingernails? How about an intelligent dictionary or, better, an intelligent encyclopedia? All yours, all solving problems you want to solve at the moment, and not some abstract, generalized problem that might or might not have bearing on your situation.

All very unexceptional, McCorduck thinks, just the sort of predictions that have been floating around the field for years, firmly grounded in what certainly, in principle, can be done and probably will be. She has other desires and is therefore gratified to read that one purpose of the Japanese Fifth Generation is to alleviate the problems of aging. She exults. For years she's been nagging for, promoting, advocating the geriatric robot. She'd all but lost hope, watching her friends in AI create intelligent physician-machines, intelligent geologist-machines, even intelligent military-spy-machines, but never anything down-home useful. Time is getting on. The geriatric robot might soon be a matter of immediate personal concern.

The geriatric robot is wonderful. It isn't hanging about in the hopes of inheriting your money—nor of course will it slip you a little something to speed the inevitable. It isn't hanging about because it can't find work elsewhere. It's there because it's yours. It doesn't just bathe you and feed you and wheel you out into the sun when you crave fresh air and a change of scene, though of course it does all those things. The very best thing about the geriatric robot is that it *listens*. "Tell me again," it says, "about how wonderful/dreadful your children are to you. Tell me again that fascinating tale of the coup of '63. Tell me again . . ." And it means it. It never gets tired of hearing those stories, just as you never get tired of telling them. It knows your favorites, and those are its favorites too. Never mind that this all ought to be done by human caretakers;

humans grow bored, get greedy, want variety. It's part of our charm.

McCorduck felt a slight jolt a few years ago when she heard Yale's Roger Schank muse in a lecture that he didn't believe a machine could be considered intelligent *until* it got bored, but he reassured her later that the art of programming was already refined to the point that a never-bored robot could be fashioned.

Now here were the Japanese, those clever people, claiming their Fifth Generation would alleviate the problems of an aging society. She read the reports eagerly: lifetime education system; medical care information; other rubbishy pieties. She flung down the proceedings in disgust. She is reconciled that she may have to turn AI from spectator to participant sport and whip one up herself before it's too late.

8

In Summary: Expert Systems as Agents of the Second Computer Revolution

Expert systems are computer programs performing at the level of human experts in various professional fields. They are part of a larger effort in computer science called artificial intelligence research. AI research in general got under way in the mid-1950s, but expert systems didn't really flower until the 1970s, in part because the necessary design principles violated a firmly held tenet of AI researchers: that intelligent behavior in human or computer was the result of grand (and tidy) general laws of thought. Since powerful general laws kept stubbornly eluding researchers, some scientists got impatient and decided to design systems that might not be so general but at least would get a particular job done, simply by knowing as much as possible of the facts, heuristics, lore, and likely strategies of the situation.

As the philosopher and logician Alfred North Whitehead observed, God is in the details. Scientifically embarrassing as all these messy details might be, they made the first expert system, DENDRAL, successful. This knowledge-based approach was tried in other fields and proved to work again, provided that the problems were carefully chosen for their suitability to the AI tools at hand, and also provided that some group of human practitioners recognized that the expert system could be an important assistant to them in their work. (At least one high-performance medical diagnosis program sits unused because the physicians it was designed to assist didn't perceive that they needed such assistance; they were wrong, but that doesn't matter.)

By the late 1970s, expert systems had caught the attention of entrepreneurs who saw that they could be used to increase productivity and hence profitability in a multitude of enterprises. Although it was pleasant to see AI step so boldly and usefully into the real world, a certain tension developed among scientists who believed all these entrepreneurial adventures would channel the youngest and brightest researchers into applications that had short-run market value but not necessarily long-run scientific value.

This was not an idle exercise in hand wringing or misguided foolishness about the necessity for pure science. The knowledge-based approach to machine intelligence is at most twenty years old, and major problems remain to be solved. Perhaps the most important is the acquisition of all that knowledge for the systems' knowledge bases, which just now must be painstakingly evoked from the mind of a human expert and recast into terms suitable for the computer. It is a long and tedious process for expert and knowledge engineer alike.

Nevertheless, even the limited success of the knowledge-based approach to artificial intelligence has inspired the Japanese to undertake an ambitious research and development program, one that aims, in the end, to mass-produce computer hardware and software for these fragile expert systems, to turn hand-crafted horseless carriages into cheap vehicles for everyone. They have labeled their exuberant new plan the Fifth Generation, because they believe these

machines will be so different from the first four generations of computers the world has experienced that they
deserve to be set apart. The Japanese, with their knowledge information processing systems, expect to set off a
world revolution in knowledge, comparable to but even
more profound than the revolution caused by the printing
press. As we are about to see, to accomplish all that, they
have begun a small but significant revolution at home.

IV

THE JAPANESE FIFTH GENERATION

1

Forty Samurai

It is early August 1982, a little more than ten months after the Fifth Generation conference. Feigenbaum and McCorduck are on the twenty-first floor of a modern but otherwise undistinguished high-rise in Tokyo, where, because of earthquakes, high-rises are unusual. On a door with a frosted glass window, typical of any insurance company or professional's office, is lettered in both English and Japanese, "Institute for New Generation Computer Technology" (ICOT). The office behind the frosted glass door has a splendid view of Tokyo, its bay, and even, in good weather, Mount Fuji. (To the young people who work here, Mount Fuji is only a promise, for the summer haze hangs heavy in Tokyo and they have only been there two months, June and July. Come back in wintertime, they say; then you'll see it.)

As is usually the case with new quarters, things don't yet look lived in. The walls are bare; the furniture is unscratched and lacks the concavities that say human bodies have been at work or ease here. The slogans, posters, and house plants—fixtures around American computer installations—are, at least after these first two months, notably absent.

Forty researchers sit in one big, sunny, pleasant room at long tables with fingertip-high partitions between those who sit face to face, but no partitions between those who sit side by side. Make no mistake, these are tables—not work stations, desks, terminal tables, or any such thing. Indeed, the only computers in evidence are over in one corner: a couple of Apple IIs, two or three minicomputers, and four terminals to a remote DEC-20 system. The researchers assure visitors that more new equipment will arrive in a month: another mini, another terminal to another DEC-20. Still, it doesn't look like a place propitious for revolution. In fact, most American computer science graduate students would turn up their noses at the austerity.

Nevertheless, revolution is the business of ICOT. It's revolution on two levels. The first is the obvious—the people at ICOT are going to bring about the Fifth Generation of computers, the second computer revolution. But very closely tied to that, perhaps a necessary precondition for it, is a social revolution, at least so far as the Japanese are concerned.

In the first place, except for ICOT's director, Kazuhiro Fuchi, everybody there—by Fuchi's demand—is under thirty-five, and in some cases well under that. Though Fuchi himself is in his mid-forties, he has long ago recognized that revolutions aren't made by the elderly, and he's insisted on this point. "Young," he says simply, "young and excellent."

This attitude is completely contrary to the way Japanese businesses and research centers are usually organized. Traditionally, the Japanese have adhered to a strict hierarchical structure based on seniority. Though Westerners will find nothing surprising in an organization built around eager young researchers, most Japanese are deeply affronted, and Fuchi is becoming something of a scientific outcast for his rash-seeming disregard of the proprieties.

The young and excellent have come from a variety of places, including the eight firms that make up the consortium backing ICOT—Fujitsu, Hitachi, Nippon Electric Corporation, Mitsubishi, Matsushita, Oki, Sharp, and Toshiba—and the two national laboratories that are also participating, the government-owned Nippon Telephone and Telegraph's Musashino Laboratories and MITI's own Electrotechnical Laboratory. The researchers have come to spend three years here for a variety of reasons. Most of them were hand-picked by Fuchi, young men who impressed him by their work on the numerous committees that deliberated before ICOT came into being; some are his former protégés. Most have come eagerly, hungry for the chance to work directly on projects of momentous significance and with responsibilities that wouldn't ordinarily be allowed them until they'd accumulated years of seniority at their various firms and laboratories.

To these scientific samurai, it's worth the considerable sacrifices they must endure. Though policies vary from firm to firm, many of the ICOT researchers understand that promotions with their cohort group in their respective companies, the normal way of moving up in Japanese firms, have for them been suspended or at least slowed down. For three years some will not share in the bonuses that often comprise 50 percent of a Japanese worker's annual salary. Those few who left supervisory positions in their firm to join the project understand that they cannot depend on returning to their laboratories at a supervisor's level. At the very least, the arduous hours of commuting have stretched out: two hours each way is typical for researchers traveling to the ICOT lab in Tokyo rather than to their respective firms. This would be hard enough for people who work regular hours, but these are researchers pushing themselves to the limits of their endurance.

None of this matters to the passionate, young majority who were stirred by Fuchi's words on the opening day of the center: "You will look back on these as your shining years," one researcher remembers him saying. "These will be great years for you. We will all work very hard. If the project fails, I will take the entire responsibility. But, of course, we won't fail."

However, a minority of researchers at ICOT hold other views. They come from firms that sent them grudgingly, firms that think the Fifth Generation project is going to be an international embarrassment for the Japanese, firms that contributed their workers only under duress from MITI. Such people are uncomfortable in the unstructured atmosphere of ICOT—who is to tell them what to do? They have adopted their firm's point of view—isn't this all much too ambitious? Do you see IBM embarked on anything so blue-sky? And worse, they find themselves doing what they consider dirty work, and so it is, the grubby business of designing and coding and trying and failing and experimenting and arguing that must inevitably take place at the start of a major project. There's been enough trouble from this minority in the first two months to provoke a delegation from the majority to entreat Fuchi to solve the problem. The dissension isn't good for morale, they warn; work may suffer. Fuchi reassures them. He hopes to convert the dissidents; he reserves the final decision to send them packing.

Even those who adore—the word is not too strong—their unusual director are often dismayed by him. A month after the center formally opened, the hardware committee met with Fuchi and showed him the fast-track two-year plan they'd devised for producing the prototype hardware scheduled for the first three-year phase. Instead of being pleased, Fuchi flew into a rage. That alone is unusual enough among Japanese managers, but what Fuchi wants is even more upsetting: cut that schedule down to a year and a half, he demands. The hardware committee is in shock. They already think themselves reckless in their two-year schedule. Fuchi will have none of it. "We *have* to manage to do this!" he says angrily. After a little while he calms down. "Go and think it over," he says more reasonably. "If you absolutely have to have two years, then you have to have them. But see if it can't be done in a year and a half. Loosen up on the quality assurance and give me a real machine in a year and a half."

Sitting with Feigenbaum across a conference table from Kazuhiro Fuchi one early August morning, McCorduck is fascinated by him and eventually reminded of Murasaki Shikibu's description of that eleventh-century hero, the shining Genji: "He brought pleasure to the eye and serenity to the heart, and made people wonder what bounty of grace might be his from former lives." Energy and intensity flow from Fuchi, touching everyone around him. He certainly doesn't talk very much, and he often leaves it to his supervisor of the international study department, a vivacious young woman, to translate what he has just said, although his English seems fluent enough when he wishes. He often speaks with his hands, eloquent gestures so that the foreign visitors can almost guess what he's said before Ms. Yumiko Okada gets a chance to translate in her smartly colloquial English. He misses nothing, watching his young researchers make their presentations, assessing the reactions of the foreign visitors shrewdly. He sometimes looks as if he's enjoying a silent, private joke.

Fuchi strikes Feigenbaum as young in spirit, adventuresome, ready to take risks. Unlike the classical Japanese technological manager who, as he climbs up the ladder of authority, gradually loses touch with the technology he manages, Fuchi commands the admiration of his staff for his deep involvement in technical projects and his awesome knowledge. In Feigenbaum's past conversations with him, Fuchi had seemed a man who despised the Japanese copycat stereotype, one that many Japanese themselves believe. On the contrary, Fuchi seems proud of native Japanese intelligence—almost arrogant about it, Feigenbaum senses. That might easily be overlooked as the cocoon of Japanese courtesy surrounds a visitor, but it's there, embodied in men like Fuchi who make it clear they believe it is no accident that Japan is on top, that no goal is too ambitious for such a gifted people. Fuchi almost seems to have taken on a personal campaign to wipe out once and for all the energetic but uncreative stereotype that shadows the Japanese.

The director's office at ICOT is well furnished in the International style, with one glass wall overlooking Tokyo Bay. McCorduck thinks it ironic that the office of the man who will command a computer revolution looks down on the very spot where Commodore Perry and his notorious black boats once threatened to demolish Tokyo (then Edo) if America didn't get exactly what it wanted in the way of trade agreements with unwilling Japan. But if Fuchi ever dwells on that incident, it isn't because he's looking out his office window; in reality this office is a ceremonial place with pristine furniture and only a few books in the otherwise empty cases. Fuchi has installed himself instead in a low-partitioned section of the main floor, where he can oversee and be immediately accessible to his forty researchers.

In short, Fuchi is a type, rare enough in the West but almost unheard of in the East, one of those who, by sheer force of will, can make something out of nothing. He's the stuff of which legends are made.

And of course legends are already growing up around him. Late in the evening (not necessarily over the computer terminals) his researchers trade stories about him. In the nature of legends, no one is quite sure which parts are true and which aren't. The stories that get repeated most are those that Fuchi's own personality makes plausible. For example, they recount the tale—though no one can verify it—that as a young man their own age, Fuchi once got so perturbed with the way things were being run at the laboratory where he worked that in fury and desperation he stalked out and stayed away for a month, coming back only after his supervisor came to his house and pleaded with him to return.

Everybody knows that Fuchi has irrevocably resigned from his former post at the Electrotechnical Laboratory, a startling step for any Japanese employee, all the more one with such seniority. A high roller, he's placing all his bets on the Fifth Generation project. The legends add that Fuchi would have been eligible for a comfortable government pension if he'd only waited two or three months to resign his position at ETL, but he spurned anything so trivial as personal financial security to delay his project even by months. This is sensational to the young researchers who have grown up in the lifetime employment system of Japan. Here is a daring leader capable of the kind of innovative thinking the Fifth Generation demands. If it can be done, Fuchi will do it. Here is a leader who can take them where they want to go. He has smashed social stereotypes; he has tossed out social traditions. Why not scientific stereotypes and traditions, too?

It is just this yeasty atmosphere of the new, the best, of "making computing history," as Fuchi will say laconically one night on the CBS Evening News, that, two years later, will cause several of these young researchers facing the end of their furlough at ICOT (and the return to their respective firms) to hope aloud that exceptions can be made, and that they can continue at ICOT.

2

Mighty MITI Gets Its Way

The Japanese Ministry of International Trade and Industry—MITI—is a government bureau unlike anything most Westerners know. It is composed of elite bureaucrats (an oxymoron in the West) whose job is to think broadly and deeply about the overall success of Japan's industries. Most especially, MITI's task is to ponder the long view. For MITI's officials themselves, this function is impelled by two personal circumstances. First, their employment is secure for a lifetime, which frees them to think into the distant future without concern for the vicissitudes of next year's elections or budget cuts that might endanger their job security. Second, each MITI official is regularly rotated among departments in the ministry so that he cultivates friendly personal relationships with the people he will be working with the rest of his life and gains an understanding of all aspects of MITI's concerns.

Compelling MITI officials to attend to the long-term perspective is their accountability for the general health of their nation's trade and industry. If things go wrong, MITI gets the blame for not having anticipated it and headed off a failure. And since Japan's survival depends on trade, MITI has a great deal of incentive and weighty national responsibility to make the best plans possible for the future. Indeed, MITI takes its task so seriously that it is known jokingly as *Kyoiku mama*, the intellectual equivalent of a stage mother who pushes her child to study, study, study.

MITI's aim is not, as Ezra Vogel reminds us, to reduce competition among Japanese companies, but to create the strongest possible companies with the greatest competitive potential. Vogel makes a useful comparison with the National Football League, which establishes rules about the size of the team, recruitment, and rules of play that produce relatively equally matched teams of powerful competitive abilities. But the league (and MITI) doesn't interfere in internal team activity or tell a coach how to do his job, though MITI does try to provide information to help the coach improve.

As a rule, MITI does not try to manage projects directly, but provides guidelines, priorities, and advice about financing, foreign exchange, and technology transfer. It sets targets for long-term growth and standards for modernization of plants, and it even promotes mergers of companies that lack the capital to meet those standards. As Vogel puts it, "They boldly try to restructure industry, concentrating resources in areas where they think Japan will be competitive internationally in the future. As wages rose to Western levels in the late 1960s, MITI bureaucrats tried to reconcentrate resources in industries that were capital-intensive rather than labor-intensive. After the 1973 oil shock they greatly accelerated plans to push Japan into service- and knowledge-intensive industries rather than energy-intensive ones."[1]

MITI has policies for both declining and emerging industries, helping ease the contractions of one and the growing pains of the other. And though it has immense power, it is the power of persuasion, rather than statute. Corporations cooperate with MITI because, first, they understand that MITI is primarily interested in the welfare of all companies in a given sector. Next, MITI provides superior information and analysis of worldwide industrial trends. Third, within a given sector, MITI and company representatives at a variety of levels meet constantly to exchange ideas and impressions and develop mutual understanding. MITI works toward harmony and agreement; its policy announcements usually reflect the consensus of the significant members of a sector.

Finally, company officials know that when the time comes for them to request licenses, permits, choice locations, and tax breaks, MITI will respond more favorably to cooperative than to uncooperative companies. MITI's displeasure can be costly to a firm; it can use delaying tactics, raise difficult questions, take a very narrow view of depreciation allowances and deductions, and even influence the banks that lend to the firms. But all this is seldom necessary.

Given MITI's own enchantment with the power of knowledge, it is not surprising that a few years ago it decided that Japan should move decisively ahead into the information age. In truth, MITI's decision was only part of a nationwide governmental decision to push Japan in that direction, allying MITI with other government ministries such as the Ministry of Health and Welfare, the Economic Planning Agency, and the Ministry of Posts and Telecommunications. Programs are planned by each of these agencies to carry out the national imperative, and, of course, the Fifth Generation will be central to fulfilling the aims of them all.

In 1978 MITI assigned the Japanese National Electrotechnical Laboratory the task of defining a project to develop a computer system for the 1990s. In typical MITI fashion, it had been decided that somebody ought to look one decade, two decades ahead. Perhaps equally important, MITI had determined it was time for the Japanese to learn to innovate on a grand scale. A new generation of computers suited these requirements perfectly.

MITI accepted the early reports on the Fifth Generation and sponsored the conference that announced it to the world. Thus the Fifth Generation was conceived, and through MITI's sponsorship it has been born.

The budget for the project is substantial, though not huge by American standards for research of this scope. MITI's announced commitment of $450 million over the ten-year period is spread rather lightly over the first three-year phase ($45 million) and then budgeted heavily for the years of expensive developmental engineering. The first phase will be funded fully by MITI. In the second and third phases, MITI expects its funding will be matched by the participating companies, bringing the total project budget to approximately $850 million. Other MITI-initiated national projects have seen higher ratios of industry-to-government spending, sometimes two or three to one. It's very possible that if the project is meeting its intermediate targets at the end of the first phase, and if the Japanese economy is strong, the total budget could well escalate to more than $1 billion.

Whether such a budget seems large depends upon what it's compared with. For instance, budgeted amounts for research and advanced development at the Advanced Research Projects Agency of the U.S. Department of Defense (ARPA) will almost surely exceed the Fifth Generation budget over the next decade, even with no special response planned to the Japanese challenge. The annual R&D budget for IBM for 1982 alone was about $1.5 billion. On the other hand, a myriad of smaller, highly innovative companies whose R&D budgets are relatively small and focused on the short term would find these figures lavish. Large firms, too, reserve only a limited portion of their annual research and development budgets for innovations; existing research projects that may go on over a long period tend to gobble up funds and develop an inertia that places them at the top of the list in upcoming budgets. From these perspectives, the Japanese Fifth Generation budget is impressive.

Equally impressive is the strategy formulated by MITI and Fuchi for managing the project. ICOT, the instant institute, drew together the forty researchers from the participating firms within two weeks of the start of the project (which itself was formed only fourteen days into the new fiscal year beginning April 1, 1982, in which MITI had said it would seek the project's funding). The project managers were selected from MITI's own first-rate Electrotechnical Laboratory, the prenatal home of the project, and from the innovative Nippon Electric Corporation (NEC) Research Laboratory.

In parallel with the formation of ICOT, closely allied R&D groups in the company laboratories have been targeted to track the scientific and technological progress at ICOT and absorb it for proprietary use. This tracking and technology transfer is to be achieved in several ways.

First, researchers will rotate out of ICOT and back to their company laboratories after three or four years. Meanwhile, no proprietary considerations limit collaboration among them while they are at ICOT, and they are routinely—perhaps once a week—sent back to their firms to report on progress. Both the rotation and the routine reports are intended to seed ideas throughout the participating firms systematically. Such cooperation might agitate a Washington antitrust regulator were it to happen in the United States. But ICOT's mission is to foster such cooperation and to educate industrial scientists actively by joint project work. ICOT gives a visitor the same feeling of openness as the major AI labs of American universities.

MITI funds for support of company groups began to flow in 1983. These funds will flow through ICOT and be disbursed by contract for work performed. The contract mechanism, so familiar to American industries dealing with government funds, is apparently unique among MITI-funded national projects. Usually funds flow directly from MITI to the firms. The contract mechanism, however, will not be applied in a heavy-handed way. Each firm has asserted one or more key areas of interest, and ICOT will respect these and work within that framework. This new structure seems to have been developed to implement a goal of major importance to MITI: to apply pressure upon Japanese industrial computer scientists to innovate, not merely to evolve existing Western technologies. Thus ICOT, with its intellectually aggressive collection of researchers, will nurture young shoots of innovative work and transplant them to the industrial labs. The point of the contract mechanism is to ensure that these young shoots receive the necessary and appropriate care so that they will grow into healthy, commercially viable plants.

Examples of company interests in the Fifth Generation project are NEC's long-standing interest in the hardware and problem-solving software associated with PROLOG machines. In contrast, NTT's Musashino Labs, the "Bell Labs of Japan," has interests in the hardware associated with the LISP programming language for symbolic processing and may build a very high-speed LISP machine. Industrial applications of the expert systems over a wide front motivate Hitachi people at their System Development Laboratory and Energy Laboratory. Fujitsu's Central Laboratory is motivated in all areas, from hardware (they are building a LISP machine to attach to existing Fujitsu machines) through software and expert systems applications. The remaining companies will soon define their own interests, with help from ICOT.

All this has been neither smooth nor entirely consensual, as we shall see. Moreover, MITI has had to sponsor the first phase of the Fifth Generation project by itself, since even the firms that were enthusiastic about the project didn't feel they could afford the large financial risk it entails. MITI has conceded the point, believing that Japan has no other choice.

3

Some Views
from the Companies

In the summer of 1982, the Fifth Generation project was
at a happy moment. ICOT had secured a $2 million bud-
get for its first year which increased to $13.7 million in the
second year, and would reach $27.4 million in the third
year. Researchers were committed for at least three years
of intense work, and their ambitions were impressive. In
their first year alone, they expected to develop two hardware systems, one a sequential inference machine and the
other a relational data base machine, both of which would
eventually be joined into one machine at the end of the
first three-year phase of the project.

How did the researchers expect in the second year to
spend an amount seven or eight times their first year's
budget? They replied that they would retain only 20 percent of it at ICOT, that 80 percent would be parceled out
to the participating firms and laboratories in the form of
contracts for specific work. Who would select these projects?
Who would select the contractors for them?

In fact, ICOT has a number of steering committees,
filled by older (if not necessarily wiser) heads, consisting
of a board of counselors, a board of directors, and a policy
committee, which itself oversees a management committee
and a technology committee. Much later, we spoke with a
key member of one of those companies, a high-ranking
manager in one of Japan's largest firms, who admitted
candidly that there were and would continue to be a
variety of problems.

"At first," he said, "we didn't like the idea of sending
our precious young technical people to such a project, but

then we realized that our company has always taken the long view, and that this is the proper place to put our long-range resources. Many things remain to be resolved, priorities remain to be set. But in three years, we're confident they will be resolved." Since his own company is considered one of Japan's most successful and innovative, his confidence did not seem misplaced.

He went on to give us further background. "At first, MITI wanted to support this project at only 50 percent for the first three years, with private firms supplying the other 50 percent of the funding, but we in the companies said no. We can't afford to support such a high-risk project, even at 50 percent, plus contribute researchers' time. When they saw we meant it, they agreed to support it 100 percent, at least for the first three years. After that, we'll see."

He reflected for a moment. "You know, MITI has the right idea. We realize not all firms feel the same way we do, and so we realize we have a teaching mission as far as the other firms are concerned. We accept that responsibility."

It's formidable. Resentment and hostility are hardly strong enough to describe the attitudes of another firm's managers toward the Fifth Generation. They told us frankly that they had not wanted to participate and only under duress (whose nature we couldn't ascertain) did they finally contribute their researchers to ICOT. They resented, they said, giving up a good researcher for three years—they chose and trained their people very carefully for many years to be good company men, and they didn't want them influenced by outsiders, which would inevitably happen at ICOT. They certainly couldn't hire people solely to send to ICOT, for under the Japanese employment system they would then be stuck with them for life. Although, like many Japanese firms, they had their own expert systems research groups going full tilt, they regarded the goals of ICOT as much too ambitious. What seemed to worry them most of all was the idea that IBM wasn't doing a project with similar goals. They saw their industrial mission as doing exactly what IBM did, only better and cheaper. But not different. They were, in short, a chaste embodiment of the belief that Japan's place in the world is to be a superb copier, but never an innovator. This firm represented the extreme; others, although not entirely enthusiastic about ICOT, at least took a tolerant wait-and-see attitude.

The manager who was also a key ICOT committee member was asked whether he thought a single large firm could accomplish the Fifth Generation's goals—his own firm, for example. "Yes," he said, "in theory it could be done by a single large firm, probably with a lot less waste and controversy. But then it wouldn't be a *national* project, would it? And of course no single firm would be willing to take a risk of such magnitude, even though most of us know that this is the proper direction for computing in the 1990s to go."

A very high-ranking official of another firm expressed nearly identical views—that he and most of his managers had been dubious at first, but now they supported the project enthusiastically and, moreover, accepted the fact that they had some educating of other firms to do.

As it happens, this particular firm has an analogous firm in the United States to which it is always compared by the press, a comparison that must feel simultaneously flattering and condescending, not unlike McCorduck's reaction when Japanese express amazement that she can eat with chopsticks and even likes raw fish. As it also happens, the U.S. firm has been historically almost rabidly anti-AI. A fresh comparison of the two caused a fair amount of laughter in Tokyo one evening, over the dinner table Feigenbaum and McCorduck were sharing with officials from the Japanese firm. "They'll come around," said our host soothingly, "don't worry. They have to." We all lifted our glasses to that.

And indeed, that American firm did come around, sooner than anybody at the table might have expected. By the end of 1983, it was running large advertisements in the *New York Times* and elsewhere, announcing its ambitions for an artificial intelligence laboratory, eventually to number between ten and twenty researchers. When the newspaper ads failed to evoke the hoped for responses, the firm dispatched headhunters into the universities to search for suitable candidates, who were told plainly that money was no object.

What had caused the turnabout? Stodgy management had been replaced by new, fresh management that saw where the future in computing lay. Unencumbered by the myths of the 1950s and 1960s, the new managers are determined to bring to their firm the best that can be had.

Unfortunately, the obstinacy of the *ancien regime* has made such a game of catchup at best costly, and possibly hopeless.

As we discussed MITI's, role that evening with the Japanese officials, our hosts observed that MITI seldom, if ever, had managed a project quite like this. It wasn't the money—$450 million isn't precisely a routine budget for a MITI project, but it's hardly unprecedented: projects in supercomputers and ceramics for the semiconductor industry are two projects MITI supports at this level. But as a rule, MITI's strategy has been to support programs that are already fairly well researched and to concentrate on bringing them through the development stage. Now MITI is in the unusual position of supporting a large basic research project and seeing it through to the world market. Our host described some of the difficulties involved with this and concluded, "Nobody knows quite what will happen."

"Except," a colleague down the table added jokingly, "MITI never fails!"

4

The Technology of the Fifth Generation

The Japanese Fifth Generation project aims to design and produce computer hardware, and software, for knowledge engineering in a wide range of applications—including expert systems, natural language understanding by machine, graphics, and robotics. In order to accomplish all this, the Japanese must improve present computing capabilities dramatically. In addition, they must make major innovations in a technology that is currently fragile, and not much past its embryonic stages.

In this section, we will discuss some of the technology of the Fifth Generation. If the technological issues are uninteresting to you, move ahead to Section 6, which is a non-technical discussion of matters that might seriously impair the success of this project.

In his speech at the Fifth Generation conference, Fuchi coined the term *knowledge information processing* as "an extended form of knowledge engineering." He added, "This, it is thought, will represent the form of information processing in the '90s." What exactly did he mean?

He meant that machines must be designed to support very large knowledge bases, allow very fast associative retrievals, perform logical inference operations as quickly as current computers perform arithmetic operations, and utilize parallelism in program structure, and hardware to achieve high speed. There must be a machine-user interface designed to allow significant use of natural speech and images. At the heart of these intelligent machines are greatly magnified versions of expert systems (explained in the section, "Experts in Silicon"). The job of scaling up this new and complicated technology is simply formidable.

All expert systems built by knowledge engineers to date consist of three main parts. First is the subsystem that "manages" the knowledge base needed for problem solving and understanding. Second is the problem-solving and inference subsystem that discovers what knowledge is useful and relevant to the problem at hand, and with it constructs—step by step—a line of reasoning leading to the problem solution, the plausible interpretation, or the best hypothesis. Third are the methods of interaction between human and machine, in modes and languages that are "natural" and comfortable for the user. Ordinary human natural language is often preferred, but the stylized notations of some fields like chemistry are also desirable for specific groups of users. Knowledge-base management, problem solving and inference, and human interaction—these have all been approached in our present expert systems via software innovations, innovations that have pressed traditional von Neumann hardware architectures to the limits of their capabilities. The Fifth Generation plan organizes its work around these three subsystems, but with a critical added dimension: for each component subsystem there is a hardware level and a software level. And between the levels the Japanese designers must define a "language" with which the software and hardware interact.

Fifth-Generation Computer Systems

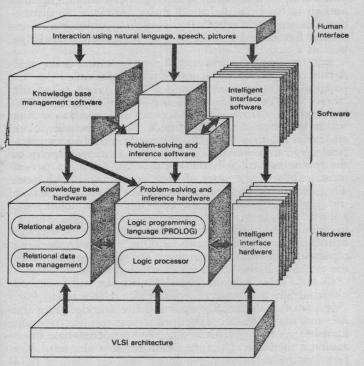

The knowledge in the knowledge base must first be represented in symbolic form, and in memory structures, that can be used efficiently by the problem-solving and inference subsystem. This representation can take many forms. One of the most common is the *object*, a cluster of attributes that describe a thing. An object is usually associated with other objects by symbolic references (*links*) in the memory. A typical kind of associative network is the taxonomy, known as "is-a hierarchy." For example, "The sparrow is–a kind of bird." In this case, both sparrow and bird are objects within the knowledge base. If the knowledge base is informed that "The bird is–a kind of animal that can fly," the knowledge-base management system must automatically propagate the little deduction that sparrows can fly. It must also be able to handle the exceptions it is told about, such as flightless birds like ostriches, penguins, and kiwis, for example, and it must also make the distinction that the dodo is both flightless and extinct, but nonetheless has its valid place in this taxonomic knowledge base as a bird.

Another common and useful representation is the *rule*. A rule consists of a collection of statements called the "if" part, and a conclusion or action to be taken called the "then" part. For example, "IF the fog ceiling is below 700 feet and the official weather forecast calls for no clearing within the hour, THEN landing is dangerous, will violate air traffic regulations, and diversion to a neighboring airfield is recommended." To find out if a rule is relevant to the reasoning task at hand, the problem-solving program must scan over the store of "ifs" in the knowledge base. That search can be immense in the size of knowledge base the Japanese plan to make possible. Here again, the knowledge-base management subsystem will be designed to organize the memory in ways that will reduce the amount of information processing to be done. Parallel processing capabilities in both the software and hardware levels of the system will also speed associative retrievals.

In the Fifth Generation plan, knowledge will be stored electronically in a large file known as a *relational data base*. The job of automatically updating the knowledge in the file and in organizing appropriate searches for relevant knowledge will be performed by the knowledge-base management software. The interaction between the hardware file and the software file manager will be handled by a logical language called a relational algebra.

The Fifth Generation prototype knowledge base subsystem will handle a modest knowledge base—thousands of rules and thousands of objects—about the size needed for current expert system applications. Each object will be allotted a thousand characters of file storage space (so that, in addition to storing the knowledge that sparrows are birds that can fly, the memory will also be able to hold knowledge pertaining to their size, weight, color, diet, range and habitat, breeding patterns, migratory routes, and so on—to call up our humble example). If knowledge about a particular object exceeds the storage capacity available, the initial object will be divided—say, into chipping sparrows, song sparrows, hedge sparrows, and so on—each as a separate object allotted its thousand characters of knowledge file space.

Within the ten-year trajectory of their plan, the Japanese goal is to develop knowledge base capacity in their systems that will be able to handle tens of thousands of inference rules and one hundred million objects! What could so much knowledge encompass? An American firm interested in the possibilities of representing large bodies of knowledge in computer knowledge bases has estimated that such a memory file could store the entire *Encyclopaedia Britannica*.

Knowledge serves as the basis for reasoning by a knowledge information processing system, but it is not sufficient in itself to discover and use lines of reasoning. Piecing together an appropriate line of reasoning which leads to the solution of a problem or the formulation of a body of consultative advice is the job of the inference process and the problem-solving strategy that employs it. Inference processes can be very much of the commonsense sort in which relevant knowledge is simply chained. A syllogism (IF X implies Y and IF Y implies Z, THEN X implies Z) is an example of such an inference process. Inference processes have been studied by logicians and mathematicians for centuries, and many different procedures for inference are known. From this logician's tool kit, artificial intelligence uses only a few routinely. Some of these methods allow for reasoning "inexactly" from knowledge that is uncertain. One, a favorite of AI, is resolution, constructed on a foundation of mathematical logic formulated in the 1960s by the logician Allan Robinson. Resolution is subtle, nonintuitive, and especially suited for computer processing.

An inference process is the tool of some problem-solving strategy. For example, the strategy for one kind of problem solving might be goal-directed backward chaining, which was described earlier in our scenario of planning a drive from San Francisco to New York by working backward from a desired set of end results at the destination through all the steps to be taken along the way to ensure that we arrive on time, see certain friends along the way, have a place to sleep each night, and so on.

The Fifth Generation envisions computer hardware engineered for logic processing, analogous to the well-engineered capabilities of earlier generations of computers to handle arithmetic processing. At present, we speak of computer capabilities in terms of millions of arithmetic operations per second. Japanese planners want their machines to handle millions of logical inferences per second (LIPS)—one logical inference equaling one step in a syllogistic, or IF/THEN, sequence of reasoning.

All scientists and engineers must place their bets for the future on what is known in the present. The Japanese are betting on resolution as the best inference method for which to target their logic processing hardware. This is an approach that has great credibility in Europe. A computer programming language called PROLOG, for "programming in logic" (invented in France, polished in England), has a somewhat similar approach. The Japanese have chosen PROLOG as the language of interaction between the logic processing hardware and the software that implements the various problem-solving strategies (in other words, PROLOG is the machine language of the logic processor).

The initial milestone in the Fifth Generation plan is a one-user PROLOG work station capable of performing one million LIPS. It is intended to be both a prototype for later development as well as an intermediate product that may be on the market by 1985. This prototype would give an order of magnitude in improvement over software-based PROLOG implementations on today's common mainframe computers like the DEC-2060. The final target for this subsystem is extraordinarily ambitious, however. It aims for an inference supercomputer that can perform one hundred million to one billion LIPS. Such incredible speed can be achieved only by the insightful use of a great deal of parallel processing in the computer hardware—a major advance over the von Neumann architecture now in use.

Most knowledge-based systems are intended to be of assistance to human endeavor; they are almost never intended to be autonomous agents. A human-machine inter-action subsystem is therefore a necessity in the Fifth Generation design. The Japanese intend to make this inter-action as natural as possible for users in both language and mode of interaction. This means language understanding—the ability to speak directly to the machine—as well as image understanding—the ability to show it pictures.

To realize these objectives across the spectrum of human knowledge and images is one of the most difficult of the long-term goals of artificial intelligence research. But if constraints are applied to the amount of vocabulary and areas of subject matter the subsystem is expected to handle, the problem becomes tractable, though very difficult, still. The Japanese have recognized this. Effective processing of the electrical signals that represent speech and pictures, first of all, requires specialized hardware to determine the most basic features of the words and images. But that's only the beginning. Software capable of inducing an understanding of the language being spoken or the image being shown must be developed, and it must be able to use the knowledge base efficiently to create a correct context; it's much easier to understand what's being said or seen if you know something about the subject matter. (These other technologies are discussed in more detail in the next section.)

That's the essence of the Japanese plan: hardware and software for each of three subsystems—knowledge base, problem solving and inference, and human-machine interaction. There's no need here to go into the nature of the ancillary software that's planned or the intricacies of the tactics that constitute the experiments to be done to approach the technical goals. That discussion forms the basis of a text for computer scientists.

The realization of visionary engineering goals usually requires much time and much money. The Japanese are accustomed to investing both in their major technology projects. The Fifth Generation project is structured over a ten-year period. The first three-year phase is targeted for climbing the well-known "learning curve"; for building the research teams and laboratories, learning the state of the art, forming the concepts that will be needed in the later work, and building hardware and software tools for the later phases. The single-user sequential PROLOG work station is one of these tools. The work station itself will be a prototype of later machines as will be its problem-solving software. Early expert system prototype applications will be written. Three will be selected from a variety of areas such as medical diagnosis, equipment failure diagnosis and repair, intelligent computer-aided design (CAD) for integrated circuit designers, intelligent CAD for mechanical equipment, and intelligent software production aids.

The second phase, four years, is one of engineering experimentation, prototyping, continuing experiments at significant applications, and the initial experiments at systems integration (making the subsystems work together smoothly). The first thrust at the major problem of parallel processing will be done in these years.

The final phase of three years will be devoted to advanced engineering, building final major engineering prototypes, and further systems integration work. The earlier work on CAD for VLSI will be used at this stage to assist the design of hardware. Experiments with some difficult applications will be attempted in this period; good engineering requires that one smash the system upon the rocks of hard reality and then learn how to fix it to ensure that it's robust and reliable. Finally, in the last phase, the results of the R&D will be distilled into a set of production specifications for the commercial products that are to be marketed by the participating companies.

5

Other Technologies
the Fifth Generation
Will Embrace

Since the Fifth Generation is so far-reaching, it demands dramatic improvements in other technologies that support the main-line KIPS goals. Essential to the future of the enterprise, for example, are extremely high-speed processors, capable of processing by orders of magnitude faster than anything now available.

Artificial intelligence made its debut on first-generation machines and has been implemented subsequently on second- and third-generation machines, but not yet on fourth-generation supercomputers.

Some computer scientists argue that this hasn't been necessary because AI programs have been designed to behave like non–von Neumann machines would behave anyway, illustrating the lag between computer structures (the actual machines themselves) and computer concepts (the way the machines are put to use). However, to design a program for a von Neumann machine and intend it to behave in a non–von Neumann fashion seems unnecessarily awkward and eventually limiting to the Japanese, which is why their Fifth Generation architecture may abandon the von Neumann scheme.

The Japanese aim for chips with 10 million transistors. Chips in current production carry a few hundred thousand transistors at most. Such processors are being developed in the course of another MITI effort, the SuperSpeed Computing Project, and will be adapted into the Fifth Generation machines. In addition, the Fifth Generation depends on access to knowledge bases in many locations, so its technology will ultimately be fused with the most advanced communications technologies the Japanese can design.

The whole area of intelligent interfaces—the ability the machines will have to listen, see, understand, and reply to human users—will require extensive research and development in natural language processing, in speech understanding, and in graphics and image understanding. All these have been concerns of artificial intelligence research from virtually its beginning some twenty-five years ago, and basic research in each of these fields has made reasonable progress. Still, state of the art in each is primitive compared to what the Japanese have in mind.

Because nonexperts will be the largest group of users, natural language processing is one of the most important research goals of the Fifth Generation. Research here will cover speech wave analysis, phonetic and syntactic analysis, semantic analysis, and pragmatic analysis, which derives understanding by extracting themes or foci in a given sentence, detecting focus shifts, and so on. For speech output, sentence generation will also be studied. Text analysis is also considered a part of natural language processing by the Japanese, although they are quite aware that the techniques used for large-scale text analysis are different from the techniques needed to smooth the way for an individual user to talk to his machine.

"In Japan as elsewhere the recent rapid progress in word processing techniques will no doubt increase the volume of text data and documents that have to be handled by computer to an intractable level," a group of

Japanese scientists reported at the Fifth Generation conference. "Sooner or later, as the problem of extracting useful information becomes more severe, we will have to turn to computing power in order to process these huge amounts of documents at reasonable speed. Our research on intelligent man-machine interface will help to solve this problem." Present artificial intelligence research suggests this can be done—in a prototype system, intelligent automatic analysis has been successfully applied to a wire news service in the United States, for instance—but the sheer scale of the automatic analysis planned by the Japanese dwarfs any existing systems.

Natural language processing will also be put to use in the development of a highly ambitious machine translation program (initially between English and Japanese) with a vocabulary of 100,000 words. The goal is 90 percent accuracy (the remaining 10 percent to be processed by humans). The translations will be part of an integrated system that takes part in each of the processes from compilation of the text to printing the translated documents.

All this research in natural language processing will proceed in three stages, beginning with an experimental system, followed by a pilot model implementation stage that is connected with the inference and knowledge base machine, and concluding with prototype implementations. At that point the machines will be expected to understand continuous human speech with a vocabulary of 50,000 words and 95 percent accuracy from a few hundred or more speakers. The speech understanding system is also expected to be capable of running a voice-activated typewriter and of conducting a dialogue with users by means of synthesized speech in Japanese or English. The machine's capacity to respond intelligently to users, known as its question-answering system, will first be designed to handle queries in the computing field, but it is expected to be a prototype for such systems in many professional fields: in addition to the query system's 5,000 or more words of vocabulary, it will have 10,000 or more inference rules to call upon.

Picture and image processing are considered almost as important as language processing, especially as they contribute to computer-aided design and manufacture (CAD/CAM) and to the effective analysis of aerial and satellite images, medical images, and the like. Here again the research will take place in three phases, beginning with an experimental phase to tackle such topics as the hardware architecture of "feature extractors"—for example, to distinguish the boundaries of objects—display generators, and the image data base. The second phase will produce a pilot model, and the third and final phase of research will be concerned with the implementation of the prototype and its integration into the Fifth Generation machine, along with studies of various applications. One obvious application is in robotics, where the goal will be to construct robots that can see, understand, and act under novel circumstances. The bulk of the Robotics R&D, however, will be done in a Robotics National Project. Eventually, the image understanding system is expected to store about 100,000 images. In this, as in voice recognition, the Japanese are building upon superb research and development that they themselves did in the 1970s during the Pattern Information Processing Systems (PIPS) National Project.

In short, the Japanese have studied the results of a quarter-century of AI research and have concluded that many of its areas are ripe for serious, methodical—and ultimately sensational—development. They are confident it can be done and that they're the ones who can do it.

6

What's Wrong?

The plans of the Fifth Generation project are audacious, some would say to the point of recklessness. The science upon which these plans are laid lies at the outermost edge (and in some cases, well beyond) what computer science knows at present. The plan is risky; it contains several "scheduled breakthroughs." There are major scientific and engineering challenges in every aspect of the work, from artificial intelligence through parallel architectures and distributed functions to VLSI design and fabrication.

The project demands early successes to maintain its momentum and funding, and that could be a problem. Conversely, meeting or exceeding the goals of the first three-year period might well propel the Japanese ahead of their timetable and will no doubt result in increased support from the participating companies.

Central to the success or failure of the project are the Japanese managers, both government and industrial. Although Japanese managers have taken on a samurai-like glamour in the past few years, thanks to enviable world-wide successes, they are in general conservative and risk-aversive. Yet here they are, charged with managing a very ambitious, high-risk project based on technology they hardly understand (through no particular fault of their own: managers everywhere tend to lose touch with technological innovation as they move up in the hierarchy).

Japanese managers have traditionally not been rewarded for successes so much as they have been penalized for failures. They are understandably firm believers in the old Japanese adage "The nail that gets hit is the one that sticks its head up." But failure is inherent in risk taking, and the Japanese must recognize this, reverse tradition, encourage risk taking, and reward it even when it fails.

Most of the breakthroughs the Fifth Generation project must achieve are basically innovations in software concepts (independent of whether these are realized in software or in silicon). The key ideas in the approach to knowledge information processing systems came out of the software world, not the hardware world—ideas about the creation, maintenance, and modifications of large and complex symbolic data structures in computer memories and the discovery of symbolic lines of reasoning. These ideas are at the level of aggregation that software scientists and engineers find congenial but would baffle most hardware engineers. A quick fix to the problem is to work on the intermediate territory of the so-called firmware—intricate and detailed "programming" of the hardware switching functions that sit at the bottom of the computing process. This is not a desirable final solution, however, since interpreting and executing the "firmware program" consumes time and slows down the machine. Japanese computer specialists and managers are not, and never have been, comfortable with software—it's intangible to them, and its production is notoriously difficult to manage "on schedule and on budget."

The Japanese lack experience in knowledge engineering and expert systems from which to draw as they begin to work out the details of what to build. ICOT and the company labs will have to move quickly to program not the mere three called for in the published plan, but ten or more exemplary systems to give themselves the necessary experience.

The Japanese lack a large corps of trained computer scientists. (We do, too, but not as severely.) Their university-level training in computer sciences is mediocre—the best is just adequate, and the rest is bad. Ph.D. candidates number in the tens, and nobody respects their degrees much anyway, because most postgraduate education in Japan is *in situ* at the great corporations or, for a fortunate few, abroad in American universities. The problem lies in Japanese university-level education in general, which we'll examine in its own right.

Finally, from a viewpoint of the AI specialist, skepticism and criticism have been focused on two elements of the plan: the priority given to the high-speed logic processor (do we really need all those millions of LIPS?) and the choice of PROLOG as the machine language of the logic processor.

In the American knowledge engineering experience, there have been few applications whose success was limited by the number of inference steps per second that could be performed. Limitations in performance tend to arise, rather, from limitations in the quantity and quality of knowledge available to the machine (too little and not well refined); the facility with which it can be managed and updated; and the speed with which it can be searched and accessed. Thus, the early focus on the inference subsystem in the Japanese plan, rather than on the knowledge base subsystem, is puzzling.

The PROLOG language has features as well as flaws. One good feature is a logical calculus, called first-order predicate calculus, known to have certain elegant and universal properties for the representation of knowledge. Its flaw is that the knowledge so represented is often opaque, incomprehensible, and arcane. A second good feature of

PROLOG is that it solves problems by proving theorems in first-order predicate calculus using computationally fast methods (that can be made even faster by using parallelism). The user never has to be concerned with the details of the problem-solving process. But PROLOG detractors see this as a serious flaw. The major successes of AI have come from mastering the methods by which knowledge can be used to control the search for solutions in complex problems. The last thing a knowledge engineer wants to do is abdicate control to an "automatic" theorem-proving process that conducts massive searches without step-by-step control exerted by knowledge in the knowledge base.

Such uncontrolled searches can be extremely time-consuming. The parallelism that can be brought to bear is a mere palliative, a Band-aid, because the searches become exponentially more time-consuming as the problem complexity increases. One can't keep up with exponential growth simply by lining up thousands of parallel processors.

7

What's Right?

Often in science and technology, the most important part of the creative act is asking the right question or placing the right long-term bet. This act, which may consume only a small fraction of project time and money, is crucial to the ultimate success or failure of the work. The rest is the necessary perspiration that brings the inspiration to life.

The time is right for a major initiative in the industrialization of artificial intelligence, and the Japanese are seizing the opportunity to move out briskly ahead of the pack. The move has been preceded by a thorough planning effort. The Fifth Generation plan of October 1981 is a strategy and not a set of tactics. Appropriately, it sets forth goals that stretch out over a long period of time. It is not, and could not be, a how-to-do-it manual. Its achievement is that it has focused attention on the right set of issues, properly structured. That's important in a complex and difficult project, for it is all too easy to squander resources and time milling about smartly without plan.

Creating the knowledge industry, with hardware, software, and knowledge system applications, is a great bet. Indeed, it is one of the few great bets sitting out there now in the information processing industry, ready for a major push toward exploitation. Of course the traditional modes of numerical calculation and data processing will continue to develop and prosper. But these will see steady incremental growth, not explosive growth. The exponential growth will be seen in symbolic computation and knowledge-based reasoning by computer.

MITI's key economic insight is correct. For an island trading nation like Japan, wealth is created by the margin of exports over imports. In the knowledge industry, the value of the exports is enhanced by indigenous resources—the intelligence, education, and skill of people—and the value of imports is minimal (computers are not material-intensive). Further, the KIPS will significantly enhance the productivity of many other industries, thereby indirectly contributing to the value added.

The creation of ICOT, the pooling of talent in a cooperative endeavor, plus the well-coordinated transfer of technology between ICOT and the parallel labs of the firms, seems inspired.

MITI's concern for nurturing the innovative talents of Japanese computer scientists appears to be well placed. In the first of the "tactical" addenda to the Fifth Generation plan, dated May 1982, ICOT (undoubtedly speaking for MITI) expresses this worry about the future: "In Japan, research and development has hitherto been aimed at catching up with the technologies of the U.S. and the advanced European nations. With Japanese technical achievements, however, the U.S. and the advanced European nations have become wary of providing leading technologies, and we fear that the old style of catching-up research and development will become more and more difficult." This is undoubtedly correct. Trade wars are under way, and blockades are inevitable.

The ten-year planning horizon is excellent. Ten years is

a long time in the information processing industry, almost inconceivably distant from us. Most of the people in the industry were not even in it ten years ago. Only two prototype expert systems had been built. Very expensive mainframes had to be shared among many users, for the idea of a personal computer—small and cheap enough to have at home, yet powerful enough to be useful—seemed like science fiction. Pocket calculators cost hundreds of dollars, and video games were no more than a primitive laboratory toy. The Japanese had yet to produce their first commercially viable microelectronic chip. As we live through it, we tend to underestimate the speed of technological change.

The Fifth Generation plan is difficult and will require much innovation; but of what sort? In truth, it is more engineering than science. Though solutions to the technological problems posed by the plan may be hard to achieve, paths to possible solutions abound. The Japanese are rich with excellent engineering talent and adequately supplied with cutting-edge computer scientists. This mix of talents enables (but of course does not guarantee) a good chance of success.

Ehud Y. Shapiro, a world authority in the language of PROLOG who comes from the applied mathematics department of Weizmann Institute of Science in Israel, was the first non-Japanese researcher to be invited for a working visit to ICOT, where he spent four weeks exchanging scientific information with ICOT workers. In January 1983 he reported, "People who believe in the unpredictability of scientific progress and revolutions find a planned revolutionary project to be almost a contradiction in terms. But sometimes ideology has to give way to reality: the Japanese project is both well-planned and revolutionary. It did not invent the concepts of logic programming but it is certainly the first, and perhaps today the only one, who grasped the immense potential in this approach, and gathered the critical mass of resources necessary to utilize it on a large scale.

"There are thoughts and attempts throughout the world at responding to the Fifth Generation project, but as I see it, this battle is already won. The eventual success of the project will follow not from the amount of money invested in it, the number of people working on it, not even from the individual excellence of these people. It will follow from the coherent vision of its leaders, the genuine enthusiasm that they generate, and from the promising path of research they chose.

"Any response to the project may match the amount of money or other resources invested in it, but will fail to come up with the same sense of direction and devotion that hold the Fifth Generation project together. One such example is the British response, which basically says: Let's keep doing what we do today, but with much more money. Money will increase the progress of research, but by itself will not result in a new generation of computers."[2]

8

What's Real?

The Fifth Generation project is hard—challenging in every dimension of the information processing science and technology. But as we have said, *TEN YEARS IS A LONG TIME!* In the magic world of computing, the world of "Always More for Less," where the More is doubled and the Less is halved every two or three years, ten years is virtually forever.

The Japanese undoubtedly will have a partial success. Managers of the Fifth Generation project have said that it would not disturb them if only 10 percent of the project goals were achieved; others have remarked that the ten-year planning horizon should not be taken too seriously, that the project goals are so important that an extension over another half or full decade would not be unreasonable.

Partially realized concepts that are superbly engineered can have great utility and be of great economic benefit. At the very least, a partial success can preempt the area and make it not worthwhile for others to enter playing catchup.

It may be the case that the first 20 percent of the technical achievement will skim off 80 percent of the economic gain that there is to be realized. If this were to be true, firms in other nations might never find it in their economic interest to enter the arena. Being late might put them out of the contest. Consider this: though videotaping was invented in the United States, the lengthy and expensive research and development process for the consumer-oriented video cassette recorder led to an all-or-none market share result, with the American industry getting the "none." Even the VCRs that carry American household brand names like RCA and Sears are made in Japan.

No matter how partial its success may be, the Fifth Generation project will provide a decade-long learning experience for a new generation of Japanese computer scientists. They will be called upon to confront and perhaps solve the most challenging problems facing the future of information processing, rather than reengineering traditional systems in a way that has provided Japan with an edge in the high technologies market, if hardly ever the leading edge. Since the fundamental ideas, as we have said, are software concepts, they will be living with and learning advanced software concepts in a way that has never been done before in Japan and has never been widely done in the United States or Europe.

The Fifth Generation project, in its short life, has emplaced the technology transfer mechanisms necessary for Japanese industry to move effectively to bring its developments to market. Right now, the United States has a substantial lead over the Japanese in virtually every area of Fifth Generation work. But *Fortune*'s article on the Fifth Generation project concludes with this observation: "Even if the U.S. retains its lead in AI research, there is no guarantee that the laboratory work will end up in products. Computer research tends to seep into the American marketplace slowly except when companies perceive a competitive threat. Assuming that ICOT can do even a fraction of what it intends, the results will show up quickly in Japanese computer products. So the U.S. computer industry could be outmaneuvered unless it takes the Fifth Generation seriously."[3]

To repeat, one thing that is real is that the United States, and to a more limited extent the United Kingdom, has a lead at present in this area of information processing technology. If the Japanese did not have a well-planned, well-organized, and well-funded effort, that lead would perhaps be ten years. But because the Japanese are moving now, the real lead is perhaps less than three years. That is still a large lead by the normal standards of Silicon Valley and Route 128, where six-month leads confer competitive advantages and twelve-month leads are cherished. But our business-as-usual attitude, our near-term R&D planning horizons, our fratricidal competitive zeal and paranoia over proprietary rights, and our planning vacuum at the national level are causing us to squander our valuable lead at the rate of one day per day. To an economic planner and to an executive in the information processing industry, that should be cause enough for alarm that expresses itself in decisive commitment to action.

9

The Japanese and Expert Systems

Feigenbaum's warning to the assembly at the Fifth Generation conference that they were planning a major computer system based on techniques that they hardly had any experience with was not to be answered, fully and finally, by Fuchi's polite retort that Japan was, in his view, something more than a child in this area, and, anyway, the Japanese are good learners.

In May 1982, when Feigenbaum received a copy of ICOT's first "tactical" addendum to the conference *Proceedings*, he immediately noted that ICOT had incorporated the selection and development of three expert systems from a diverse spectrum of problem bases into the mid-range objectives of the project.

He was not surprised. In a few short years, the Japanese

AI researchers had matured, both in their quiet, imperturbable self-confidence and, as well, in the speed and insight with which they analyzed and responded to any criticism that they thought might matter. As recently as the late 1970s, Japanese visitors to Feigenbaum's Stanford laboratory had conveyed (affected perhaps?) an air of inferiority about their work. With elaborate and sincere apologies, they would ask Feigenbaum's comments on work that, in fact, needed no apologies; work that, on the contrary, was excellent and original.

In the area of problem selection, in particular, they had gone from zero to good taste almost overnight. Problem selection—the selection of a domain in which to attempt the building of an expert system—is an art. Problems must be chosen that fit the state of the art in knowledge engineering. If they fit precisely, well and good. If they're slightly beyond the present tools, they push the state of the art. But if they're far beyond what everyone else is doing, little can be accomplished, and time and effort are wasted.

A few years before, engineers from Hitachi called on Feigenbaum with a list of possible candidates for the expert systems treatment. There might have been thirty-five items on the list, and those were rather vaguely explained. But all the visitors wanted from him was advice on whether each project was likely or unlikely (some "warmer-colder" judgments). A year later, they returned with their list pared down to six, those problems beautifully analyzed. One in particular intrigued him: the debugging of an integrated circuit fabrication line. Here the problem was slightly different from the other candidates that had been put forward for expert systems treatment, where the issue was replication of human expertise. In the IC fabrication line problem there was no single human expert who held—or could hold—all the expertise necessary to make this complex industrial process function with high yield. Thus the problem was one of integrating expertise from many different experts. Rumor has it that Hewlett-Packard is working on a similar expert system. But it was the Japanese who identified the problem as a splendid one to work on, and it was a good indication of their growing sophistication in knowledge engineering.

Another Japanese project, under way at Hitachi, which also suggests imagination and growing confidence, concerns the problems of managing large construction projects. Such projects are usually risky, and PERT charts embroidered with probabilities aren't really helpful because much of what the people managing the work know and can report about risk is qualitative rather than quantitative. But if symbolic reasoning instead of formulas were used, an expert system could provide qualitative knowledge that can assist in good management on a risky project.

A visit to Japan in midsummer 1982—post–Fifth Generation conference—suggested that the Japanese are embracing expert systems research enthusiastically. In addition to the research formally sponsored by ICOT, anywhere from ten to fifty knowledge engineers are working on expert systems and the AI research underlying them at each of Fujitsu, Hitachi, Nippon Electric Corporation (NEC), Nippon Telephone and Telegraph (NTT), and the Electrotechnical Laboratory, all in the greater Tokyo area. Other efforts are under way elsewhere in Japan.

Most of these expert systems are similar to those in the United States. But the Japanese have also chosen to design expert systems for two areas that, so far, are theirs alone. They are working in the pregnant area of crisis management, in which little work exists elsewhere. (There is research at Rensselaer Polytechnic Institute on crisis management by computer, but it relies on management information systems, not expert systems.)[4]

First is the nuclear power reactor crisis. If a Three Mile Island–like event suddenly occurs, there's no time to do a mathematical simulation of the situation. What is needed is the rapid exercise of the carefully prepared "art of good judgment" that is the hallmark of the expert system.

Second, and similarly, a Japanese firm is working on an expert system for the management of an electric power grid crisis. Again, if something goes wrong, it takes several minutes to do the numerical simulation of a power grid to decide upon the appropriate corrective action. But skilled grid managers have seconds, not minutes, to protect a power network. (Incidentally—and not so incidentally—the Japanese firm estimates that it could sell 10,000 of these expert systems worldwide, because there simply aren't enough human experts to go around.) The embodiment of human expertise, carefully captured and honed, in a computer program that knows what to do in a crisis, whose expertise can easily be improved and updated as equipment and circumstances change, and that doesn't get bored or distracted between crises is the ideal solution for dozens of crises-waiting-to-happen situations in today's highly technological world.

MITI-sponsored research from a few years ago in another advanced area is also having a delayed payoff in its potential applications in the machine-user interface subsystem of the Fifth Generation project. That program, to develop Pattern Information Processing Systems (PIPS) to process and interpret visual signal information, is a difficult challenge that has all the problems associated with natural language processing, including understanding context, as well as special problems concerning depth and shading and edges and corners and so on. PIPS was never exploited as a commercial product, and most Western computer scientists assumed that it had been a technological failure. It had not. Feigenbaum was to see some late PIPS models, for instance a PIPS for motion tracking, a difficult problem in computer vision. It monitored TV pictures of people walking down a passageway in a Tokyo subway and in real time tracked the paths that they were taking. That's certainly on a par with any other pattern-information processing work going on in the world. PIPS was a marketing failure, but not a technological failure. (It was even, by MITI standards, a strategic failure. Although it taught the Japanese many things about visual processing, it produced no hardware until very late in the project. Some Japanese suggest that this accounts for Fuchi's decision to produce a prototype piece of hardware as soon as humanly possible.) But Japanese scientists understand the success they had with PIPS, even if few others do, and it plays a core role in the Fifth Generation project which will, as we have already observed, accept pictorial as well as voice and written input.

One cannot help but be struck by the general industriousness of the Japanese. They have pulled themselves from nowhere to somewhere, and often to world predominance, simply by hard work. Their quick study in expert systems is typical, one of many examples that could be cited in computing alone, not to mention a host of other fields. McCorduck also observes that not only are the people she meets in Tokyo hard at work doing science, but somehow, sometime, somewhere, nearly all of them have managed to learn English, too. A young Fifth Generation researcher discloses that he practices on his daily commute, plugged into his Walkman, sounding out his English pronunciation in concert with the cassette. In the crowded train to Tokyo station, nobody remarks on such a thing.

The Japanese miracle puts her in mind of the curious but telling fact, unearthed by Donald Keene, that one of the first English-language books to be translated into Japanese in the nineteenth century—and a runaway best seller—was a book called *Self-Help*.

10

The Problems
of Compatibility

Feigenbaum and McCorduck chanced to arrive in Tokyo just as the scandalized Japanese were digesting the news that a score of executives from Hitachi and Mitsubishi, two of their most prestigious firms, had been indicted in a scheme to steal trade secrets from IBM. The initial shock of seeing on TV the spectacle of top executives in hand-cuffs had worn off, and Japan was experiencing some deeper emotional reactions.

There was, for example, a doleful letter to the editor of one Japanese newspaper which detailed the computer sin, added the sins of steel dumping by Mitsui in the United States, and concluded that the Japanese were now "hated all around the world." The writer added, "I wish I lived in a poor but honest country again."

There was a persistent feeling among the Japanese that the matter was both ordinary and extraordinary at the same time. "Everybody does it" so it was ordinary; but the Japanese had been naive enough to get caught. They had been caught—the extraordinary aspect—because the U.S.

government had decided to make an object lesson of them, to force Japan to yield in trade negotiations that were then under way at the U.S. Commerce Department, and, some thought, as a revenge for Japan's quick embargo the year before on California fruit infested with the Mediterranean fruit fly.

A Hitachi executive who subscribed to the ordinary-but-naive theory told Feigenbaum that the problem was simply that Hitachi didn't have a sufficient number of lawyers to guide them. Stealing was stealing, Feigenbaum observed mildly.

A bizarre theory from the opposite camp had Ronald Reagan conspiring with IBM to give the economically beset American people a new rallying cry: instead of "Remember Pearl Harbor," Americans could now cry, "Remember Silicon Valley" as they boycotted Walkmans and digital watches and Toyotas, putting their dollars instead into domestic products at last and thereby exhuming the American economy.

In connection with the Fifth Generation, a journalist for *Asahi Shimbun*, Japan's largest-circulation newspaper, suggested that the computer scandal had caused a crisis of confidence in Japan. How could the Japanese embark on something as ambitious as the Fifth Generation project, he wanted to know, if they had to steal secrets from the United States to stay competitive? He could not be persuaded that the two were not necessarily connected.

Hitachi executives fretted that the Fifth Generation would eventually produce machines that were incompatible with IBM's. Feigenbaum's reassurances that conventional computers would continue to be used for data processing while the Fifth Generation machines went on to perform more intelligent work (or, more precisely, that the new machines could simply link into the data processing machines whenever large amounts of data were to be processed) failed to comfort.

Eventually a constructive attitude emerged, expressed in an editorial in the *Japan Times*, which wondered whether being compatible with IBM was, after all, the only role for the Japanese computer industry. Might it not be time to try some other path?

The question is not without pertinence. The great argument for IBM compatibility has always been the bargain it is—users of any IBM-compatible machine can be sure that their costly software, developed over thousands of man-hours of labor, will always be, if not efficient, or even convenient, at least usable. IBM-compatible machines eliminate the expensive and risky business of reprogramming software that is known to work, recoding files that have historically conformed to IBM's way of doing things. Thus the cost of any departure from IBM's standards has always seemed so formidable that few have had the courage to go their own way.

But if Japan has correctly assessed the future, the crisis of confidence some Japanese felt as the result of the trade secret scandal is unwarranted. If MITI succeeds in its overall goal of achieving world leadership in the information processing industry in the 1990s, across the spectrum of technologies from integrated circuits to the most complex kinds of software, it will be IBM's worry to be compatible, not Japan's.

11

Why Are the Japanese Doing All This?

We have dwelled on some of the technological reasons why the Japanese have produced their plan for a new generation of computers. We have talked about the advantages that accrue to knowledge workers when they have the help of computerized expert systems. But Japan also has significant social, intellectual, and economic reasons for embarking on this most ambitious project, and in the long run they will be the most compelling.

The eminently correct Professor Tohru Moto-oka of Tokyo University opened the Fifth Generation proceedings with a speech that immediately named the big issues. "In the 1990s," he said, "when Fifth Generation computers will be widely used, information processing systems will be a central tool in all areas of social activity, to include economics, industry, science, culture, daily life, and the like, and will be required to meet those new needs generated by environmental changes."[5]

If this seems sweeping and somewhat grandiose, it might be instructive to substitute "written language" or "the printed word" or another amplifier of human intelligence for "information processing systems" and see not only how well it fits, but also how it suggests the changes to come. The world was very different before humans invented the method of recording their language called writing, and it changed still again when that writing could be distributed far and wide, and cheaply, thanks to the printing press. The quantitative amplification—it is fair to say the magnification—of the human intellect that intelligent machines represent is about to bring a qualitative change in human affairs that we can hardly imagine.

But the Japanese *have* tried to imagine such a world. They have picked out specific areas where the Fifth Generation will make a large difference.

First, it will be a means of increasing productivity in low-productivity areas. Computing has already had such an impact in secondary, or manufacturing, industries. But other industries such as goods distribution and public services have remained almost the same (and some might argue that they have declined). In particular, the Japanese have suffered from low productivity in white-collar work. So has nearly everyone else, but the Japanese feel it especially because their language doesn't lend itself easily to mechanical means of reproduction such as typewriters. The first writing the Japanese ever saw was Chinese, and though their language had practically no relationship whatever to Chinese, the Japanese adopted that form of writing and have had to live with it ever since. In any case, the Fifth Generation will offer natural Japanese language processing in systems that can handle nonnumerical data, like documents, graphics, and speech.

The Fifth Generation systems will be intelligent assistants to managers, acting as consultants with inference and learning mechanisms of their own which can also connect to nationwide, even worldwide, data and knowledge bases for the high-level expertise necessary for making important decisions.

Again, Moto-oka cites a key economic insight: Japan is land-poor and resource-poor but "Japan's plentiful labor force is characterized by a high degree of education, diligence, and high quality. It is desirable to utilize this advantage to cultivate information itself as a new resource comparable to food and energy, and to emphasize the development of information-related, knowledge-intensive industries which will make possible the processing and managing of information at will."

A certain amount of pious lip service is paid to international cooperation—the Fifth Generation can smooth international exchanges through the development of translation and interpreting systems—but then Moto-oka introduces a theme that runs throughout the project, a theme that is far more important than it first seems.

"Although we have mainly followed the lead of other countries in computer technology up to now, it's time for us to break with this outmoded tradition and center our efforts on the development of new computer technology based on our own conceptions, so that we can provide the world with new technology with a view to promoting international cooperation." The form such cooperation might take is vague, but there is no doubt about which nation will provide the technology to make it happen—who, in short, will lead.

The Japanese speculate that the Fifth Generation will help to save energy and resources. We live on a planet with finite resources, after all, and one way of conserving those resources is through better information that allows us to minimize or optimize our energy consumption, improve the efficiency of our energy conversions, stimulate possible new sources of energy, reduce energy consumption in production through computer-aided design and manufacturing, extend the life of products through damage detection and automatic repair, and reduce the movement of people by propagating distributed systems or, as we in the United States have come to call it, the electronic cottage.

And they envision the Fifth Generation will be put to use in coping with an aging society. By 1990, 12 percent of Japan's population will by sixty-five years or older (in the United States we are already there). An aging society suggests, among other things, that medical and welfare costs will increase, together with a relative reduction in the labor force. Thus the Fifth Generation can improve and streamline medical and related information processing systems for health management, help develop systems for enabling the physically handicapped to become active, contribute computer-aided instruction systems for the lifetime education of the aged, and develop distributed processing systems for enabling people to work at home.

The Fifth Generation will expand human abilities. Until now, the Japanese argue, increasing productivity has been accomplished only through improvements in the efficiency of human labor. Now intelligence, not merely physical labor, will be amplified.

Decision-support systems will provide high-level information for increasing the effectiveness and reducing the time and costs required for making decisions. The Japanese are used to group decision making, and they see their Fifth Generation as a means of smoothing that consensual process. They envisage the general development of knowledge industries to promote stable, consistent, and sophisticated judgments in politics, administration, and industry. Decision-support systems will not be only the tools of moguls of industry and government. Home decision-support systems will allow ordinary people to plan their family finances, schedule their activities, and "design their lifestyles" in a rational way.

"With these achievements, activities in all facets of society will be affected and within a margin of safety, more advanced, humane behavior will be possible, thus allowing for a more balanced society." As utopian as such a sentiment sounds, we should hesitate before we scoff too much. Sociologist Daniel Bell puts it this way: "Beginning a little more than 150 years ago, modern Western society was able to master a secret denied to all previous societies—a steady increase in wealth and a rising standard of living by peaceful means." Previous societies had sought wealth by war, plunder, and other painful means, but Western society had discovered productivity, which is the ability to gain more than proportional output from a given exertion of labor or expenditure of capital. In short, everybody could get more for less, though not everybody got as much more as he or she wanted.[6] Productivity has revolutionized society and though industrial productivity has not been without its costs, it has made us wealthier, which has brought with it a glorious cornucopia of benefits which few of us are willing to give up, no matter how hard we complain about the costs. Those who don't have that wealth want to share in it.

But perhaps the best answer to the question of why the Japanese are doing all this comes from Sozeburo Okamatsu, a MITI official who told an American journalist: "Because we have only limited resources, we need a Japanese technological lead to earn money for food, oil, and coal. Until recently we chased foreign technology, but this time we'll pioneer a second computer revolution. If we don't, we won't survive."

12

The Myths of Japan 1: Copycats in Kimonos

Westerners labor under a number of misapprehensions about Japan, which take the form of mythical assumptions about the Japanese people. Among those American computer scientists, engineers, and sales executives who have heard about the Japanese plans for the Fifth Generation project, most dismiss the idea and quote the old myths. In general, they assume, the Japanese are simply incapable of the level of innovation a project like the Fifth Generation requires, for everybody, including the Japanese themselves, knows myth number 1. *The Japanese may be wonderful copycats, but they're incapable of producing original work.*

As with most stereotypes, there is enough truth in this myth to prevent most people from looking beyond it to discover a more complex reality. It is certainly true that in the postwar decades the Japanese have taken technology first developed elsewhere and improved upon it to the point where they have driven its originators out of business: cameras, watches, consumer electronics come at once to mind. But this borrowing and improving upon is an old and unremarkable habit of every nation, especially Europeans and their former colonies. We've swapped ideas in technology (and art and science and literature and language and food) for centuries without expecting it to be otherwise, and without feeling the least embarrassment in the process. Usually, these changes have been gradual, and they have seldom been perceived as a threat.

Given all this, the Japanese stereotype of uncreativeness endures. Even Edwin Reischauer more or less accepts the stereotype, but in *The Japanese* he writes: "These traits of relative weakness in theoretical innovation but great strength in practical application were characteristic of the United States too during its period of catching up with Europe. Americans have taken a leading place in science, scholarship, and thought only in recent decades. As Japan draws abreast of the West, the same change may occur there."[7]

Many Japanese themselves accept the stereotypes. One night Feigenbaum, his wife, Penny Nii, and McCorduck are guests at a traditional dinner in Tokyo. Their hosts are managers of one of the largest computer companies in Japan, and inevitably the conversation gets around to East versus West. "You Westerners," says a Japanese executive quietly, "you are the hunters of the world. You go out and find things, hunt them down. We Japanese are the cultivators, the agrarians."

McCorduck smiles at this but says nothing. Her host goes on.

"We don't innovate. We don't hunt for something new. We're most comfortable with what we know, but we do that beautifully." He repeats his formulation once more: "You are the hunters; we are the cultivators."

McCorduck thinks to mention that the agricultural revolution was a significant event in human history, and it's thanks to it that civilization began, but it has been a long day and she's in no mood for even polite dispute. Her host offers the beer around the table.

"No," says Feigenbaum, "as a matter of fact, what I'd really like is a cup of coffee."

"The rice isn't here yet," his wife says, meaning the meal isn't yet over, though everyone feels gorged on the parade of elegant delicacies that have been brought in by the kimono-clad hostess (*waitress* just isn't the word).

"I know," Feigenbaum says affably, "but what I feel like just now is a cup of coffee."

His hosts oblige, though since this is a traditional restaurant, coffee isn't so easy to come by. At last a cup of instant coffee arrives, with apologies.

A younger colleague of the man who has made the hunter-agrarian comparison begins to laugh. "My friend here is absolutely right," he says with good humor. "What you just did—order a cup of coffee when nobody else was having coffee—no Japanese would dream of doing that. Have you ever noticed when a Japanese family or group goes out for dinner, everybody orders the same thing? That's the way we are. It's our culture." Thus the words of a young man who's done graduate work at both Stanford and M.I.T.

Westerners go further and claim that this lack of innovative spirit prevents Japan from ever producing a genius. Two observations can be made about that. First, no one would claim that computing suffers by being worked at by geniuses, but the secret to producing a new generation of computers is not so much genius as a large amount of hard work and superb organization. IBM has rarely produced a genius either, but that doesn't prevent it from being preeminent in computing right now. (Ironically, one of IBM's rare geniuses is Dr. Esaki, who is Japanese.)

The second observation is less pleasant. The Japanese have often simply failed to receive the recognition they deserve. For example, most Western textbooks generously admit that the calculus was invented independently and simultaneously by Newton and Leibnitz, but the earlier independent invention in Japan by Seki Takakazu (1642–1708) goes unmentioned. The Japanese receive scant recognition for their literature. English-speaking students still learn a history of the novel that parallels the rise of the European bourgeoisie in the eighteenth and nineteenth centuries, even though the magnificent novel *The Tale of Genji* was written in the first quarter of the eleventh century.

In fact, one study shows that Japanese schoolchildren have an average I.Q. score that is eleven points higher than that of their American counterparts.[8] The *New York Times* counseled American parents to react calmly, point-
out that this is all probably a matter of nutrition and

But perhaps these arguments miss the real point. How are the nations that produce certified geniuses doing? Could it possibly be that in the postindustrial society the best way to accomplish useful things is through concerted effort by a large group, instead of the inspired work of one outstanding genius? The Apollo project to put a man on the moon was not the work of a solitary genius, but a series of well-orchestrated efforts by many well-trained and knowledgeable people. The same is true of successful firms, government agencies, military adventures, and performing arts. Our myth of a glorious rugged individualism, whether in the log cabin or inside the human cranium, is dear to us, but it is a fiction that doesn't stand up to inspection under twentieth-century circumstances.

Richard Dolen, a computer consultant who has the advantage of being able to read the Fifth Generation plans in their original Japanese, writes: "In the field at hand, the papers of the working groups show a mastery of the gist of previous research in the field. Although many of the researchers are newcomers to the field, so that their knowledge of some of the techniques is more vicarious than experiential, this is not a defect in ability, nor one which is irremediable."

He goes on to observe that an industry such as computing advances by the combined efforts of three types of persons: persons of genius, experts in the field, and many persons of lesser ability. It is likely that persons of genius are distributed equally over Japan and the West; the West has a rapidly narrowing superiority of experts in the field (with only half the population of the United States, Japan still graduates more electrical engineers annually); and the average work day and work week of the Japanese computer technologist seems to be longer than that of his Western counterpart.

On the inability of the Japanese to be as creative as Westerners, Dolen says, "Even were these arguments substantial, they seem more relevant to affect the conduct of the average shopgirl or office worker rather than the quality of research of the computer scientist or senior research professor, whose abilities alone place him or her in the 99.9th percentile. These are the persons least likely to follow average patterns of behavior, especially where creativity is concerned." Besides, he adds, the com
about the lack of Japanese creativity seem to b

from popular Japanese magazines which publish articles by creative Japanese who decry social habits that discourage creativity.[9]

Still the Japanese acknowledge this stereotype about themselves, and although some accept it, it rankles others. Scientist after scientist working on the Fifth Generation project mentioned it and claimed for the Fifth Generation the chance to erase that myth once and for all. They intend to change the myth by changing the facts: the kind of innovative basic research and development necessary to produce the first large-scale intelligent computers will be of the highest order.

In the first edition of this book, we concluded this section with the following: "Many Western computer scientists believe that the Japanese have already achieved a psychological coup by embarking upon this Fifth Generation. Future computers, regardless of who develops them, will inevitably be measured against these Japanese goals."

So it has been, but sooner and more decisively than anybody could have imagined. In 1983, for example, entire issues of Western technical journals were devoted to the Fifth Generation; international seminars on the topic abounded; and the Association for Computing Machinery, the pre-eminent computing professional society in the United States, announced the theme for its 1984 annual meeting: The Fifth Generation.

13

The Myths of Japan 2: Variations on the Theme

Many Westerners comfort themselves with other variations on the main theme that the Japanese cannot innovate or be creative, and therefore the Fifth Generation is nothing to worry about. One variation runs: *Everything in Japanese society points toward an unwavering mediocrity instead of peaks of excellence. Indeed, peaks of excellence are discouraged in the Japanese effort to achieve conformity.*

Here is a confusion between conformity and homogeneity, and the relationship of either characteristic to intellectual achievement. Reischauer comments on the remarkable cultural homogeneity of Japan, a consequence of several influences, but mainly a conscious effort by government through basic education policies to develop a uniform, unified citizenry. The mass media join in, including television and the newspapers, which are national and not party organs as in Europe, or geographically specialized as in the United States. But the result of all this can hardly be described as mediocre.

"One can safely say that the Japanese on average are provided with fuller and more accurate newspaper coverage of both national and international news than any other people in the world, and only an occasional newspaper elsewhere surpasses their great national dailies in either quantity or quality of news," Reischauer writes. As he observes the mass society in Japan, he says, "These mass characteristics, however, are hardly all or even the most important aspects of modern Japanese culture. Much more significant is its tremendous vitality, creativity, and variety. In the field of Western music, Japan's many symphony orchestras rank with the best in the world, as do individual Japanese musicians and conductors. Japanese architects are world famous. Modern painters and woodblock artists are tremendously prolific. All the more traditional arts are more alive today than for many decades. Japanese traditional potters have set the styles that are copied worldwide. Literature is bounding with energy. People are sparkling with artistic creativity, and young people are bubbling with new life-styles."[10]

But Reischauer is cautious. "Still, there is reason to wonder if intellectual creativeness will ever be a special forte of the Japanese. Their past history is studded with prominent religious leaders, great poets and writers, outstanding organizers and even distinguished synthesizers of thought, but not with great intellectual figures. Japanese have always seemed to lean more toward subtlety and sensitivity than to clarity of analysis, to intuition rather than reason, to pragmatism rather than theory, to organizational skills rather than great intellectual concepts."[11]

So far as the Fifth Generation computer system is concerned, that may not matter. Reischauer chides Westerners for their biases and asks whether truths realized by reason are superior to those attained by intuition, or whether disputes settled by verbal skills are preferable to a consensus reached through feeling. "It is possible that a Japan standing near the forefront of knowledge in the world may come to show more intellectual creativeness than it has in the past, but on the other hand those other traits may remain more characteristic of the Japanese and may continue to contribute more to their success."[12] Especially if they have the symbolic inference machines of the Fifth Generation to do analysis and reasoning for them, he might add. Our own impression is that their natural analytical skills are more than adequate.

14

The Myths of Japan 3:
Languages Natural and Artificial

Another myth goes something like this: *The Japanese might be able to build terrific cars, stereos, cameras, and baseball mitts, but computers are different. The Japanese can't produce software. But it's not the fault of their intelligence; it's a limitation of their language.*

The natural Japanese language is indeed difficult for Western speakers. Japanese belongs to a small family of languages called the Altaic languages, which include Turkish, Mongolian, Manchu, and Korean. By historical accident, the Japanese adopted Chinese characters to write their language, although the two languages otherwise are unrelated. But if these difficulties flummox human speakers, they aren't necessarily relevant to science, in particular to software design for computers.

Reischauer disposes of that part of the language myth this way: "Many foreigners, most of whom have precious little knowledge of Japanese, complain that the language is too lacking in clarity or logic to fit modern technological or scientific needs. . . . Certainly the Japanese, with their suspicion of verbal skills, their confidence in nonverbal understanding, their desire for consensus decisions, and their eagerness to avoid personal confrontation, do a great deal more beating around the verbal bush than we do and usually try to avoid the 'frankly speaking' approach so dear to Americans. They prefer in their writing as well as their talk a loose structure of argument, rather than careful logical reasoning, and the suggestion or illustration, rather than sharp clear statements. But there is nothing about the Japanese language which prevents concise, clear, and logical presentation, if that is what one wishes to make. The Japanese language itself is fully up to the demands of modern life."[13]

Another form this myth takes is *The Japanese are ten years behind us in software*. Western nations do lead the Japanese in software development at the moment. But the Japanese have made a national commitment to concentrate their energies and efforts on software, catch up, and overtake the Western nations. Given this explicit objective as part of the Fifth Generation plan, Westerners can be sure that their lead will be quickly eroded. But there are two important points to keep in mind. First, Westerners don't know all that much about software themselves. Software innovations are in short supply in the West as well. Second, as we have suggested, the Japanese are undertaking an entirely new kind of software, a variety that may put us years behind if we're not careful.

To be specific, our software lead is slight and for each day we do nothing, we run the risk that a Japanese breakthrough will eliminate it altogether. Right now, we are in the position of trading places—they have a lead in commitment, and we have a lead in technology. Day by day, our technology lead will decrease, and their technological excellence—which is fired by their zeal to improve their present software as well as to create some that's entirely new—will grow.

15

The Myths of Japan 4:
They Just Can't Do This
and They Know It, Too

In the first edition of this book, we said: "Among Western computer industrialists is a surprisingly large group who believe this myth: *The entire Fifth Generation effort—planning documents, conference, new Tokyo laboratory, initial budget and staff—is no more than a giant charade*. The Fifth Generation project, these skeptics say, is nothing more than a promotional effort to gather resources for improving tomorrow's computer products, not products ten years away. We have already mentioned that when asked why the Japanese would go to such elaborate lengths to achieve small changes that will come along all in good time anyway, these people have no answer. No experience seems capable of teaching the skeptics that the key to Japanese success thus far is an intelligent combination of short-range *and* long-range planning. The Japanese excel at both."

The surprisingly large group of computer industrialists we described has withered into near invisibility. Similar remarks, however, can still be heard on Wall Street. For example, in the fall of 1983, addressing an international seminar of business executives from the United States and Europe, one market analyst suggested in all seriousness that the Fifth Generation might be no more than an empty threat by the Japanese government in the hopes of resisting the American government's requests that Japan shoulder a larger proportion of the costs of its own national defense, a topic that was just then in the news. (Ignoring the fact that the Fifth Generation had, by then, been in the planning stages for three years, and an actual research project for two additional years, that still seemed a far-fetched theory.) Another analyst at the same conference declared that it was all just a matter of a couple of academics getting upset over what the business community had already concluded was no threat, and that academics were making a fuss for their own nefarious purposes. He expanded on all this in a newsletter sent out by his firm, declaring that the "cool-headed, business-like judgments" of the business community saw no threat to the American computer industry in the Japanese Fifth Generation; that "the American genius for innovation and creativity will continue to flourish and should keep the United States ahead of the Japanese."[14]

If there are any computer professionals remaining who embrace such theories of fraud and duplicity on the part of the Japanese, or complacency in the face of the potential for Japanese achievements, such people are silent. Moreover, as later events would suggest, it isn't just the American academic community that expresses alarm and is taking action. But legitimate questions still surface about Japanese capabilities, and they deserve examination.

If the Japanese are truly capable of mounting a huge project like this, the skeptics ask, why, in the summer of 1982, were some Japanese business executives implicated in a plot to steal industrial secrets from IBM? The question contains a non sequitur. The kinds of machines the Japanese expect to produce for the Fifth Generation have no counterparts in any Western laboratories, industrial or university. As reprehensible as this episode of industrial espionage was, it was particular to the problem of maintaining IBM compatibility and is irrelevant to the Fifth Generation project.

It's only a marketing trick to improve Japan's product prestige, the skeptics say, just a political move to take some business from IBM. The Fifth Generation is undeniably a marketing strategy at the same time that it is a survival strategy. But MITI has made a conscious decision to avoid head-on confrontation with IBM, and instead plans for a future when Japan will be far ahead of the American firm and on an entirely different path. They expect that by the time their international competitors are alert to the value of knowledge-based symbolic inference machines, it will be too late for those rivals to catch up. It's a gamble, but it isn't a myth.

The Japanese propose to give the world intelligent

machines. They base this proposal on research that was pioneered in the United States, but let nobody read this as still another cooptation of American technology by the Japanese. The pioneering American systems have only suggested the way. Basic research has hardly scratched the surface of the problem. The Japanese are moving on a grand scale into a field that has, at best, been a loosely connected ensemble of small, almost intimate efforts. Japanese aims are high. Their verve is magnificent. We are ill served by a foolish underestimation of Japanese national will, pride, or capabilities. We are equally ill served by racism. Still, that's an enduring weakness on both sides. At the turn of the century, Okakura Kakuzo, the curator of the department of Chinese and Japanese art at the Boston Museum, politely chided Americans for their racial follies: "Why not amuse yourself at our expense? Asia returns the compliment. There would be further food for merriment if you were to know all that we have imagined and written about you."[15]

16

Japanese Computer Science Education— an Achilles Heel?

The Japanese universities are not educational institutions so much as gates to the professions. The particular university a young Japanese attends will have a crucial influence on his future professional opportunities, and so he aims to enter the "best" university he can, though as we shall make clear in a moment, the "best" doesn't mean the same in Japan as it does in the West.

Because the university he attends is so important, a Japanese student undergoes excruciating pressures in preparation for college entrance exams during his secondary school years (and for the very ambitious, even during primary school years). Ezra Vogel remarks: "The entrance examinations measure acquired knowledge on the assumption, widely accepted, that success depends not on innate ability, I.Q., or general aptitude, but on the capacity to use innate ability for disciplined study. It is acknowledged that native ability may affect the capacity of an individual to absorb information, but in the Japanese view there is only one way to alter the result: study. Those who spend a year or more going through special cram courses in order to enter what they consider an acceptable institution are not criticized for plodding but are praised for perseverence."[16]

The pecking order among the unversities for science and engineering runs roughly this way: at the top are the major national universities, beginning with Tokyo, followed by Kyoto, then Osaka, and so forth. In a second tier there are the private universities, not only lower in the order by tradition, but in fact often skating near the edge of financial ruin, depending as they must for their existence solely on student tuitions. (By contrast, a private university in the United States seldom receives more than a third of its operating expenses from tuition; the rest comes from endowment income, grants and contracts, and gifts.) This ranking doesn't necessarily match the facts; a first-rate department might very well exist at what is perceived as a second-rate school—indeed, little pockets of excellence are a constant surprise in otherwise shabby educational enterprises. Nevertheless, everybody behaves as if the pecking order is valid, both students at entrance and employers at exit. And of course a self-selecting group of the best students pushes the universities that receive them toward being the best, though the difference between students from first-rank and second-rank universities is far less in reality than is supposed.

Having passed through "examination hell," as the Japanese call it, to reach the best university possible, students are exhausted. The first two years of university are pretty much written off as a loss. At Tokyo University, for instance, underclassmen are sent off to a suburban campus outside the city and come to the main campus only for specialized work during their last two years of undergraduate study. Upon graduation they typically move into lifetime employment with a firm or government agency (the matching of new bachelors with eager firms is a major responsibility of professors, who spend most of the fall of each year in this delicate process), and any further education they receive comes there.

In fact, employer-supplied education is considerable. Firms routinely bring in top instructors, including American professors, and invest two to three years in the education of their new employees, an investment of time—and a great deal of money—of which they feel confident, knowing that the employee will be theirs for a lifetime. "We'd rather have our students at twenty-three, and spend two or three years educating them in our company's needs, technologies, and policies, than take them at twenty-eight with a Ph.D.," one manager says. He goes on to explain that a postgraduate degree is sometimes seen as a liability—its possessor has a status ("face" to save) that prevents him from being moved around as flexibly within the firm as an employee with a mere bachelor's degree might.

In short, industry uses the university as a filtering device, acting on the assumption that the strict entrance exams will identify the brightest and most tenacious. The quality of education offered is almost irrelevant, because the firms reserve to themselves the actual training of talent.

As a consequence, computer science training in the universities is not of high quality. Two years is not enough to train a computer scientist even if all other dimensions of university education were excellent, but as it happens, they are not. A group of interrelated circumstances makes computer science in the universities neither stimulating nor up-to-date.

To begin with, since everybody moves off to firms or the government after having received a bachelor's degree, there are few graduate students around. Graduate students in the West are the prime pushers of research, keeping professors on their intellectual toes; without such students, Japanese professors are all too liable to intellectual stagnation.

University computer science laboratories are equipped at the poverty level. Since there is no tradition of corporate gift giving in the national universities, since, in fact, such gift giving would be culturally frowned upon (the private universities are somewhat less accountable), the national universities must look to the Ministry of Education for funds to buy equipment. But compared to MITI, which supports industrial research, the Ministry of Education is relatively poor and impotent and moreover must support all educational efforts more or less equally, regardless of their usefulness to the future of the nation. Funds disbursed by the Ministry of Education must be waited for in line, which can mean several years of waiting, and when they come, they are paltry. What's worse, funding approvals tend to depend more than is comfortable in science on clout, not merit. Thus, the extremely high cost of computing equipment and its rapid obsolescence causes university laboratories to fall further and further behind (a problem that hasn't been solved satisfactorily in the West, either).

Finally, the universities have a deep resistance to interdisciplinary contact which, in the computer field, is essential to the enterprise. On sabbatical at Tokyo University, Feigenbaum gave a series of twelve lectures on artificial intelligence and knowledge engineering. But the lectures were announced only in the information science department, and not in the engineering or medical schools. When he asked why, his hosts were astonished by the question.

Does this wide variance from Western customs matter in the end? It is very hard to know. The system makes no allowance for late bloomers, and practically no allowance for people who find, partway along in a career, that they have made the wrong choice. Many Western observers see all this and presume that such inherent rigidity will prevent the Japanese from innovating at the high level necessary to achieve a new generation of computers. But that remains to be seen. A mediocre university system might not matter in a culture where the firms, with their lavish support for research from MITI, take on the function of grooming young talent. On the other hand, company training might (though it need not) be less imaginative and far-ranging than university computer science training in the West. The system is certainly less likely to encourage mavericks, though as we've already seen, mavericks exist despite the system and may be about to have their day. Kazuhiro Fuchi, recognizing that university research has been extremely valuable in the West, especially in such fields as AI, has created a mechanism that, at least for Japan, is highly unusual, in that it draws the brightest people on Japanese university faculties into ICOT "working groups" and allows them to share in the grand adventure.

Still, nobody in the West should underestimate the overall cultural impact of the schools of Japan. If the universities can be termed a four-year vacation, the situation is quite different in the primary and secondary schools. One observer has written: "The great accomplishment of Japanese primary and secondary education lies not in its creation of a brilliant elite . . . but in its generation of such a high *average* level of capability. The profoundly impressive fact is that it is shaping a whole population, workers as well as managers, to a standard inconceivable in the United States, where we are still trying to implement high school graduate competency tests that measure only minimal reading and computing skills."[17]

A highly literate work force, not necessarily college-trained, is precisely what is needed for worker flexibility and adaptability in the post-industrial society, with its ever more rapidly changing circumstances. Thus even if university training is poor, Japan can count on its primary and secondary school systems to prepare the workers who can use the Fifth Generation to its best advantage.

17

One Generation Passeth Away and Another Generation Cometh

The forty young researchers at Tokyo's ICOT, vanguard of a larger group who are bent on producing a new generation of computers, are themselves part of a new generation, not only in Japan, but all over the world. For Japan especially, a large experiment in innovative computer research may be under way, but equally important, there's a large experiment in social change under way too. The old way of doing things is being cast aside by young people who have exuberantly wagered their future, not to mention their collective face, on a project so technologically audacious that its very aspirations dwarf anything in computing that has come before now. Kazuhiro Fuchi likes to compare the Fifth Generation project with the U.S. space shuttle project. Its purpose is not only to give birth to a new piece of technology, but to make sure that the technology permeates Japanese society—and anyone else's who will buy.

Naturally the older generation doesn't always welcome the newer. Contrary to our Western assumptions about the inevitable nature of Japanese consensus, the eight firms and two national laboratories composing the consortium that, along with MITI, are backing this project have offered their contributions like almsgivers: their enthusiasm ranges all the way from joyous opportunism to the grudgingly minimal, some right in the middle, ready to bolt for either extreme. Though, to our knowledge, no one has polled the Japanese public on the issue, its opinions probably stretch across the same spectrum.

But the Japanese, at least, have compelling reasons for moving rapidly into an information society and for using KIPS as the vehicle. The wisest among them understand that farsighted innovation is the only assurance they have for national survival—an understanding that lends to this project an emotional urgency that mere intellectual consensus wouldn't be sufficient to do.

Of course the Japanese don't stand eccentrically alone in their belief that in knowledge lies the wealth of the future, with computing as the central technology. Nations great and small are beginning to see that knowledge—whether in trade, or in employment, or even, alas, in weaponry—is what equalizes us, weaker with stronger, poor with rich, unlucky with lucky. Other things being equal, the nation (or firm or individual) with more knowledge has an edge; other things not being equal, the one with more knowledge can overcome handicaps of poor resources and achieve that edge.

If the Japanese are the farthest ahead in perceiving where the new wealth of nations lies, there are others stirring themselves behind. In the next sections we examine how several nations are responding to challenges and opportunities. If there is a single message, it is that the new generation not only comes but will prevail—as it always seems to do.

V

THE NATIONS

1

Wisdom, Vision, and Will

One part of wisdom is the ability to recognize when you have a good thing. Another part of wisdom is to recognize a bad thing and abandon it without a backward glance. Still a third part of wisdom is to summon the will, perhaps even give over to the obsession, to carry the good thing through to its fulfillment, regardless of obstacles.

The Fifth Generation project has probably come along at the right scientific moment, but it has certainly come along at the right psychological moment for Japan. MITI has decided that the Japanese must learn to innovate; ICOT will be exemplum. It doesn't hurt that its product will be suitable for helping the national vision along either. A visitor can easily perceive the eagerness, the exuberance, that pervades the Tokyo laboratory. Japanese computer scientists are simply itching to do something important, and as their own report declares, information processing *is* important, affecting as it does every other enterprise. If they are taking a gamble with expert systems as the basis of the Fifth Generation, they are hedging their bets carefully, planning periodic assessments that will guide their next levels of scientific and financial investment. The Fifth Generation shows every promise of becoming a national success.

Americans have almost forgotten the heady pleasure of profound national successes. We celebrated putting a man on the moon and the return of American hostages from Iran—genuine celebrations, but evanescent; our diversity of sentiment asserted itself in short order. When we put a man on the moon, many voices demanded to know why we couldn't also clean up our cities (although the two problems were incommensurate); when the hostages returned, angry voices wanted to know why veterans of the Vietnam war hadn't been given the same kind of welcome (though everybody knew the tragic answer to that).

Both Britons and Argentines had moments of euphoria during the 1982 battle in the south Atlantic, and perhaps there are Britons who believe at this moment that the battle's outcome was a national success, fortuitously coupled with the birth of a new heir to the British throne.

But to outsiders that euphoria looks less like a national success than a breathtakingly lavish anachronism. In late October 1982, Prime Minister Margaret Thatcher told the House of Commons that the Falklands war had cost Britain an estimated 700 million pounds or $1.19 billion (plus $1.4 billion in damage and loss of ships and aircraft) with $678 million per year allocated for future maintenance. But it will be costlier yet if this last battle for empire diverts funds the British mean to invest in their own Fifth Generation effort, which we shall have more to say about presently.

It's easy to criticize the excesses of nationalism, but we ought not to forget its gratifications. Poles coming out of their much beset country after martial law spoke not of the hardships, which were many, but of the deep feelings of solidarity, of the new friends, of their own sense of being Polish in the face of almost overwhelming adversity.

Now here are the Japanese, committed not just intellectually to a project they see as a splendid way of securing their leading position in the family of nations in the future, but emotionally committed, too.

It is difficult to talk rationally to a Japanese about the project. One Japanese working on it, a software specialist named Toshiaki Kurokawa, describes the emotions surrounding the Fifth Generation project as excitement, indifference, hostility, approval, and envy. "One feeling that doesn't exist is that we're crazy. In Japanese *kichigai* is a rather negative term. We are not considered *kichigai*.

But we are considered ambitious. In the computing industry young researchers are, in general, excited by this project." But, he goes on, the senior people, particularly the managers, raise questions: the project's aim is ambiguous, the goal is too difficult, the Japanese have had no experience in managing such a difficult project, and so forth. "In this regard," Kurokawa says, "it's interesting that MITI laid down a guideline that the researchers to be recruited for the Fifth Generation should be under thirty-five years old. This guideline hasn't been strictly applied, but it's had a big effect, I think."

Since the Fifth Generation is a scientific and technological project, perhaps the closest American parallel to its joyous, try-anything-now spirit is found in California's Silicon Valley start-up companies. But in Silicon Valley, the motive is personal profit. Personal profit is not an ignoble motive, but it doesn't really compare to the exhilaration the young researchers at ICOT feel in pursuit of something more transcendent, a goal for the good (and perhaps the salvation) of their nation.

The last time Americans had such motives—when they weren't out to beat anybody so much as they were out to save themselves—was the New Deal. Then too youth was fixing up sins of omission and commission by the older generation. George Ball has written in his memoirs: "It was *épater les bourgeois* in political and economic terms or—more precisely for us—it was *épater les vieillards*, a form of exercise that inevitably lifts the hearts of anyone under thirty. The old order had discredited itself; we would conjure up a new and better one in its place. . . . In those days of unlimited expectations our basic credo was simple: Nothing that had been done till then was good enough nor was there anything we could not do if we set our minds to it."[1] For all its excesses and even its failures, the New Deal attracted a generation of men and women who would provide America with some of its noblest hours.

The Fifth Generation project has just enough similar ingredients to do the same for Japan. What the Japanese lack in experience they will make up for with vision and will. That vision is forward-looking to a more peaceable and richer future for us all, instead of backward-looking to a martial past which the world does well to outgrow. It certainly takes into consideration competition and change. The Japanese perceive that their KIPS will make drastic changes in their lives, but they are cheerful about it: "That's all right," says Toshiaki Kurokawa, "because we have changed our life-style so much from World War II!" So much and so often, he might have added.

Thus, almost regardless of the technological outcome, the Japanese seem destined for a national success. But the technological outcome is likely to be favorable, too, in the long run. As we've argued, there's a manifest destiny in information processing, in knowledge systems, a continent we shall all spread out upon sooner or later. The difference is that the Japanese already have the wagons loaded and are rumbling off down the trail. Or, to change the comparison, we might recall what Goethe once said of Napoleon: he went forth to seek Virtue, but, since she was not to be found, he got Power. Doubtless the Japanese will be glad for either, and gladder of both.

2

Well, Then: Why Isn't Everybody Doing This? or, England's Tragedy

It was early in July 1953, a wonderfully rare hot day at the end of the summer term at Oxford. Two punts were being poled languidly down the river Cherwell, filled with high-spirited young men who were on their way to a twenty-first-birthday picnic for Beresford Parlett. Parlett, who would later become a professor of computer science at the University of California at Berkeley, was an Englishman with an affinity for American friends, and it happened that his punt carried the college's American contingent of Rhodes Scholars, men who were studying economics and mathematics. Among them was Alain Enthoven, later to be assistant secretary of defense for systems analysis and, still later, a professor of economics at Stanford

University. Enthoven stared meditatively at the punt ahead of them which contained, by everybody's estimate, the brainiest young men in the college. They were all "reading Greats"—studying the Greek and Latin classics. "There," said Enthoven, fixed on the punt ahead of them, "*there* is England's tragedy."

When McCorduck considers the history of artificial intelligence in England, she is put in mind of Parlett's poignant birthday recollection. Perhaps *tragedy* is not too florid a word when a nation's brainiest young people study ancient civilizations under the quixotic impression that it will prepare them to make decisions on behalf of their nation in the last part of the twentieth century. All knowledge is not equal at all times. But how else to account for England's obstinate refusal to take what has been offered again and again; on the contrary, her willful repudiation of a series of opportunities that the Japanese were forced to create for themselves?

Those who disagree with McCorduck invariably begin by quoting Santayana on the virtues of studying history: if you don't know history, you're condemned to repeat it. She smiles politely. Surely some appropriate attention to the rise and fall of Troy is worthwhile. An afternoon with the odes of Pindar can be wonderfully refreshing. But all things in moderation (itself a Greek aphorism), and she sometimes thinks immoderate attention to the Greats is the only plausible explanation for the series of missed opportunities and perverse decisions that are the leitmotiv of British AI. The argument that those responsible for the debacle were not those who read Greats but those who studied science seems to imply that the brainiest boys don't go into science. Not true. The brainiest boys in England have often gone into science, despite the difficulties.

Then again, the line between tragedy and farce lies in the eye of the beholder, and honest surveyors could come to different conclusions about AI in Britain. Perhaps the best description of all for it is melodrama, because the cliffhanger isn't over yet. For all of this, the British do have one advantage over the Americans. The Japanese Fifth Generation project is generally perceived in England as the audacious challenge it really is. The squabbles come in how to meet the challenge. If, in the end, Britain sinks in tragedy, farce, or even melodrama, it won't be for lack of native talent.

The first inkling that a computer might be capable of intelligent behavior came from the brilliant Cambridge logician Alan Turing. Turing had studied mathematics at Cambridge in the early 1930s, and though he was gifted, he was erratic: he took only second-place honors when he graduated because he found it difficult to put his mind to things that didn't immediately capture his interest. Still, his gifts were honored, and he was elected at age twenty-two to a fellowship at King's College, Cambridge. In 1937 he published a paper that mathematicians agree is so singular that it would assure him a place in the mathematical annals if he'd done nothing else. Among the other things, this paper proposed an abstract machine that would be realized a few years later in enormously more complex form as a computer. Nothing like this machine existed when Turing wrote his paper, yet he managed to describe a model so general that it would embrace all the real computers that were to come.

After critical work on code breaking and computer building during World War II, Turing went to the National Physical Laboratory in Teddington, where he worked on the design of the Pilot ACE, another pioneering British effort in computer building. Restless at the slow pace of progress at the laboratory, he asked for a sabbatical which he spent at Cambridge. The result of that year's sabbatical in 1947 was a lucid little paper called "Intelligent Machinery" which discussed ways that "machinery might be made to show intelligent behavior." Many of the ideas in the paper are naive and ill formed, but by no means all of them: some suggestions he makes for going about the development of intelligent machinery were just those ways used a decade later to produce the first intelligent programs (though independent of Turing, since that paper was unpublished for thirty years).

After his sabbatical, he was even more unhappy at the National Physical Laboratory (and justifiably: the Pilot ACE, designed by 1947, was not commissioned until 1958 when it was already an embarrassing dinosaur). By 1950 Turing had gone to Manchester University, where he worked on the design of a new machine and published an essay called "Computing Machinery and Intelligence" which received wide attention. There he once again addressed the question of whether machines could think. He proposed what came to be known as "Turing's Test," in which an interrogator is separated from the person (or machine) under interrogation and can communicate only by teletype. Turing suggested that if the interrogator could not tell for certain whether he or she was communicating with a person or with a machine, the machine could indeed be said to think. In addition, he collaborated on a chess-playing program ("a caricature of my own play," he described it) that would later be adapted as the first program capable of playing a complete, though slow and poor, game of chess.

Turing was perhaps the most brilliant, but not the only, British subject who thought about artificial intelligence. From the late 1940s, a loosely connected group of friends and associates met in a group called the Ratio Club, where they discussed many aspects of machinery and brains. Indeed, from time to time Turing also had joined them.

First at a modest level, and then more vigorously, artificial intelligence research efforts were established at several universities, most notably Manchester and Edinburgh, and later Sussex, Essex, and University College, London. At Edinburgh a large research group began making rapid and admirable progress in problem-solving programs, robotics, and high-level language research. Edinburgh became a rising star; its lively group of scientists was producing results that were the equal of almost any AI laboratory in the world.

One of the central figures at Edinburgh was Donald Michie. He was indisputably brilliant, a young associate of Turing's during the World War II cryptanalysis work. But he also had an uncanny ability to rub people the wrong way. During the late 1960s and early 1970s, the American cousins were vastly entertained by tales that floated across the Atlantic (doubtless inflated in transit) recounting the uproars that always seemed to have Donald Michie at their center.

But in 1973, matters got less entertaining. A report was issued by the Science Research Council, as the government funding agency for science was then known. It had been written by Sir James Lighthill, a famous applied mathematician, and in it Sir James "evaluated" artificial intelligence. Demonstrating neither understanding nor sympathy, Sir James declared the work sadly wanting at best and bordering on charlatanism at worst. In either event, it deserved no further support. Many researchers, both in Britain and abroad, believed the report must have extrascientific motives, and the most plausible of those was to garrote Donald Michie professionally. Michie, being something of a Rasputin when it comes to surviving attempts on his professional life, is still managing quite well. What really happened as a consequence of the Lighthill report was that artificial intelligence sustained a body blow in Great Britain (and, incidentally, in Australia as well). The superb robotics project at Edinburgh was largely dismantled and many of its young and able researchers scattered. For Lighthill had not taken a charitable view of the early robotics research. Since robotics is about to play a significant role in Japan's soaring productivity advances, Lighthill's report was a costly one to a nation whose industrial productivity is a grim joke. Lighthill overlooked any potential in expert systems—more forgivable, because few people appreciated their possibilities in 1973—but he gave ammunition to those whose budget-cutting zeal assured that no significant research could take place.[2]

Among the Edinburgh researchers who scattered was Patrick Hayes, who planned to stay in the United Kingdom and work on artificial intelligence as best he could under the circumstances. But Hayes came up against another problem. Since, as he puts it, "British higher education is going to pieces,"[3] he found himself with no place to go. He could find a junior position, but there were no senior positions to be promoted into; those who had the few senior positions might not be producing, but they weren't budging either. Hayes, like several other key researchers, finally succumbed to an American offer; as later did Michael Brady, now associate director of the M.I.T. AI Laboratory; as did David Warren, designer of the Edinburgh Prolog System, now at SRI; and as did Derek Sleeman, formerly of Leeds University and now with the Stanford computer science department.[4]

3

There Always
Was an England

A dispassionate observer might be inclined to think that Japan and Britain have some qualities in common. They are both densely populated island nations lacking essential natural resources. Japan lost a major war; Britain lost an empire and has not yet found a role, in Dean Acheson's acute phrase. Relative to other nations, both enjoy a national homogeneity, exemplified in national newspapers and other mass media, that can be potent when channeled toward a common goal (though the Japanese have much the more).

There are odds and ends: both countries have ceremonial royal families, drive on the wrong side of the road, esteem fish and fine gardens, and consider wintertime central heating effete.

Japan seems to have better public education, at least if the performance of schoolchildren in tests is any indication, but Britain has North Sea oil and a language it has imposed on the four corners of the globe. Both countries have long and honorable traditions of valuing knowledge, culture, and education.

A dispassionate observer might then conclude that all the reasons the Japanese think a Fifth Generation project is worth their while are apt for Britain, too. The dispassionate observer would not be alone.

For example, in 1980 Donald Michie and a group of his colleagues proposed a research institute, to be named for Alan Turing, who had died in 1954, which would function as a national laboratory to design future generations of information processing systems. But this idea was not taken up by anyone with the cash to finance it, especially not the government, which was asked to provide support amounting to a million pounds per annum for five years until the laboratory could begin to earn revenues from joint projects with industry.

When the U.K. delegation returned from the Fifth Generation conference in Tokyo in the autumn of 1981, some of its members began raising genteel alarms. Various committees and panels met to discuss matters, and in January 1982, under the auspices of Britain's Department of Industry, a meeting was held to brief eighty industry leaders. The meeting was termed secret, and in a sense it was, since nobody would allow himself to be quoted for publication. But it was less secret than exclusive; it excluded the press, and it excluded most of the people who knew anything about artificial intelligence in Britain.

Among the people not invited was Donald Michie, who had not only been a bona fide AI pioneer, but had also built Britain's first expert system. Also not invited was Alex d'Agapeyeff, who was the first chairman of the British Computer Society's special interest group on expert systems. Michie told *Computing*, a weekly trade newspaper, "The fact that I was not invited to the conference was not a personal slight, but a pattern whereby government decision making in technical areas has yet to learn to bring in people technically qualified." D'Agapeyeff said, "There is difficulty over who the government is choosing to listen to. Some people are jumping on the Fifth Generation bandwagon who do not really believe in the expert systems approach."[5] (An industrialist who attended this conference told Feigenbaum that the exclusions had been deliberate. Michie was, he said, a well-known troublemaker and would only have caused friction. It might be true; or it might be an after-the-fact excuse for sloppy planning.)

A week later, the editorial page of *Computing* urged the U.K. to act. But with asperity, *Computing* reminded its readers that there were always the usual reasons for doing nothing: the Japanese might be on the wrong track; coordinated planning was never a forte of U.K. industry and might prove impossible; the Americans might be offended. Nevertheless, the editorial said, it was time for long-range planning, and this was an opportunity that might never come again.

Indeed, it looked as if *Computing* had mounted a small campaign on behalf of AI in general and expert systems in particular. In early January an article entitled "The U.K.'s Dying Generation" had described the impact of the Lighthill report and the exodus of three leading AI researchers to the United States. Now, in the same issue as the editorial just quoted, there was another article entitled "U.K. Ignores Its AI Pioneers," which, with a bit more hyperbole, covered the same territory. It also complained about the miserly level of funding from the Science and Engineering Research Council (SERC). As far back as July 1980, the article went on to say, a group of experts in knowledge-based systems had petitioned the SERC for a "long range exercise in technically informed monitoring of Japan's Fifth Generation." A reply dawdled back six months later, sufficiently vacuous to prompt Michie to write again, charging that the SERC had neither drawn upon the advice of experts nor even selected them as Britain's delegates to the Fifth Generation conference in Tokyo. Instead, it had sent computer scientists with no AI experience. (The Japanese sent a personal invitation to Michie anyway.)

The next week, a front-page headline in *Computing* disclosed that the secret meeting had contained a stunning announcement: the British government was prepared to spend 250 million pounds over the next five years to develop its own Fifth Generation system. If true, this would effectively match the Japanese government's investment and compress its timetable in half. It seemed incredible. It was. In the fine print, the sum floated tantalizingly beyond feasibility studies that were yet to be undertaken.

By July 1982 even the *New Scientist* had joined the discussion. "It could all be science fiction," the article said of the ambitious Fifth Generation, "but then the bureaucrats who run Japan have been very good at translating ambitious policy aims into results: witness their successes over the past 30 years in electronics, and making cars and steel."

By now the *New Scientist* could report that a committee of electronics specialists had been set up to advise Britain's minister for information technology on how the British should respond to Japan's challenge. The committee's composition had a decided anti-academic bias, the *New Scientist* observed, then quoted a government official's salty Anglo-Saxon: "A lot of the discussion [about the Japanese project] is by menopausal academics who have been shit-scared by the University Grants Committee. They're shouting about the threat from Japan as an excuse to get more money for their projects." But the *New Scientist* demurred: that attitude ignored the fact that the universities are doing most of the work in Britain on advanced computers, and the companies are well behind. Expert systems would be left to a small number of private firms that are starting up, one- or two-person software efforts that do not include the British computing industry as a whole.

For not everybody there is enchanted by the Fifth Generation. In the companies one heard talk that in fact the Fifth Generation was a subterfuge: the Japanese might talk about intelligent machines, but what they were really interested in was improved disk drives and chips. Better not give money to AI people—they always wanted to work on 1992 things when what was needed were 1982 things. Industrial Britain should keep a rein on AI's foolishness.

Among all these voices was a small song heard in the British computing press. Too late, it said. We could have matched the Japanese, but now we can't. The human brain drain has wrecked whatever chances the artificial brain might once have had in Britain. And it is true that accounts of AI research in trade papers like *Computing* sounded more elegiac than repentant.

Significantly for both Britain and Japan, at the end of 1983, Japan requested and was permitted to take Britain's place as the second largest shareholder in the World Bank, after the United States, which is the largest. Bank analysts agreed that the realignment reflected economic reality and was, in fact, overdue.

4

Exhuming the Body

Contrary to the splenetic outburst of Whitehall's spokes-man quoted by the *New Scientist*, the Fifth Generation conference inspired some cogently argued reports which circulated in the U.K. during the first half of 1982 and relied equally on views from companies and academic institutions. They said the same thing: the U.K. should launch its own Fifth Generation project, based partly on human experts the U.K. already had on hand, emigrants it could surely lure back home if they could be convinced a serious, well-coordinated, and well-funded effort was a reality, and a bootstrapping plan to identify and support talented students in the universities early. The various panels agreed that the Japanese had the right idea, the problems were ripe for attack, the time was auspicious to begin, and pointed to the competition posed by Americans and Europeans as well as the Japanese. This is a splendid old international game, played to perfection by national military groups. The simple idea is to show that the compe-tition has it, or soon will, and so should you. Scientists, being relative amateurs at the game, don't play with the same self-promoting flair of the military, but play they do: at the same time British computer scientists were brandish-ing the American AI effort at their government, an exer-cised group of American computer scientists cited the distribution of supercomputers at British universities as a reason more American universities should have them too. We earnestly hope the sociologists of science are busy keeping track of all the instruments of the Fifth Generation, this book included, as they exert their tugs and pulls on scientific research the world around.

For example, the Alvey Committee, an official government committee to advise on British research in information technology, released a report in mid-1982 admitting frankly that its formation was a response to the Japanese challenge. It strongly recommended that the U.K. undertake research that would be "essential if we are to preserve and strengthen our capability and competitiveness in IT [information technology]." The four major areas ripe for research in advanced information technology, the committee declared, were software engineering, man-machine interfaces, intelligent knowledge-based systems, and VLSI. "There is solid consensus amongst industrialists and other knowledgeable people in the IT community whom we have consulted that the areas which we have identified are key to the future development of IT in this country. . . . We believe that the thrust of the programme which we recommend, will be widely welcomed and supported. We urge that it be implemented speedily."

Briefly, the Alvey Committee's recommendations were for a national program for Advanced Information Technology at a budget of 350 million pounds (about $567 million) over five years. Government would contribute two-thirds of the direct cost of the program, and industry should provide the remainder, as well as the much larger sums needed to translate the results of the program into marketable projects. The program should be collaborative among industry, academia, and other research organizations. A high level of government support was essential, the committee argued, for without it, collaboration would not be possible, nor full dissemination and exploitation of research results by all levels of the business sector, including small businesses. Most interesting, the committee called for a strong central directorate, headed by a director "hand-picked for the job" who would have "enough autonomy to get on and run the programme."

The committee went on to make almost identical arguments to those the Japanese had made in their own Fifth Generation announcement, except in this case the arguments were couched ominously: "The issue before us is stark. We can either seek to be at the leading edge of these technologies; or we can aim to rely upon imported technology; or we opt out of the race. The latter we do not regard as a valid option. Nor is reliance upon imported technology practical as a general strategy, though we cannot be completely self-sufficient either.... The only sensible option, in our view, is to share in the future growth and development of the world IT sector, by building up our technological strengths in specific targeted priority areas, which will maximise our prospects of exploiting the opportunities available. Our programme is geared to meet this requirement."[6]

In early July 1982, Alex d'Agapeyeff, a computer consultant in the U.K., chaired a London conference sponsored by SPL International, a large British software firm, to discuss the Fifth Generation. The participants included well-known people in AI, both within the U.K. and from abroad. Speakers covered a wide variety of topics from the technical to the commercial aspects of the Fifth Generation.

Donald Michie, for example, asked in colorful, not to say homiletic, terms: "What then do the intrepid knowledge engineers have for characterizing and scientifically measuring the new bomb which they are building—the knowledge bomb? The question has a succinct answer: *next to nothing!*" True enough. Michie had just been arguing for "the development of a sound and well-quantified theory of knowledge" to go along with the Fifth Generation effort, and he expounded on the value of theory: "Since Newton's time the practical bridge-builder has had a sound scientific theory of matter and motion known as mechanics; the steam engineer now has Carnot's thermodynamics; the aero-designer has fluid dynamics; the agricultural breeder has statistical genetics; the communications engineer has Shannon's theory of information."

Unfortunately this seems to argue for a rather awkward cart-alongside-the-horse approach. Although it's doubtless true that Newtonian mechanics has been immensely helpful to practical bridge builders, the boy Newton (and the Roman legions long before him) wandered across many a practical, standing bridge without so much as moistening a toe before physics ever got around to explaining theoretically why bridges stand. Animals were bred successfully before statistical genetics entered anyone's mind, and the Wright brothers were innocent of fluid dynamics. The theory of knowledge will one day be interesting, important, and germane to the practical design of intelligent machines, in fact may one day mark AI's finest hour, but the efforts of two thousand years of Western philosophers who have had to tackle the problem in the abstract have so far proved unenlightening.

Michie was surely aware of all this. What was he really arguing for? A hint is supplied in Michie's claim for American AI research that just such a working view of cart-alongside-the-horse exists, a virtuous and equal regard for science as well as technology, theory as well as applications. Perhaps by comparison to the vast distance scrupulously maintained between clean British science and leprous British engineering, it looks that way. Or perhaps he was trying to bridge another division, the one perceived between practical persons of industry and government and impractical persons of academia, as the quotation in the *New Scientist* makes manifest. Or perhaps it was London versus the provinces, or U versus non-U; the characteristics of British factions, which do exist, and seethe with fury at each other, surpass the understanding of outsiders.

In any event, after the technical talks at the July conference, Colin Crook, a British computer entrepreneur, spoke about the commercial possibilities of the Japanese Fifth Generation and concluded, as nearly everybody has, that it is likely to work. He particularly admired the fact that although the Japanese have a ten-year plan, there are provisions in it for exploiting intermediate results—products, processes, and concepts—in the market as soon as they appear. In his opinion and that of the research team of his investment firm, the plan addressed the most relevant areas for commercial exploitation in the next twenty years: VLSI, knowledge engineering, communications and networks, personal computers, software, and so on. He ended with two questions: Could the Japanese summon the creative energy to do it? And what should everyone else do?

The question of Japanese creativity is open and more complex than it once seemed. The question of what everybody else should do is yet unanswered. It wasn't answered after SPL's conference, and insofar as the British are concerned, nobody can be unduly optimistic that the U.K. can reverse decades of bickering and carry out a coordinated national plan.

But that island nation has always been full of surprises. Two years after the Protector, Oliver Cromwell, died and was given a lavish state funeral and burial in Westminster

Abbey, the government reversed itself and condemned him to execution as a traitor. The remains were exhumed, hanged at Tyburn, and separated skull from torso with eight whacks of the executioner's ax. A nation with such distinctive patterns of changing its mind, however late in the game, cannot be counted out.

5

Pounds for Principle, Pennies for Polo

Government support for research and development in the U.K. is relatively slight, and what little there has been has gone disproportionately to physics, probably because physicists traditionally dominate the committees that control British government allocation of research funds. Physics can be considered the polo of science, a glorious game but nothing for a middle-class shopkeeper to get into. Nevertheless, Britain has stubbornly kept up appearances, buying polo ponies when the family car was broken down, the shop needed new inventory, and Mum new uppers. It is an old but sad fact of life that people with limited funds must make choices, and Britain's haven't always been wise.

If there is to be little government support of consequence for research, what hope there is for Britain rests on private or industrial support. But Britain is the only major Common Market country to have experienced a decline in privately funded research and development between 1967 and 1975—down 11 percent in those years. It's largely thanks to this indifference on the part of private industry that the percentage of Britain's GNP spent on basic research also fell from 2.32 percent in 1964 to 2.09 percent in 1975.[7] No one expects any changes in these trends.

Now it happens that relative percentages for Japanese research and development during those same years were almost identical to Britain's. What accounts for the fact that Japan was doing so well while Britons were going to seed? A major factor has to be that Japanese companies did not, until recently, consider it profitable to invest in basic research and development. Instead, they purchased foreign technology and adapted and perfected it for large-scale production. But technology is no longer a cheap buy, and in addition, Japanese national pride has become involved. As a consequence, Japan now has about as many people engaged in nonmilitary research as the United States does, and the Fifth Generation is only one example of such an undertaking.[8]

England, on the other hand, neither imported technology to repackage nor produced it in original forms in any significant amount. Suppose the British wanted to think about such things, to respond, for example, to Donald Michie's warning that "whereas a pint or two of petrol may be enough to re-start a car, it will not take it very far in an international rally race." Then they would have to follow Michie's advice: "We should, therefore, look to the future. Quite a radical shake-up of ideas will be required, not only among government departments but also, be it noted, among the more conservative university departments."[9]

But who would do the shaking? There is no real British equivalent to Japan's MITI, to coordinate or guide, even if Britain's hostile factions could sit down and talk to each other. Philip Gummett, a sociologist of science, observes: "To return, finally, to the question of machinery for science policy, it must be emphasized that there is in Britain no adequate national institutional focus for thinking about the state and direction of science and technology as a whole. If, as for instance Henry Kissinger has argued, science and technology will be the principal resource of advanced industrial states in the coming decade, this is an omission which Britons should be really sure they wish to accept."[10]

Perhaps it is unfair to single out the British failure in artificial intelligence when Britain has done so badly elsewhere in computing too. British VLSI is not formidable. British mainframes are not best sellers. With the exception of the British development of the French language PRO-

LOG, British programming languages have been inconsequential on the world scene.

The only reason for dwelling on the British example is that it demonstrates what it was like to have had everything in place to excel, and yet by mismanagement, by misperceptions, by *folies de grandeur* and other delusions, the British instead have demonstrated how to turn a nation from a winner into a loser. In England's tragedy there is an obvious lesson for Americans.

By the same token, it is instructive to see how a winner manages. Japan is unique, and its circumstances cannot be duplicated exactly. Most of us outside Japan wouldn't even wish that. But it has done some things so extraordinarily well that it not only deserves congratulations; it deserves close examination.

6

La Belle France et La Cinquième Génération

Some of the most elaborate plans for entering the new age of information are being drawn up by the French. Support in France for science research and development in general is scheduled to increase in the next few years by 6 to 8 percent a year over inflation, since the French aim to upgrade their capabilities in many areas. But electronics has received special attention. Beginning with the Giscard government, and accelerating under the Mitterand government, a special plan is being put together to integrate and coordinate electronics nationwide in France, from chip manufacture to telephones, from software engineering to artificial intelligence and robotics. The ultimate goal of this plan, of course, is to make France a world leader in knowledge information processing.

In early June 1982, when heads of state of seven major industrialized nations met in Versailles, their host, France's President François Mitterand, greeted them by reminding them that many of the problems they were meeting to address paralleled problems that have occurred before. "The past bears witness that the first phase of each of the two previous industrial revolutions in the West was characterized by rising unemployment, protectionism, and inflation," he said. Despite objections by U.S. President Ronald Reagan that government planners could not predict the technological future, Mitterand asserted that technology would have a major impact on society, stressing telecommunications and computing in particular. He estimated that by 1990, 20 percent of mass production would be carried out by robots. "We must devise the means to manage this transformation to make sure that technology will not destroy jobs at a faster rate than it can create them."

Having sounded the warnings, he then went on to criticize economic austerity programs that hinder technological development: "We must now respond to the technological revolution by encouraging private and public industrial investments." He asked for global cooperation to achieve research goals in several fields, and proposed cooperative programs to help introduce computers into schools in the developed countries, and pushed a French plan that aims to bring high technology, in particular computing, to the less developed countries. Finally, befitting a son of France, he suggested that France sponsor a modern-day electronic equivalent of Diderot's *Encyclopedia*, an idea that had also surfaced at the Japanese Fifth Generation conference.

Insofar as international cooperation is concerned, he might have saved his breath. But Mitterand was voicing a widely felt French sentiment about the future: everywhere, the French are acknowledging the central importance and the pervasiveness of information technologies. For example, the state-owned French telephone company, once a global joke, is leaping headfirst into the electronic age by providing information services for telephone subscribers by means of home terminals. In September 1982 it began giving away those terminals to subscribers in the northwest city of Rennes at the rate of ten thousand per month. These terminals not only give ordinary directory service but suggest the nearest location of a service a user might want, hours of business, and so forth. The telephone system even makes some guesses if the user isn't quite spelling a name right. The same kinds of terminals offer shopping services and airline schedules to subscribers in a Paris suburb, and a farming community has electronic access to social security rights, building permit procedures, and agricultural laws. Other cities will go on line in the near future.

This is partly what Jean Claude Hirel, the government's director of electronic and information industries, meant when he addressed a group of French information technology specialists recently and said that not only was computing going to affect industry, but information technology would be "diffused throughout our country." He promised full support from the Ministry of Research and Technology to assure that diffusion and promised that France aimed to be first not only among Third World countries, but elsewhere, too.

To help fulfill that promise, the French have been paying close attention to the Japanese Fifth Generation and are making plans to respond to it. A group known as SICO, for Club Systèmes Informatiques de la Connaissance, composed of scientists and industrialists from both the public and private sectors, has met to plan a specific French response to the Japanese challenge. SICO, formed under the auspices of INRIA, the French national information sciences laboratory, issued a group of recommendations at just about the same time the Alvey report appeared in the U.K. Those recommendations included the immediate acquisition of American-manufactured VAX and Lisp machines for research purposes—one recommendation that didn't sit well with the government's policy of buying at home and, at this writing, has yet to be carried out. But there were other recommendations, too, that boiled down to concerted French action to design and manufacture software and hardware to compete with Japan's, particularly in knowledge-based systems. In fact, knowledge-based systems are in place or under design in at least two French firms, Schlumberger—the oil field instrumentation specialist—which considers artificial intelligence important enough to have established its own AI group, and ELF Aquitaine, which has contracted with an American firm to provide an expert system for oil-drilling process.

So for the French it isn't altogether just talk. Perhaps

the biggest headline magnet of all is the World Center for Information Technology and Human Resources, the brainchild of author Jean-Jacques Servan-Schreiber. It was conceived under the Giscard government, but it has had enthusiastic blessings (as well as nearly $9 million budget in its first year, an amount that is scheduled to go up by nearly half again in its second year) from the Mitterand government.

The Center has been established in Paris, and its mission is to train people from abroad and develop and distribute information technology to the less developed countries. The assumption is that Third World countries need not recapitulate the historical experience of the industrial countries, but can bypass the heavy manufacturing phase and move directly into the electronic age. This accords well with the French government's policies of rapprochement toward the Third World and is also expected to push France forward in its high-technology competition with the United States and Japan.

These alone would be awesome responsibilities for any single institution, but Servan-Schreiber speaks cheerfully to the press of using computers deliberately to shape social and economic change, to conduct "social experimentation" that will benefit the young, the unemployed, the aged, and any group that could possibly come to mind. Though two American computer scientists joined the Center temporarily, and others from the United States maintain loose ties, the very effusiveness of the Center's claims and aims raised skepticism from the beginning. Nevertheless, a computer literacy project has started in Senegal under the Center's auspices. "Wait 'til the first time they get dust in the floppy disk," one dubious American computer scientist said, "then they'll wish they'd paved the road out in front instead."

Dispute didn't even take that long. The Center's conflicting goals have already caused two Americans, a Swede, a Norwegian, and a Chilean to resign, protesting the distortion introduced to Third World missionary work by French industrial self-interest. Resigning as the Center's chief scientist, M.I.T. professor Seymour Papert complained about political interference in scientific goals and the use of the Center as a remedy for the French economic crisis. Papert also declared that rather than benevolently and respectfully offering the new technologies to the Third World, France is embarked on a neocolonial adventure.

But perhaps the biggest problem facing the Center is money. Its generous budget recalls Marie-Antoinette's proverbial cake when university departments of computer science have no bread to speak of, and there is a fair amount of cynicism about the government's fiscal priorities among the very French computer scientists and industrialists who are charged with carrying out France's grand plan to become a world leader in computing and electronics. Mitterand's criticism of austerity programs that hinder technological development sounds hollow to many.

The French grand plan does seem to mimic the Japanese plan in a variety of technological, if not fiscal, ways, but it also has some particularly Gallic touches. There is a minister of free time, whose task is to guide France into the new economic order of automation and computing, which the French believe will bring a shorter work week. Since, in industrial societies, workers get bored, suffer stress, and turn to alcohol, crime and drug abuse when they no longer work full time, the minister of free time is charged with providing constructive alternatives to those bad habits. Even more Gallic, the French are squabbling and threatening each other with legal action over terminology. The French, like the British, show that they understand where the future of their country's economic survival lies. Whether they can overcome the enervating arguments that seem to accompany almost any French undertaking remains to be seen.

If they do not, it will not be for lack of leadership and vision at the top. A year after the Versailles summit meeting, where Prime Minister Mitterand had first declared the importance of science and technology to the new age, he arrived at Williamsburg, Virginia, for the next meeting, ready to make the same arguments. This time his proposals were more welcome, and he succeeded in obtaining commitments for greater collaboration among the member countries in scientific and technical research, at least on projects in which the free-trade countries could see no commercial threat.

Both the British and American science advisors admitted surprise that science and technology had been pushed to such prominence a second time among the European,

Japanese and American heads of state, and both science advisors expressed hope that international cooperation might indeed take place. Although the projects proposed spanned science and technology, including their social impacts, and even included a possible collaborative effort on advanced robotics (jointly led by France and Japan), there was no specific response to Japan's Fifth Generation challenge.

7

The Ins and Outs
of the Knowledge Game

From Singapore to the Emerald Isle, nations and their governments are suddenly awakening to the role information technology will play in their future economic growth.

Singapore, to take one example, traditionally looks out for interesting businesses for its people. The government there often acts as a venture capitalist, financing the beginning stages of new enterprises that it judges can keep that small nation prosperous and independent. Recognizing that most of the value added (and therefore the profit) in computing comes from software, the nation of Singapore is going into the software business. High profits aren't the only attraction: software requires no imported materials—a consideration for a nation that must import even its water—and the factory is the human mind.

For a start, three government-funded software companies have been set up. To staff them, Singapore is sending its brightest young people to graduate school in the United States, then returning them to intensive on-the-job training at one of the three firms that are engaged in a $100 million project to computerize the Singapore government. That job would have been done anyway; Singaporeans have chosen to make an apprentice program out of it for their young people as well. The Singapore National Computer Board, a government agency, not only watches over the three software firms but also administers the plan.

Ireland, too, sees information technology as important to develop and is offering generous tax breaks to computer companies that establish themselves in the Irish Republic. In addition, the Irish supply young engineers on very favorable terms to these new companies, in the belief that any investment the government makes in their on-the-job training will be amply repaid by a stable and employed population in clean new technologies that will be central in the future.

The German computing firm Nixdorf sent an observer to the Fifth Generation conference in Tokyo in the fall of 1981; he returned with a high assessment of the Japanese chances of reaching their ambitious goals and argued that his firm ought to consider entering this field. But the Germans are acting conservatively. Though some AI research is going on in German universities, the government is unlikely to take any initiative to meet the Japanese challenge.

The European Common Market has proposed a plan dubbed ESPRIT, for European Strategic Program for Research in Information Technology, which would be a joint venture among EEC countries to cooperate in microelectronics, robotics, advanced production techniques, artificial intelligence, and software engineering, but, until recently, the usual national factionalism has prevented agreement on how to accomplish all this.

But sheer desperation promises to alter the quarreling among the Europeans. In 1978, Europe had a $5 billion surplus in balance of trade in electronic equipment. By 1982, that had plunged to a nearly $12 billion deficit. This dramatic drop seemed to be one reason why, in late 1983, a five-year crash program, financed at $1.5 billion, was actually taking shape. ESPRIT was coming alive. In the words of one member, "I have never seen such a sense of urgency in any international undertaking." It was the result of a year's study by members of Europe's largest electronics companies and outlined what they believed were achievable goals in microelectronics, software, artificial intelligence, office automation and computer-aided manufacturing. A twenty-member international steering committee hoped to eliminate the factional problems that had plagued European cooperation in the past.[11] Meanwhile, complementing ESPRIT, is a joint venture among Britain's International Computers Ltd., France's Compagnie des Machines Bull, and West German's Siemens, which in 1984 set up a jointly funded center in Bavaria for artificial intelligence research.

Finally, readers over forty will be curious to know about the Soviet Union. Ever since Sputnik, Westerners have heard ominous warnings about the armies of engineers marching out of Soviet universities each year, trained from the cradle in calculus and other technologically useful topics, eager to out-calculate, out-engineer, and generally outfox the softies in the West. Given the conspicuously poor performance of the Soviet-designed and -installed missiles in Lebanon in the summer of 1982, and the technological problems attending the European gas pipeline, where are those armies now?

Of course they exist. If their education hasn't been quite as formidable as it once was touted to be, the Soviets are endowed with as much in the way of human brainpower as any other nation. But nothing will stifle brainpower faster than a rigid political and economic system that fails to produce even what all agree is essential to the national welfare. Computing is a perfect case in point.

In earlier days, Soviet computer scientists seemed almost admirable in their austerity: what they lacked in advanced hardware that the West had, they made up for in clever programming. But AI in particular began to founder. Feigenbaum, who was an early-bird Soviet computer watcher, especially as it pertained to AI, and who made two trips to the Soviet Union in the 1960s, gradually lost interest in what he perceived as pretty boring stuff.

Recently, a staff reporter for no less than the *Wall Street Journal* was invited to the Academic City at Novosibirsk, a new city built in Siberia in the late 1950s and early 1960s with the very purpose of encouraging scientific research that could eventually be developed into new technologies. He found an almost antiseptic relationship between science and industry: science goes its own very abstract way, and even if it didn't, industry wouldn't listen.

Political considerations continue to play a large role in Soviet science. Not only are certain fields prone to fall in and out of favor (in the past, genetics and cybernetics have been banned as anti-Marxist, though they are currently politically acceptable), but individual scientists make decisions about their lives with political threats hanging over them. (One Polish scientist remembers his father's counseling him earnestly never to go into a field where the government might have any say whatsoever; he works in a field of extremely abstract mathematics and has given his own son the same advice.)

The Computing Institute at Novosibirsk claims to have developed computers and programming for industrial automation, but most factory machinery is so old that it can't be adapted to computerized control. The Soviets themselves estimate that it will be the 1990s before computer control is widespread in Soviet industry. There may be further delays because the Soviets are ideologically opposed to salespersons, and therefore scientists must themselves leave their laboratories and go from factory to factory, trying to persuade reluctant managers to take a chance on new ideas.[12] There's some irony in the fact that a centrally planned economy, which could benefit the most from fast and accurate information flow, is so backward at installing the very instruments that could actually make rational planning a possibility.

Americans surmise that what the Soviets can't grow at home they will steal, especially whatever can be applied to weaponry. But in fact espionage is a last resort. It's relatively easy to buy used equipment on the open market abroad, and if reverse engineering—pulling apart a piece of technology to see how it works—is too time-consuming to be useful in the superheated computer marketplace (which is why the Japanese computer manufacturers got involved with the clandestine purchase of IBM's secrets), it's serviceable enough for Soviet purposes. Finally, there *is* espionage. Security measures are a necessity, but the best protection, as the Japanese are busily demonstrating, is to achieve world leadership.

This section has explored the response of a variety of nations to the challenges posed by the new age of knowledge and to the challenges of the Japanese Fifth Generation. We began by asserting that it takes more than technological prowess to enter this competition. It requires wisdom, vision, and will, all of which permit a nation to admit mistakes, aim for realistic goals—which is often a euphemism for more modest goals, but in this case can just as well mean more visionary, splendid goals—and summon the will to surmount inevitable obstacles that stand in the way of great achievements.

For most of the nations we have looked at, the problems have not been technological. They have resulted instead from shortsightedness on the part of those who had the power but lacked the vision to understand where their long-term interests might lie. Britain, and even France, have at least one incalculable advantage over the United States, which is that their governments have officially acknowledged that Japan's challenge will not be met by mere hand wringing, denial, or other forms of self-delusion. Though here and there in the U.S. government there are those who really understand the problems, it is a genuine possibility that the United States, through a combination of myopia, complacency, and general inertia, is ready to recapitulate what it has already experienced with Japan in steel, autos, and consumer electronics. That alone should make us wonder how smart we humans really are.

VI

THE
AMERICAN RESPONSE

1

Americans Stir

In January 1981, Professor Arvind of MIT returned from Tokyo with an early report on the Fifth Generation Project, the same report Feigenbaum had put in his "to read sometime" pile at Stanford a few months earlier. Arvind showed it to Michael Dertouzos, a professor and director of the MIT Laboratory for Computer Science. Dertouzos recollected in notes: "I panic. My colleagues are (way too) relaxed about it and tell me that I am over-reacting." One of the things that troubled Dertouzos was the similarities between the Japanese plan and long-range plans at MIT. "I felt as if somebody had been reading our mail," he would joke later, "and I was born European—gentlemen don't read each other's mail!" In this, he didn't really mean that the Japanese were copying MIT's plans (or if they were, that was all part of science, where ideas are open to anybody). What he believed was that these plans were the only ones that made sense for long-range research in computing, and so, naturally, Japan was going to arrive at the same plans at MIT, or anybody else who thought the problem through carefully.

Despite the indifference of his colleagues, the Japanese plan gnawed on Dertouzos's mind, and in November of 1981, he sent letters to the chief executive officers of

Honeywell, IBM, Intel, Data General, Digital Equipment Corporation, Control Data Corporation and to the Defense Department's Advanced Research Projects Agency, warning them of the danger. In this letter, he raised some questions, particularly about the impact of the Japanese activity on U.S. computer science research, about the "apparent lack of a correspondingly aggressive, ambitious and integrated long-term plan among our own companies," and about the utter lack of research by the U.S. computer industry in several of the areas targeted by the Japanese plan. "Are we worrying without cause or is this sufficiently important to pull us together for a corresponding discussion?" Dertouzos offered MIT as a site for any such discussion.

As it happened, some of those CEOs were indeed taking seriously the Japanese challenge in computing, not only in research, but in manufacturing as well. Both IBM and Digital replied to Dertouzos that their people were keeping an eye on the Fifth Generation. William Norris, president of Control Data, had already conceived of a meeting to discuss cooperative efforts among computing firms, and invited both Dertouzos and Gordon Bell, a vice president for engineering of Digital, to address that meeting, which would be held a few months later, in February 1982, in Orlando, Florida.

For many of the top executives assembled, it was their first encounter with the Fifth Generation. Among them was Richard DeLauer, Undersecretary for Defense, who listened with rapt interest.

Dertouzos laid out what he saw as the major issues. The Japanese development was as "natural as it is inevitable" he argued, for "It matches their technological orientation and lack of natural resources with a technologically intensive resource that all can possess and no one can deplete—information! For the U.S., this development is critical, for it strikes at the heart of our technological leadership. In blunt terms, it forces us to ask whether we would like to see, ten years from now, our computer industry in the same shape as today's Detroit." But, he went on to say, this challenge could be transformed into a valuable opportunity, if the U.S. met it properly.

Then Dertouzos outlined his notions of a successful response. It must work well within our own free enterprise system; it must be a "U.S. positive rather than a

Japan negative approach," it must strive to improve productivity, and it must focus on long-term high technology research and development. He made some concrete proposals: substantial short-term tax credits for long-term research projects; a consortium of leading non-profit research institutes to serve as identifier of, and clearing house for, research efforts in the cooperating companies to help reduce duplication of effort, and so forth.

Dertouzos remembers the meeting as very exciting, and full of a common sense of urgency and desire for cooperation. Afterward he rode to the airport in a minivan and found himself looking around at the talented people in the van (and calculating their net worth, which he figured into the many millions) who were bubbling with ideas; he thought that the meeting had been a great success.

His assessment was correct. The Orlando meeting, held by invitation only and closed to the press, would have two significant results. First, it would lead to the formation of the Microelectronics and Computer Technology Corporation, a consortium of electronics manufacturers, about which we shall have more to say presently. Second, it would help focus some plans in the Advanced Research Projects Agency (ARPA) of the Defense Department that were already in their nascent stages, but at that early time, lacked momentum.

Partly as a result of his presentation in Orlando, Dertouzos was invited to brief the Defense Department's Defense Science Board in October 1982. Here he emphasized the hardware and system architecture challenges posed by the Fifth Generation. He made an "impassioned plea," as he would later describe it, for the Japanese challenge to be taken seriously, for it would have significant military, commercial and geopolitical consequences. Again, he pleaded for a national program as the only sensible way to meet the challenge. Afterward, he was informed that the Defense Science Board had been impressed, that there was general agreement as to the seriousness of the problem and the approach Dertouzos proposed, and that furthermore, there was sentiment in the Defense Department that a new program should begin. "As you know, it takes a lot of persistence to initiate a new program, but there is much support for what you propose and if we all keep pushing, we should be able to make it happen."

Dertouzos heard these encouraging words nearly seven

months to the day after ICOT had formally opened its doors, plans and financing securely in place.

But if there was some stirring, it was confined to a small group and barely touched most American computing professionals, even the ones likeliest to be affected. For example, the Fifth Generation seemed to McCorduck to be one of the most important announcements ever made in the brief history of artificial intelligence, and she expected everybody connected with AI research in particular and computing in general to share that excitement. In August 1982, just after she and Feigenbaum returned from their first visit to ICOT, Feigenbaum went to the meeting of the American Association of Artificial Intelligence in Washington, D.C. When he returned, she quizzed him eagerly: what were the AI professionals saying in the halls about the Japanese plan? Feigenbaum reported the bad news: they weren't saying anything at all. No praise, no hostility, no interest whatsoever. Not for the first time, McCorduck entertained some serious self-doubts about the importance she had attached to the Fifth Generation. Not for the first time, she went back to the Japanese documents to remind herself what epochal announcements those documents contained.

Why were Americans so slow to catch on to the significance of the Fifth Generation? The answer is complex and many-sided, but an illuminating analysis came from George E. Lindamood of the Tokyo office of the U.S. Office of Naval Research. In September 1982, just after McCorduck had once more settled her own doubts, and just before Dertouzos would address the Defense Science Board, Lindamood had arranged a special session at the Sixth International Conference on Software Engineering, held, as it happened that year, in Tokyo, where senior members of ICOT described the Fifth Generation for foreigners attending the software conference.

Lindamood reports: "The reaction of many of the guests was incredulity; a few were outright hostile. After recovering from my initial shock at the behavior of some of my fellow countrymen (who were, after all, guests at a presentation arranged especially for them), I tried to figure out what was evoking such a strong reaction. In discussing it later with my colleagues, we concluded that it was probably the vagueness of the ICOT plans for achieving what everyone admitted were very ambitious research goals."

No American researcher, Lindamood thought, would dare present such ambitious and costly research goals on the basis of such vague plans; and if he did, not only would he not receive funding but would likely jeopardize his credibility for acquiring future funds. The Japanese, on the contrary, argued that their "vagueness" was necessary, unavoidable, and even desirable in long-term projects of basic research.

"Thus," Lindamood concluded, "the reaction of the audience in Tokyo last fall may not really have been directed at the 5G project itself nor even at the challenge to American supremacy in computer science that it represents. Instead it may have been prompted by the conditions under which American scientists must try to respond."[1]

In other words, a series of circumstances, which we will examine in this section, seemed to have pushed Americans into an obsessive caution, with concomitant skepticism toward those more daring. It was as if what had once been a debonair, plucky and almost rash youth had settled into a middle age of crabby prudence. Then again, it may have been a number of other things, or maybe it was everything in combination. What seemed clearest of all was that the Japanese had seized the initiative, and anything Americans—or the rest of the world—might do would only be in response to the Japanese challenge.

2

Are There Any More American Heroes?

One winter weekend in late January 1982, just before the Orlando meeting, McCorduck and her husband, a computer scientist, were houseguests of Gwen and Gordon Bell in the Massachusetts countryside. Gwen Bell had shown them around the superb Computer Museum, which she directs, and her plans for it were appropriately scaled: it's to be not just a computer museum but a museum of information processing, the new age's American Museum of Natural History.

Over the evening's wine, while Gwen Bell was patiently needlepointing her way through a book of designs based on integrated circuit layouts and turning those designs into handsome pillows, McCorduck suppressed her covetousness for one of them by turning to Gordon Bell and bringing up the subject of the Japanese Fifth Generation. She wasn't sure he'd even heard about it; hardly anyone she'd then talked to had.

But Gordon Bell, vice-president for engineering of the Digital Equipment Corporation, was alert at once. Five DEC researchers had been part of the American delegation to the Fifth Generation conference in Tokyo. Bell, unlike many of his industrial colleagues, took the Japanese announcement with utmost seriousness. He knew a lot more about it than McCorduck did. He began assessing its technical features, sometimes admiring, sometimes critical; he spoke, as he always does, in half sentences, the words exploding from him, his arms sweeping like a traffic cop's (for Bell, ideas have always come like rush hour), laughing, groaning, pounding the couch beside him for emphasis. His mood would swing from euphoria ("What *vision* those guys have!") to gloom ("Will there even *be* an American computer industry in ten years if we don't make the right response to Japan?").

The next morning he installed McCorduck in his study and put before her as much as she could read of his private notes on Japanese computing. Since Bell has a reputation for being more eloquent in body English than in ordinary English, she was surprised to find the notes perceptive, lean, and often funny. Always clear.

Gordon Bell was alarmed. And his alarm was significant. When the great creative designers of computers are named, those individuals whose ideas have changed the character of computing, Gordon Bell appears on everybody's list and at the top of many. He's best known for the architecture of Digital's PDPs-4, -5, -6, and -10, pioneering mini and midsize mainframe computers. These machines brought scientific computing to the laboratory. They performed with acceptable and useful power but sold for tens or hundreds of thousands instead of millions of dollars. The beauty of Bell's designs for these machines lies in the fact that miniaturization was accomplished by virtue of the architecture itself and the software Bell helped design to run the machine, because the large-scale integration of components had not then taken place. Thanks to Bell's fecund creativity, Digital's PDPs consistently led the market for price and performance.

In the late 1960s, Bell left Digital to join the faculty at Carnegie-Mellon University, but still consulting at Digital, he was chief architect of the PDP-11. The PDP-11 quickly became a favorite of laboratories all over the world; its elegance of design, ease of handling, and economy spoke to programmers the way a Toyota speaks to drivers. He eventually returned to Digital as its vice-president for engineering, but he kept close ties with his university colleagues.

Over the rest of the winter of 1982 and into the spring, Bell continued to worry about the apparent indifference of most of his fellow industrialists to what he considered a grave long-term threat to their industry. Even among those who took the threat seriously, there seemed to be no agreement on the right action. One idea was a joint venture among several companies, but what form should that take?

Two different interindustry groups were coalescing. One, the Semiconductor Research Cooperative, was an industry-supported program that planned to funnel money into university research laboratories to develop new devices and would consider its support a prepayment of royalties to the universities that patented and licensed their developments. By the fall of 1982, its members included just about every American semiconductor manufacturer except AT&T, but most centrally, it included IBM.

The second group, the Microelectronics and Computer Technology Corporation, known as MCC, which had been conceived at the Orlando meeting, had far fewer members and a much more uncertain future. Late in the spring of 1982, flying to a meeting of this newly forming group, Bell and Bruce Delagi, DEC's strategic planning manager, who had attended the Fifth Generation conference and shared Bell's concerns, began to talk about how they might shake their fellow industrialists out of their day-to-day preoccupation with small, steady improvements in products they already had and offer them something that would capture their imagination for the distant future. With MCC's inception, Bell saw an opportunity to create a Japanese-like cooperative program for advances that looked far beyond mere product development. In his mind, MCC should undertake the research that was too expensive for a single firm and too technologically difficult for a university laboratory to handle.

"Well, we made our pitch," Bell says now. It certainly captured some imaginations. The MCC was incorporated on August 12, 1982, with an ambitious agenda. It would concentrate initially on four advanced, long-range technology programs, including microelectronics packaging, advanced computer architectures (an eight- to ten-year program to focus on architectures for knowledge-based systems, artificial intelligence, and their applications—in short, an American Fifth Generation[2]), CAD/CAM growing out of the achievements of the advanced architecture group, and a program to gain an order-of-magnitude improvement in the effectiveness and applications of software.

The grand design envisioned an annual budget for MCC in the $50–$100 million range after the start-up period, and participants would be either shareholders, who would fund one or more technology programs, or associates with more limited involvement.

Yet despite Bell's passionate vision—and his record for having had so many right ideas in the past—by the year's end, the MCC had signed up only Digital Equipment Corporation, Control Data Corporation, and Sperry. A pack of potential members, including Xerox, Intel, Hewlett-Packard, Texas Instruments, and IBM, stood aloof. Even if individuals in those firms were convinced that Bell was probably right once more, MCC raised as many questions as it answered. Where was all that money to come from? Each of the firms is financially stretched just to keep up with its day-to-day commitments. Where were the people to come from? What would the attitude of the Justice Department be toward the possible violation of antitrust laws? Visionary plans aside, how was it really supposed to happen?

Moreover, the MCC was struggling up mountains that wouldn't even be molehills in Japan. For example, a study subgroup of MCC unanimously recommended that the

laboratory for development of post–von Neumann architectures be located in Palo Alto, to take advantage of
expertise at Stanford and other institutes that already
have some experience in that area, but MCC's board of
directors was cool to the idea, fearing that technologists
from eastern and midwestern computing firms would,
having spent a two-year furlough in the Sun Belt, elect to
stay there forever.

And then in late January 1983, MCC announced it had
a new president and chief executive officer, Admiral Bobby
Ray Inman. A former Quiz Kid and a college graduate at
nineteen years of age, Inman had first come to public
attention as the new head of the National Security Agency,
succeeding a man most people had never heard of to a
post in an agency that was equally unknown to them. But
the NSA is the United States' most powerful and ubiqui-
tous intelligence agency and, as a consequence, perhaps
the government's most sophisticated computer user.

Bobby Inman had gone public to soothe angry feelings
after a subordinate told both an entrepreneur and a professor that the NSA had the right to monitor the work of
computer scientists working in cryptology and to forbid
them to receive patents or publish freely in the normal
scientific journals if such practices seemed contrary to
national security. The entrepreneur was stupefied and
enlisted his senator and then the media in his outrage.
Academics were furious at what they saw as an infringe-
ment not only of their academic freedom but of their
constitutional rights as well. Inman stepped in and acknowledged both sides to the conflict. He then called for a
"dialogue" between the intelligence and the academic
communities, which resulted in an uneasy but voluntary,
and, so far, workable self-censorship on the part of scientists.

But Inman seemed to see the cryptology issue as symp-
tomatic of many much larger national problems. Carrying
the idea further, he used a phrase in an address to the
American Association for the Advancement of Science
that would be quoted far and wide: America's technology
was hemorrhaging, not leaking abroad, and in the name
of national security, that hemorrhaging must be stanched
at once.[3]

But the MCC cannot have the power that the NSA has, or
even the CIA, where Inman was most recently deputy
director, to suggest national policy or influence legislation,
much less claim funds. Although Inman's appointment

convinced some more firms to join the MCC, bringing the total participants to ten, Americans have no MITI to finance and coordinate such an effort and no experience in doing it themselves. No ICOT-like central laboratory exists to direct the research and parcel out the projects.

Could Inman be a charismatic leader like Fuchi, driving everything with his energy and vision? Could he reduce the mountains to their proper size by persuading participating firms that certain risks must be taken, and even sacrifices made, for the long-term common good? Would the firms that had stayed away from MCC and its Fifth Generation-like goals now be persuaded to risk funds? Would Inman, like Fuchi, attract some forty—or more—bright youngsters, ready to make immediate financial sacrifices, to wager their futures, because they believe that what they will be doing is important enough to themselves and to their country to make sacrifices and wagers? Inman's considerable skills are political, not technological. Fuchi is not nearly the skilled bureaucrat that Inman is, but Fuchi has the technological insight and command: he will not be found in his handsome bureaucratic office but on the floor of ICOT, guiding his young researchers.

Are there any more American heroes?

3

IBM and AI

Various misgivings were voiced at the October 1981 Fifth Generation conference about the Japanese plan. A number of objections to the specific plans were raised; a number of questions were asked about the human capacity to bend social institutions to new needs. By the time of the last session of the conference, which was a summary panel with representatives from the United States, the United Kingdom, and

France, as well as Japan, it seemed the most important issues had been aired, even if they couldn't yet be settled.

Professor Tohru Moto-Oka of the University of Tokyo, who had been chairing the session, looked out into the audience. "We have a lot of requests," he said, "to ask the opinions of people from industry who are present here in large numbers. In particular, there are many people from U.S. industry, including IBM. Would any of them like to give us some comments?"

Herbert Schorr, the leader of IBM's delegation, rose to answer. "Well, we're happy to be invited. As it has been expressed by other people, we're very impressed with your openness and the thoroughness of your plans. I think some of the comments you have made summarized the situation quite well. It's a very forward-looking project, and I think you've done a very interesting planning exercise, and I think some of the things that have been said about the project have been expressed by yourself and Professor Fuchi. You have a starting point for a project on basic research, a good plan, we hope. It's the manufacturers who tend to be a bit more conservative, as we saw in some of the remarks repeated by the Hitachi and Fujitsu people, but I come from the research division so I can be a little more appreciative of the progressive nature of what you are attempting. I think you have a project in basic research that, as has been stated over and over again, is high risk. I think a lot of things will succeed and we will be prepared for some things to fail. I think that should be expected. I look forward to coming back in one or two years, whenever you're ready to present some more results, and I would be happy to see what those are."

It took a moment for the audience to realize it had heard a statement so noncommittal that it verged on being altogether free of content, and then Bruce Delagi, manager of strategic planning from Digital Equipment Corporation in Massachusetts, got up to speak.

"As long as you've asked. As Professor Feigenbaum mentioned, Digital is currently using expert systems for internal industrial applications. I might say personally, not as a representative of DEC or of Mr. Reagan, that I respect the organization of this project, its clear goals, checkpoints, and perhaps most importantly, a vision that allows many people to contribute in a coherent way to a major undertaking. I marvel at the ambition of the goals, even though I am from a manufacturer. I suspect that even partial success will be significant." Delagi concluded with a suggestion that the Japanese gain as much experience as they could in expert systems research as soon as possible.

In the difference between these two statements lay the difference between two American manufacturers' attitudes toward AI. DEC was not only an enthusiast but a user itself and had a long and mutually beneficial relationship with the American AI community (and, for that matter, with academic computer science in general). IBM, on the contrary, had a long and—it's irresistible—checkered history of official skepticism about the whole subject of AI.

In the first edition of this book we described Yorktown Heights, the largest of IBM's research centers, as censorious of, if not downright hostile to, the idea of artificial intelligence. We went on to remark that what had once been marketing strategy (never allow people to think computers can be considered intelligent in case they get nervous and cease to buy the product) has ossified into corporate dogma. Over the years, little sorties had been made by IBMers into the world of artificial intelligence—Feigenbaum himself had been interviewed by at least two of these task forces—and they had returned home to research headquarters shaking their heads. AI was not to be taken seriously.

Officials of IBM objected to this characterization, and in part, their objections are justified. As they pointed out, Yorktown Heights has had research in progress on natural language, speech recognition and robotics, in some cases since the late 1960s. If, as recently as 1980, the sales side of the corporation was running full-page ads to assure Americans that machines would never be intelligent, it wasn't the responsibility of Yorktown Heights, the purpose of which is research. Our characterization reflected a widespread view among workers in artificial intelligence.[4] Let us simply say that IBM's embrace of artificial intelligence has been less than ardent, which strikes old-timers as amusing, since some of the first successful AI problems ever solved had been done under IBM's corporate roof.

In a seminal meeting in 1956 at Dartmouth College, where the very term *artificial intelligence* was selected for the field, one of the four organizers was an IBM employee named Nathaniel Rochester, who was then a research manager at IBM's Poughkeepsie laboratories, the predecessor to the Yorktown Heights labs. Rochester would carry back from that meeting an idea he passed on to one of his newly hired Ph.D.'s, Herbert Gelernter, who turned it into a full-fledged computer program that proved plane geometry theorems and was a wonder for its time.

Another participant at the Dartmouth conference was Arthur Samuel, formerly of the Poughkeepsie laboratories but by 1956 a roving gatherer of computer intelligence in Europe. Samuel had developed a checkers-playing program that soon started playing better checkers than he himself could (by 1961 it played championship checkers, and it learned and improved with each game). Samuel used this checkers-playing program as an entrée to the European laboratories he visited, which allowed him to share research progress in a topic in which IBM had absolutely no corporate interest, while in return he learned what was going on in European computing.

Alex Bernstein also participated in the Dartmouth conference. Bernstein had persuaded his boss at the applied science division of IBM to allow him computer time to work on a chess-playing program. IBM's original justification for permitting Bernstein's work on chess was the hope that if he was successful, business executives would be persuaded that computers could be used to solve problems even as difficult as those in business. In fact, Bernstein eventually succeeded in writing a program that played a respectable beginner's game, and he was soon flooded with publicity—the *New York Times*, *Life* magazine, and *Scientific American* all wrote about him—which gave both IBM stockholders and management acute indigestion.

4

The Discreet Charm
of the Bourgeoisie

Large corporations are not unlike large mercantile families. They are both in their way perfect emblems of middle-class values and virtues. Under normal circumstances they change slowly—by accretions, by movements along a predictable continuum. They thrive on the slightly, but not greatly, unexpected. To the adventurous they seem pickled in their own respectability, but for all that they endure.

At the beginning of the 1980s, IBM was the most middle-class of corporations, even to the point of inspiring novel-length sagas of its history. Nobody would have described the firm as particularly innovative, except the handful of technologists who were privy to IBM's hardware manufacturing and packaging technologies (which are brilliant). But it was Main Street steady—it could be depended on to be middling and okay and uncontroversial and unsurprising. What it offered instead of surprises was stability.

In computing it was widely believed that IBM purposely chose to arrive second with a new product. Let others stub their toes (or worse) on new technology; IBM would offer it only after the bugs were gone, only after IBM could guarantee its splendid and very desirable service, consisting of well-written documentation (describing what the software does and how to make it work) and endless house calls until the product worked smoothly. What's more, IBM always insisted on compatibility—software from one set of IBM machines would work on any other IBM machine. Though that policy made computer specialists joke that you could find a 1953-vintage machine chugging away inside the very latest model if only you looked deeply enough into the code, compatibility saved customers many millions of dollars in software costs as they moved from less to more powerful machines, and customers were always grateful and usually loyal to a firm that saved them money.

When IBM surveyed its competition, it looked at corporations that seemed to be little chips off the old block. The phrase in computing circles was IBM and the Seven Dwarfs. It was from the Dwarfs that IBM expected challenges, and these it would meet with its own mighty resources in its own good time.

As an example of such conservatism, there was the market for supercomputers. Though rumors to the contrary floated about like spring pollen, IBM had not so far announced its own version of the fourth generation of computers, the so-called supercomputers. These were machines of awesome capacity, able to execute 100 million instructions per second; even more important, they had a modicum of parallel processing, which meant that sometimes they could carry out many similar operations in parallel instead of sequentially, as the first three generations of machines had done. Their capacity was so great that they actually required little satellite computers to help with the input and output processes, and their architecture reflected a variety of solutions to the problems of large-scale data flow.

Supercomputers were sold by Dwarf companies: Cray Research, Inc. (the Cray-1), and Control Data Corporation (the CYBER 205). (Experimental fourth-generation machines had been built by the University of Illinois and the Burroughs Corporation, but these had been dismantled.) IBM had left the field to Cray and CDC (and to Japan, which was flexing its supercomputer muscles), judging that the market was rather limited for supercomputers. Indeed, by mid-1982 only some fifty supercomputers were operating in such places as oil companies, the U.K. Meteorological Service, the Los Alamos Scientific Laboratory, and other such computational gluttons.[5]

It could be argued that in the early 1980s the supercomputers occupied the niche that the original first-generation computers had occupied in the early 1950s. That is, they were so costly ($10–$15 million) and so powerful that only a very special group of users could afford them or make use of them. But then you'd have to add that by the end of 1953 the outlook for first-generation computers was much less rosy: thirteen companies were manufacturing computers then, and IBM and Remington Rand led the field with a total of nine computing installations between them. Thirty years later, those same computers (vastly diminished in physical size and cost but not in power, except that they were much easier to use) were being marketed to eager home consumers. You couldn't help but wonder if supercomputers might follow the same route and if, this time, the journey would take thirty years.

IBM seemed unconcerned. If the American public developed a taste for supercomputers, there would be time enough to move into the market. IBM always pursued what might be called the Paul Masson theory of research and marketing: "We shall do no research or marketing before its time." If IBM's attitude to a home-grown technology such as the supercomputers (a mere amplification of the von Neumann machines everybody knew and loved) was this conservative, it was no wonder that its attitude toward Japan's off-the-wall proposal was cool—to put it tactfully.

What the Japanese were suggesting with their Fifth Generation plan was new and very different from the machines that IBM had made its fortune on. Worse, the Japanese were unabashedly describing their proposed machines as artificial intelligence machines. Still, it was instructive to recall that the great calculator companies— Friden, Marchant, Comptometer—had themselves fallen to the new technology of the computer when they had failed to see its value.

There were signs. If IBM's conservative strategies had saved its loyal customers money, the price to IBM had sometimes been intolerable in terms of new markets that the company chose to ignore. For example, IBM had disdained minicomputers, leaving that market to DEC for years, until it woke up to the fact that DEC was making a lot of money selling minis. Apple had pressed ahead with personal computers years before IBM had finally entered that market. IBM had lumbered into office automation only long after other, smaller companies had darted in first. It chose a Japanese partner for marketing simple put-and-place robots, although its own more sophisticated robots, to be marketed in the near future, are causing comment by Japanese robotics specialists about strong

competition, especially in the robots' programming languages, sensor technology, and connectivity with sophisticated computers. IBM chose not to go into hand-held
calculators at all.

It wasn't that IBM had no bright ideas of its own.
When you spoke privately to IBM researchers, they claimed
research at their many laboratories was superb. But 90
percent of those bright ideas somehow just lay around
without even being developed. IBM is a corporation with
its own technology transfer problems from research to
development.

All these are signs of conservatism, caution, and conven-
tionality, characteristics of the bourgeoisie to be sure. But
the bourgeoisie has its charms.

A high-ranking executive who formerly worked for
IBM—one of the relatively few to leave IBM's benign
corporate household—recalls that when he first visited
Japan on behalf of IBM in the 1960s, he was mightily
impressed by the lavish banquets and copious sake that
accompanied them. A lovely young woman would kneel
just behind each of the visitors, filling the sake cups after
even so much as a sip. The evening, as a consequence,
would get jollier and more glowing, the jet-lagged visitors
never quite able to gauge how much they'd had to drink
since their cups were perpetually full. When their host
judged that the visitors were suitably mellow, the conversation would turn suddenly from the social small talk that
had been going on to hard questions of substance about
IBM's newest (and inevitably confidential) technology. That
tactic is probably the second-oldest subterfuge of the human race, and like the oldest, it hasn't altogether lost its
efficacy. But the IBM man caught on after the second
banquet. Thereafter, he took advantage of his Occidental
heft as compared to the slightness of his Oriental hosts,
drank them under the table, then asked the hard questions himself.

And when, in the summer of 1982, a great scandal
broke out over industrial espionage between the United
States and Japan, the target of the espionage was IBM,
not one of the corporations of Silicon Valley's feverish
beau monde. They might be next week's, next year's secrets,
and not the secrets of a decade hence, but somebody had
thought they were worth paying a great deal of money

for, which spoke to one of the most fundamental bourgeois values of all.

The Japanese aren't alone in their eagerness to get (or probably their methods of getting) information about IBM. IBM has its professional watchers, even as the Kremlin, Beijing, and Washington do, and their purpose is the same: to divine from a variety of sources just what Big Blue (as it's sometimes known) is going to do, and to sell that information to clients. These professionals claim they do nothing illegal, but they do concede they have unusual ways of getting confidential information, such as inferring from a help-wanted ad that IBM is about to move into a new aspect of communcations, or pondering IBM's own scientific journals (chancy, because publication there is often a consolation prize for working on a project the company has decided against).[6]

IBM dominates. Its reliability and its service are priceless comforts in a frenetic world. And who can argue with its strategies? When it finally decided, for example, to go into personal computers in 1981, in its first year alone it captured 17 percent of the personal computer market. There are also signs that it is getting perturbed by its image as a symbol for the growing conservatism of American industry: a testy senior vice-president complained to a *Wall Street Journal* reporter: "I'm sick and tired of dealing with the perception that our technological advantage is deteriorating," Jack D. Kuehler was quoted as saying, "As far as I'm concerned, we take a back seat to nobody in technology. And more importantly, that technology lead is growing, not shrinking."[7]

A little bit of laughter could be heard from the laboratories and boardrooms of the surviving Dwarfs, of the original Seven, but it was tinged with nervousness. The nervousness had less to do with IBM's repudiation of its middle-class torpor than with some vexing problems they saw coming from across the Pacific.

5

Today I am a Wimp

Not long after the Fifth Generation conference, a number of Dwarfs signaled that regardless of IBM's indifference, they themselves were seriously concerned about the implications of the new Japanese initiative. Feigenbaum and others who had attended the Tokyo conference were invited to travel around the country and address some of their technical staffs to brief them on what was under way.

Since McCorduck is, by now, an old hand in the land of artificial intelligence who remembers it long before it was appearing in every magazine and newspaper, its equity positions argued in the financial pages, its applications detailed in widely circulated news and business magazines, and its heroes canonized in glossy profiles, and since she holds all the interests, prejudices, and predilections of any old hand, she dropped in on one of these talks to do some reality testing of her own. The firm she happened to pick was a middle-sized Dwarf, neither the largest nor the smallest, which for purposes of this narrative will be known pseudonymously as Dopey.

McCorduck was somewhat puzzled as to why Feigenbaum had been invited there. By now the Fifth Generation conference proceedings were pouring off copy machines as fast as you could sneeze, and even more interesting, Tohru Moto-oka, the titular head of the Fifth Generation project, had talked at this very laboratory a month or two earlier. What more needed to be said? But it emerged that Moto-oka's presentation had been so opaque that most of the technical staff had come away from it convinced that the Japanese didn't know what they were talking about.

Nevertheless, a stubborn few who had studied the Japanese report in detail were convinced that despite Motooka's opacity, what was stirring in Tokyo was worth worrying about. In short, Feigenbaum had been invited to incite as much as to inform.

He gave a formal presentation in the morning, which was partly an explanation of expert systems and partly an explanation of the Japanese plan for the Fifth Generation project. His audience was quiet but attentive, gasping only when some technical detail struck their fancy, such as the goal for 1992 to build machines capable of one hundred *million* to one thousand *million* logical inferences per second (today's machines can handle ten thousand to one hundred thousand LIPS). But they were silent to the news that the Japanese expected their own machines to be the core machines of the 1990s and that they hoped to make transition from the old-style machines to the new as painless for others as possible.

After his presentation, Feigenbaum began the questions himself by answering a question he was always asked: Are we Americans capable of concerted action in the face of the threat the Japanese pose? "I'm not optimistic," he answered himself. "We use the excuse of antitrust, but really, we're a competitive country. It's bred into our bones; it's our ethic; whereas the Japanese understand cooperation." Still, he went on, we do have instances of such cooperative efforts—for example, the Apollo project to put a man on the moon.

It was time for the audience to ask its own questions. Somebody wanted to know what the U.S. government was doing. Nothing, Feigenbaum replied. Very few people in the government took this seriously. What was IBM doing? Nothing. Everyone laughed.

The rest of the questions were similar—aggrieved, despairing, curious, even humorous. Somebody described it later as gallows humor, and McCorduck thought that was apt. What it most definitely wasn't was penetrating. There was to be an informal presentation in the afternoon, and time for more discussion. McCorduck hoped things would look up.

But the afternoon session was depressingly similar and ineffective. There were all those earnest, intelligent people who really understood the problem, the threat to their industry, the opportunities that might be missed, the challenge that had been posed, and yet they seemed stymied. Another visitor confided to her with a growl: "These are Band-aid questions begging for Band-aid answers, and the patient's in a coma." She could not disagree.

Somebody raised the possibility of an interindustry group that might do something, but the chief engineer was not optimistic. If competitiveness and secrecy weren't bred into their bones, they would still have to worry about antitrust.

Feigenbaum offered the Stanford campus as a neutral ground where industry and academic knowledge might be pooled. But would Texas Instruments, which takes the Japanese symbolic inference machine seriously, be willing to cooperate with Digital Equipment, which also takes it seriously, even at Stanford? Would Hewlett-Packard confide in Control Data Corporation? Would Honeywell? Then again, would an industrial project intrude on academic freedom? And where would the money come from? No single corporation has the kind of money to spend on a long-term project like the Japanese have received from MITI. Everyone could see the problems, but nobody could see any solutions.

Later, McCorduck drove her rented Toyota back to the airport and heard a popular song: "those certainly depressin', low-down, mind-messin', workin' at the carwash blues." That seemed to sum up a plausible future for her country. On board she sat next to a representative of Kirin Beer. In New York at last, she called her husband, hoping he hadn't yet had supper, and discovered that he and a colleague were about to go to Midtown for sushi. Under the watchful eye of a Manhattan sushi master, she ate her dinner and pondered the day's events. Were they all corny improbabilities, or is it the end, the wimpish end, of the American century?

6

Blame and Reappraisal

The American Century, declared in 1943 by an exuberantly optimistic Henry Luce, seems in danger fifty years
later of coming to a premature close. To live through
what may be its waning few years is a melancholy experience,
and it raises many questions about why the chief business
of the American people, namely business (as Calvin Coo-
lidge once observed), is doing so badly. Nearly everybody
has a pet theory for all this. Japan is blamed for being too
competitive; circumstances at home are lamented, from
our legal to our educational systems; our history and national philosophies are examined and found wanting since
they stress so much that is superficial and so little that is
profound. In one of the most important competitions the
United States has ever engaged in, it seems to be losing.
But the difference between blame and true cause is subtle.
This section will try to examine—and distinguish between—
the two.

For the last decade or so, the business pages of newspapers have hardly been distinguishable from the sports
pages. The home teams haven't been doing so well, and
their descent to the cellar seems to be accelerating.

At first it was only the offbeat sports—cameras, let's
say—whose sales were off. But then the major leaguers,
such as televisions and stereos, began getting clobbered.
Even that quintessentially American product, the baseball
mitt, also fell to the Visitors.

Matters seemed less sporting when steel and automobiles threatened to succumb. Twenty years ago, foreign
autos had 4.1 percent of the domestic market, and foreign

steel 4.2 percent. Today, imported steel accounts for 14 percent of the American market, and imported autos take between 27 percent and 30 percent.

Still, the average American consumer has found it hard to feel sorry for either the steel or the automobile industry. We bought Japanese cars because they suited us better: the Toyotas in our garages were a pleasure to drive, being reliable, fuel-efficient, and unlikely to rust out from under us like the American heaps we'd just replaced. Steel seemed a more remote problem—even its own managers didn't want to have anything to do with it. No steel barons went on TV to tell us if only we'd come back and try again, things would be different this time. On the contrary, they were eager to grab a chance to mismanage oil instead.

In the tradition of the Monday morning sports pages, observers have replayed every situation. They tell us that the home teams, once World Series, Superbowl, World Cup shoo-ins, are losing because:

1. The Visitors only copy us—but do it better, putting the savings they realize from bypassing research expenses into better development and marketing instead.

2. American firms take only a short-run view of profit making, whereas the Visitors have double vision and look at both short-run and long-run profitability.

3. American firms use quantitative methods for decision making, which favor analytic precision and detachment over insight and judgment based on experience.

4. The Visitors use both top-down and bottom-up management, whereas American management and labor have traditionally viewed each other as adversaries, to be outmaneuvered and not cooperated with.

5. The government just has too many regulations to let the free market operate properly.

6. The Visitors always settle everything amicably (or deviously) among themselves, whereas we're always in court.

7. Inflation is killing us.

Some readers might observe that missing from these seven laments is any mention of tariffs, trade barriers, protectionism, or the like. As most observers do, we consider protectionism foolishly shortsighted on anybody's part. Moreover, we blush to hear it from the mouths of our negotiators. We were once the premier practitioners of gunboat diplomacy, and our present cries of anguish and protests against what we consider unfair treatment must sound peculiar at best. Is there a Japanese trade negotiator alive today who, recalling Admiral Perry's sortie into Edo Bay, doesn't sometimes retire to his hotel room after a round of talks with the put-upon Americans and have a good laugh?

7

We Taught Them Everything They Know

That the Japanese only copy and don't innovate is a charge we've met before, a complacent myth some people still believe and reckon will prevent the Japanese from achieving the high level of innovation necessary to develop the Fifth Generation. Although we have dealt with the issue in a general way, it might help to cite some specifics.

Jordan Lewis, a professor at the University of Pennsylvania's Wharton School, has studied the relationship between American economic growth and Japanese technology and makes the persuasive argument that the story is really one of attitudes rather than technology. Consumer electronics, for example, regarded as a mature field by American firms in the 1960s, was viewed with greater insight by the Japanese. For the immediate market, they produced a superior color television tube, the Sony Trinitron. But they also looked at what might tempt consumers in the future. They hit upon the home video recorder, a device that had been invented in the United States but had never been developed here for lack of a perceived market potential. The Sony Betamax went through four generations and fifteen years of development before it succeeded as a consumer product, but the Japanese stuck with it. Sony's newest success, the personal stereo, the Walkman, is a product that literally invented its own market.[8]

In memory chips, a vital component in computers and other electronic equipment, the Japanese have pulled ahead decisively. Leaving both Americans and Europeans struggling in their dust, the Japanese produced cheap and reliable 64K RAM chips (64,000-bit storage random access memory chips) and are well on their way to dominating the next generation, the 256K RAM chip, as well. By early 1982 an agreement had been reached between Hitachi and Hewlett-Packard—an agreement proposed by the American firm—whereby Hitachi would supply Hewlett-Packard with the technology to manufacture the new chips under license. However we may care to interpret this novel arrangement, the important point is that Hewlett-Packard, one of America's most innovative companies, is gladly "copying" from the Japanese.

Given these instances (and there are others) it takes some self-delusion for us to cling to the "Japan as copycat" myth much longer. We've noted that the Japanese themselves chafe under this reputation and now intend to dispose of it once and for all. One of the driving forces behind the Fifth Generation, one that can't be overstressed, is the deeply felt national determination to show the world that the Japanese are capable of innovation of the highest degree.

8

Short Run, Long Run, End Run

And what of the second magic reason for Japanese success, that American firms take only a short-run view of profit making, whereas the Japanese look at both short-run and long-run profitability? Jordan Lewis, for one, agrees with this charge against the M.B.A. fast-track mentality of most American managers. But there seems no use railing against the M.B.A.'s when they are responding rationally to the more subtle pressures of equity holders and the tax structure. Vogel says, "The [Japanese] company's capacity to think in long-range terms is made possible in part by their relatively greater reliance on bank loans than on the sale of securities to meet their capital requirements. Since stock now accounts for less than one-sixth of a company's capital needs compared to one-half in the United States, stockholders lack power to pressure for showing a profit each year, and banks are as interested in a company's long-range growth as the company itself. When companies are able to pay interest, the banks want to continue to lend them money, for banks are as dependent on quality companies to lend to as companies are dependent on the banks for borrowing. Indeed, when quality companies with their own capital want to cut costs by repaying loans, the banks try to make it attractive to continue borrowing."[9]

And where do Japanese banks get the cash to press into the hands of diffident industrialists? For one thing, the savings rate in Japan is 20 percent of personal income, as opposed to a U.S. rate of about 5 percent. This translates to four times the leverage for capital investment and four times the potential to accelerate their economic growth.

Harvard's Robert B. Reich points out many problems with the tax structure in the United States, which serves the goal of long-range development very poorly. For example, the steel industry enjoyed a "breathing space" beginning in 1969, which included tax credits among other protectionist measures. But nobody offered those tax credits to the steel industry on the condition that it restructure itself toward greater productivity and competitiveness. The American steel industry has moved rapidly into other fields—oil, for example—instead of trying to rebuild and upgrade old plants, or build new plants, or undertake new research, and so on. Reich comments: "This is not to suggest that steel, or any other industry in distress, should necessarily reinvest in its original product. Diversification into a more competitive industry may be a far superior adjustment strategy. But adjustment assistance is often provided to distressed industries on the assumption that they need it to regain competitiveness rather than simply to maintain overall corporate profitability. At the very least companies receiving such assistance should be required to specify the investment strategy they will pursue, and the public should have an opportunity to decide whether that strategy merits public support."[10]

Here it's instructive to compare Japanese and American steel industry responses to the new challenge from steel suppliers in Latin America and Southeast Asia, who have the advantages of much lower wages, state-of-the-art technology, and easy access to raw materials. The Japanese are restructuring their steel industry, moving away from bulk steel to the manufacture of new types of stainless and specialty steels where they can maintain their advantage. American steelmakers are demanding new tariffs.

Finally, to return to the tax code, Robert Reich points out how it promotes mobility of capital, but not the utilization of unemployed labor or underused public works. Thus when an American firm or industry begins to decline, Americans pay not only in terms of tax assistance to that declining industry, but also in tax assistance to the unemployed whom the sinking industry draws into its undertow, and the suddenly unsupportable schools and community services. "At the very least," Reich says, "adjustment policies should ensure that tax deductions, accelerated depreciation, and tax credits not retard worker and community adjustment. Perhaps tax benefits should be provided for reinvestments in 'human capital' and renewed contributions to local tax bases."[11]

In *Theory Z*, UCLA professor William G. Ouchi points out how the lifetime employment of an executive in a Japanese firm gives that man—and, to be sure, it is always a man—a compelling reason for considering the long-term fortunes of his firm. As an executive, he is carefully schooled in many aspects of his firm's business and becomes a corporate generalist. American firms, on the contrary, must deal with a management turnover that can reach 25 percent in a year. If a given American firm fails to promote its young managers fast enough, they go someplace that will. This, however, encourages functional specialization rather than generalization. And managers who are strangers to each other must then rely on each other to be "professional," that is, to respond in standard ways to problems. This in turn leads to a bureaucracy—inflexible, insensitive, and inefficient.[12]

9

Quantification and Its Discontents

Is it then the fault of American business schools, which have taught "science" when business is really an "art"? Lewis, for one, argues that the quantitative decision making taught in American business schools is basically risk-averse, though he goes on to suggest that American firms have chosen those risk-averse procedures because they accorded with all sorts of needs that are both internal to the firm and external to the social and economic environment. For example, he describes the General Electric Corporation's adventures with quantitative decision making in the 1960s. The firm was then considering growth opportunities in computers, nuclear power, and semiconductor electronics. "At the time, markets and technologies for the first two options were presumably closer at hand and thus easier to quantify than the third. General Electric proceeded to drop semiconductor electronics and invest heavily in computers and nuclear reactors. Since then the company has left the computer business, nuclear power sales have tumbled, and semiconductor electronics has become a major growth industry." Perhaps so. But if GE had been able to make a go of it in computing, nobody would have remembered the less wise decision to drop semiconductor electronics or the unexpected (and perhaps unpredictable) flop nuclear power has turned out to be in the United States.

More important, Japanese students have been studying side by side with American students in business schools and have learned to use the same decision-making tools. But they have returned home to use them in a very different society.

10

Proceed Always with Ambition and Youthfulness

This brings us to the top-down and bottom-up management practiced by the Japanese. Ouchi's *Theory Z* describes the shape of Japanese management, its intricate social ties and assumptions, its reliance on trust, intimacy, and integrity. The Z firm shares decisions (and authority), develops interpersonal skills, provides broad incentives for sustaining a long-term work relationship including stable employment, participatory management, and an atmosphere so pleasant that it carries beyond the work place and into social relationships outside work.

Lewis also praises "bottom-up" management, making the point that although major innovations can change an industry, most change takes place through small incremental differences, and those come from employees whose experience on the shop floor and in the field is crucial. New ideas come from such sources only when employees can be sure that they will be listened to respectfully.

Whatever the health of top-down management in the United States, bottom-up management has fared badly. Studies as early as 1952 and 1953 demonstrated the advantages of using workers' ideas to improve productivity, not only in electronics but also in coal mining. If business schools were teaching quantitative methods, they were also teaching participatory management, and practitioners chose to take one and not the other. Historical differences between labor and management often have been cited as an insuperable problem, with roots in nineteenth-century conflicts that can never be resolved. But if we look at who our international trade competitors have been since that time, we see that change is quite possible. Japan, for one, has changed itself from labor-intensive to capital-intensive and is about to change to knowledge-intensive industries. West Germany has experienced a similar set of changes both in industrial management and in politics.

The blame for American inflexibility is by no means entirely management's. In 1955, asked to write a thoughtful piece about the future, George Meany, then head of the newly federated AFL-CIO, was at pains to point out that all American workers wanted were money and benefits, that they had no desire and no place in management councils. George Meany headed the AFL-CIO until late 1979 and did not change his mind or his policy.

On the floor of the Honda factory in Saitama outside Tokyo, there are signs in both English and Japanese. Here is what they say:

1. Proceed always with ambition and youthfulness.

2. Respect sound theory, develop fresh ideas, and make the most effective use of time.

3. Enjoy your work and always brighten your working atmosphere.

4. Strive constantly for a harmonious flow of work.

5. Be ever mindful of the value of research and endeavor.

We shall leave as an exercise for the reader the construction of a set of comparable rules for an American factory floor. Advanced students may try them for a British factory floor. Only professionals had better attempt them for a Soviet factory floor.

11

The Lawyer or the Engineer?

Surely, then, the problem is overregulation. Senator Paul Tsongas of Massachusetts provides an interesting insight on that topic: "As someone very involved with the Chrysler Loan Guarantee Bill a few years ago, I spent hour upon hour listening to American auto manufacturers testify about the millstone of U.S. regulation. They blamed everything but the Edsel on regulation. I felt very sorry for them at first. Then I discovered that the Japanese and the Germans had to meet the same regulations. I realized that the American manufacturers either knew they were crying wolf, that they were being deceitful, or they were deluding themselves. I prefer to think they were lying because, if they really believed what they were saying, they cast their competence as managers in such a poor light."[13]

Certain studies show that pollution abatement regulations reduced general annual productivity growth in the United States by 26 percent between 1973 and 1976, with the effect of health and safety regulations being half that. Of course these studies do not take into account the improved quality of life for workers and residents nearby, or even the long-range effects of such regulations, which might make the numbers look very different. While some companies in the chemicals field, for example, threw their resources and energies into fighting every regulation tooth and nail, 3M and Dow Corning re-engineered their production processes to capture and use previously discarded wastes, often with *net* cost savings. But only 20 percent of American firms have chosen this path.

Automobile emission regulations were imposed in Japan long after they were imposed in the United States, but Japanese auto manufacturers met standards in Japan and the United States well before their American competitors. The story is similar in steel.

Air quality standards are more stringent in Japan than in the United States, but otherwise those standards are similar. However, once regulations are set in Japan, they are enforced by persuasion instead of coercion; by conflict resolution instead of litigation.

Again, Senator Tsongas: "In 1980 the Honda three-door Civic failed a 35-miles-per-hour, head-on collision test conducted by the National Highway Transportation Safety Administration. Many American cars passed. How did the U.S. auto industry respond? Rather than press the obvious competitive advantage the test results offered, the American companies objected to the test as unwarranted. They went to court. The Japanese reacted differently. Rather than hire lawyers, Honda must have hired engineers. Last year, the Civic passed the test."[14]

12

No Trust, Antitrust

The Japanese talk to each other. They talk at dinners, they talk at meetings, they talk over the telephone. They share one language—and that is meant in the metaphorical as well as the literal sense. Their cultural homogeneity is precious to them and is fostered actively by everything from the government to the mass media.

Westerners, on the other hand, are heterogeneous. And a number of studies have shown that regardless of the idea or the setting, a new idea spreads more slowly among people who have different beliefs, values, education, and social status. If an environment is discordant, the problems of introducing and then maintaining innovative behavior are magnified.

Americans, then, have many differences. Instead of talking to settle them, we meet in courts. It's startling to realize that the number of civil law suits filed in the federal courts has increased seven times faster than the population over the last twenty years. We are an enormously contentious society, and we are getting more so. When we rely solely on litigation to resolve our conflicts, we assume that trust will not work. We have no national vision to sustain us, no common interests that transcend our differences.

American law firms complain indignantly about what they perceive as a freeze on lawyers' visa applications, a policy instituted by Japan's Ministry of Justice that effectively prevents American lawyers from practicing in Japan. "The inability of American lawyers to service American clients in Japan is a bar both to American investment and market penetration," says Sherman E. Katz, a Washington partner in the New York–based international law firm of Coudert Brothers. But the Japanese distrust our adversarial proceedings. American technical and entrepreneurial people share that sentiment, and it's not uncommon to hear them say, "We can do it if only we can keep the lawyers away from it." Lawyers are trained always to consider the worst case, to assume that the adversary is a rascal, and to achieve the best for their own client by fair means or even foul. This hardly is conducive to the best for national interests, the best for an industry, and often isn't conducive to the best for anybody but the lawyers.[15]

In the name of antitrust, Bell Laboratories has been threatened with legal regulation that might very well prevent it from doing what, historically, it has done best, which is basic research. Bell Laboratories is responsible for the transistor, for voice recording, the solar cell, radio astronomy, lasers, and some computer innovations only peripherally connected with telephones. But Representative Timothy Wirth proposed legislation in 1982 by which Bell Laboratories would concentrate instead on much more narrowly focused product-related research. Whatever short-term savings might accrue to the telephone subscriber must be weighed against that subscriber's long-term interests as a citizen of this country.

One Bell Labs official describes the whole antitrust episode this way: "It's a peculiar experience. You wake up one morning feeling fine, and the phone rings. It's your doctor. What's wrong? you ask. Well, we don't exactly know, he says, but we think you're sick. But I feel great, you say. All the same, better get down to the hospital, he says. You go to the hospital. Get into bed, he says. But I'm fine, you say. No, you're not, you're very sick, he says. We're going to have to operate. But I'm fine, you protest, just as they're clapping the anesthesia over your mouth."[16]

Antitrust surely has its purposes, but it shouldn't be a suicide pact between a nation and its industry.

13

That Leaves Inflation, Right?
An Excursion into
Industrial Policy

One explanation for the great American plateau (if it isn't in fact a decline) is inflation. Since inflation makes the future so unpredictable, it's argued, it hardly matters how much money gets spent on research and development because nobody will put the results of that research into productivity. Jordan Lewis shows that the proportion of U.S. industrial research and development funds devoted to basic research has varied inversely with inflation, at least over the last twenty years. Moreover, higher inflation rates inhibit capital investment by raising the cost of new facilities to prices well beyond those to be replaced. Inflation may be the villain behind Wall Street's demands for short-term gains. The 1973–74 energy crisis only magnified practices that were already well established.

It would be splendid if we could cure inflation once and for all, and nostrums are as numerous as those for the common cold—and about as effective. Moreover, once the dramatic drop in the inflation rate under the Reagan administration took place in 1982, there was no sign at all that such a drop would very much affect the issues that really mattered. It began to look as if inflation, burdensome though it was, was no more than a scapegoat for problems that were really brought on by an utter absence of industrial policy in the United States, whether for declining industries, such as steel and automobiles, or for emerging industries, such as electronics.

Reich, for example, suggests that our losses to Japan, Inc., can be laid to our unwillingness to put aside our ideologies about a "free market," put aside our fears about planning, and confront our problem plainly: our lack of a coherent industrial policy.

We shall have to stop professing astonishment that the Europeans and the Japanese follow self-interested trade policies quite unrelated to our laissez-faire free market catechisms. Quite simply, Western Europe and Japan function differently.

Chalmers Johnson of the University of California has identified four major conditions in all developing Asian societies, including the Japanese, that he believes account for their stunning victories in global markets. First is stable rule by a political elite that does not accede to short-range or special interest demands that might undermine the long-range goals of the society. Second is cooperation between the public and private sectors under some pilot institution (in the case of Japan, MITI) with *much* initiative from the private sector. Third is heavy and continuing expenditures on education, and the relatively even distribution of income throughout the society—a condition that obtains in Japan far better than it does in, for example, the People's Republic of China. Finally, governments in the developing Asian countries understand and use without hesitation the intervention of the price mechanism in the market. All these are parts of Asian industrial policy, and in the case of Japan, industrial policy furthermore encourages personal savings (by giving Japanese wage earners large incentives to save), work productivity, and orderly change when the time for change comes, as it inevitably must.

Of course the fully free market is an illusion, as each session of Congress demonstrates. We offer subsidies and bailouts and fiddle with the tax laws obsessively, all of which make a mockery out of the "free market." In Robert Reich's words, "Because neither government nor business can admit to the intimacy of their relationship, both sides treat it as an illicit affair, hiding it from public view and thereby thwarting any attempt to give institutional legitimacy to those aspects of the relationship that promote adjustment."

But when our free market delusions shatter against the reality of the perfectly understandable self-interests of other nations, we only know how to demand protection, which everyone agrees is short-term at best.

As an alternative to protection, Reich suggests "managed

adjustment," a partnership of government, labor, and business to ease inevitable national economic transitions out of declining industries and into emerging ones. Such agreements have worked in Japan and West Germany because they are based on contracts in which all parties agree in advance to certain shifts of industrial resources. Such agreements tie industry adjustment to worker and community adjustments, diffusing the social costs that changes always carry with them.[17]

The Japanese aren't angels. But somehow workers and employers alike can be persuaded that beyond their immediate goals are larger ones that will ultimately benefit everyone. How this is done in Japan is explicitly described in Ouchi's *Theory Z*, and there's nothing very mysterious about it. A structure of reconciliation—talk, talk, talk—builds mutual trust among all parties, a sense that everyone's in this together, and what is deeply harmful to one segment of the group will eventually be harmful to all; but large goals can be mutually agreed upon and achieved together.

Americans find the company songs and canned pep talks that come over the public address system and the company uniforms of Japanese firms almost embarrassingly corny. We imagine ourselves beyond such things. But college alma maters and national anthems are corny too, yet they can move us to tears by touching something noble and precious, our sense of belonging. This is the spirit that dwells in Japanese industry.

Jordan Lewis concludes: "American businesses, government agencies, individuals, and others have come to rely increasingly on rules and regulations that purport to govern our relationships. But many of the procedures we have created to protect ourselves from each other have also masked our mutual interests and inhibited the collaboration necessary for our common gain. Publc and private measures that reduce conflict and build mutual trust are thus likely to make important contributions to our economic progress."[18]

Declining industries aren't the only ones with problems. Emerging industries also need an overall national policy. It is startling to realize that 30 percent of U.S. research and development is funded by the Pentagon alone. Of research that has no immediate commercial application, government funding exceeds two-thirds of the total. Even in industrial laboratories, managers lament the nearly non-existent transfer of technology from research into commercial products because we lack a systematic means of moving basic research into development. Some would argue that we also lack the capital. But once again, that problem could be met by farsighted changes in the tax laws. The income from municipal bonds is tax-free to their holders because municipal bonds are perceived as a social necessity but an otherwise unattractive investment. Why not industrial R&D bonds along the same lines?

Pentagon support has been generous and sometimes enlightened, as we shall see further on, but the goals of defense and those of commerce aren't identical. The U.S. Defense Department is not chartered to concern itself with competition within American industry. Pentagon programs are often exasperatingly brief and subject to political shifts, which are dangerous for or antithetical to good marketing of innovative products.

In contrast, Japan's MITI allows, encourages (and in the case of the Fifth Generation all but coerces) firms to cooperate in specific basic research projects, but once the basic research is completed, MITI insists that the firms compete in marketing.

There is no American MITI responsible for gathering detailed information about world market trends, the competitive strategies of our trading partners, and the long-term outlook for particular U.S. industries. The secretiveness of both declining and emerging American industries presents difficulties, especially since American firms depend on surprise rather than long-term investment and marketing. Nevertheless, as securities analysts have shown, that information can be gathered. No such group works at the U.S. Department of Commerce. In addition to its information gathering, MITI acts as a forum for special interests to meet and discuss mutual problems and arrive at long-term solutions. Americans end up in court, which is costly and not likely to produce optimal long-range solutions.[19]

It is not as if we have a choice about change. It is, as Reich asserts, the stuff of history. The choice we do have is how we adjust to change, for some choices are easier, fairer, and more effective than others.

In a way we do understand that there is such a thing as the national interest. Unfortunately, the only model of that idea we seem comfortable with is what we call national defense. Public spending on everything from highway building to education can be rationalized as "defense" safeguards against some dreadful threat from the outside, a Sputnik, a Gulf of Tonkin, a missile gap, a window of vulnerability, or worse.

"If you can think of a good defense application," one Pentagon official said to Feigenbaum, "we'll fund an American Fifth Generation project." There are compelling defense applications, as we shall see. But the emphasis of this book has been that the economic and intellectual benefits of intelligent machines are just as compelling.

14

Where There Is No Vision, the People Perish

For former flower children and other blithe spirits who crashed to earth during the economic contractions of the 1970s, the lessons Japan has to teach must seem a bit dreary: diligence, study, application, duty, responsibility, suppleness, patriotism, and playing the game with intensity. (Vince Lombardi might have been a Japanese sage with his "Winning isn't everything, it's the only thing." He's misquoted—common to the oral tradition—but that's what we wanted him to say. In fact he said, "Winning isn't everything, but wanting to win is.")

The Japanese still believe in hard work. So did we, not so long ago. It was enshrined in our popular poetry and aphorisms: "Genius is one percent inspiration and ninety-nine percent perspiration," said Thomas Edison; and Edgar Guest, arguably the most widely quoted and worst poet America has ever produced, wrote inspirational verses such as this: "Somebody said that it couldn't be done/But he with a chuckle replied/That maybe it couldn't, but he would be one/Who wouldn't say so till he'd tried." As a people we were once moved by that. We still are—a little.

Yet we have allowed something to go wrong, and we don't know how to fix it. Everybody seems to understand that the world is changing, yet nothing seems urgent enough to prompt us to change along with it. We only pull ourselves together at the dramatic gesture, the imminent threat, or the sudden catastrophe.

John R. Opel, the president and chief executive of IBM, gave a talk in the late spring of 1982 where he gave details of our dismal national tailspin, citing, for example, the fact that over the last twenty years, the average combined verbal and mathematical scores on Scholastic Aptitude Tests administered to college-bound youngsters have fallen by a total of 90 points. Half of all U.S. high school students take no mathematics after the tenth grade, only one junior or senior in six takes a science course, and only one in fourteen makes that physics. He too lamented our national lassitude and concluded, "What we need now is another such shock of recognition; an awareness in community after community across the land that we face an urgent national problem and a resolve to overcome it."[20]

Well, now, anyone who has read this far will surely have gathered that *we* feel such a shock has been delivered to the world and, as it happens, in the form of a new generation of computers, Mr. Opel's own specialty. We too should like to welcome a new, better-educated generation of young people equipped to meet the Japanese challenge with all the verve and imagination it will certainly demand. But as we are about to see, the United States has some severe problems to overcome before it can hope to realize that dream.

15

In Youth Is Our Salvation

Americans have traditionally looked to their young people to save them from whatever trouble the country seems threatened with. Most obviously, the old send the young to war. But the notion that in youth lies our hope and our salvation continues to shape our history and certainly our mythology. The exuberant youth, who always shows the old how foolish and inconsequential their traditions are, is the miniplot of countless television commercials, and conversely, the theme of sermonizing rebukes from social critics who worry about such things, especially as the population, demographically speaking, gets older and older. But still we believe, for in the main, our belief in the power of youth has served us pretty well.

The faith is spreading. We've seen here that Fuchi, for one, has inverted the seniority system that permeates Japanese society and has given power to his young researchers that's undreamed of under normal circumstances in Japan. Surely, then, if Japanese computing is a threat, our own youth will save us—and if not youth, then the young in spirit, because, again, according to our mythology, entrepreneurs are as successful as they are youthful. A perfect enunciation of that faith was expressed in 1982 when President Ronald Reagan presented a record defense budget to the U.S. Congress for its approval. Reporters inquired where he thought companies would find technical workers if his defense budget passed, particularly since increases in defense had deeply affected government support of education. He smiled his most winning smile and said, "Give industry the money, and it will find the people."

They're to be found, one supposes, under cabbages. To win a defense contract, a company must demonstrate that competent technical talent is at hand, if not already employed by the firm itself. If a company doesn't have a particularly good cabbage patch, it forgoes bidding. Other companies "bet on the come," as the phrase in defense contracting has it, and hire additional personnel in the hopes that a contract will materialize, a practice that is not only wasteful but that exacerbates the shortage problem. Gypsy engineers, who a few years ago could move from defense contractor to defense contractor, something like high-class migrant workers, now find that they're priced out of the housing market in states like California and Massachusetts, so they stay put.

Perhaps Americans ought to consider a vast professional retread program. Inspired by the example of the Japanese, who on a per capita basis have fewer than one-twentieth the lawyers and one-seventh the accountants, but five times the engineers as the U.S., we might diet down to those proportions ourselves. Since it takes some time to simplify all legal processes (and it might meet with some resistance, as involuntary diets often do), a pilot program could be set up to engage Ph.D.'s in English, who would be only too glad to be gainfully employed at anything. The surplus lawyers and accountants would eventually fall into place, and English Ph.D.'s, lawyers, and accountants could be retrained as engineers. Not only would this exceptionally attractive scheme solve the pressing engineer shortage, but economically marginal workers could move into high-productivity jobs.

Persiflage aside, the education of our engineers—the youth who are to translate our hopes and dreams into working apparatus—is in deep trouble. Nowhere is it in more trouble than in computing.

16

A Discipline in Crisis

Every two years for the past decade or so, the chairmen of the departments of computer science in U.S. and Canadian universities have gathered for a few days in Snowbird, Utah, a mountain retreat whose altitude makes the heart sing and the blood effervesce, and have talked over their common problems. After each meeting they have descended from Little Cottonwood Canyon with this engraved on their tablets: *Computer science is a discipline in crisis.*

Since everything from the national parks to hairdressing is "in crisis," it's tempting to dismiss this as just one more panic, but in fact the computer scientists have something to worry about. If, as the Japanese maintain, computing is the discipline that affects all disciplines, then perhaps *crisis* is not too strong a word. Specifically, the problems are with people, equipment, money, and even philosophy.

We must dispose of philosophy at once. Whether studying the phenomena surrounding computers is a natural science like physics, or an artificial science like mathematics, or fancy engineering, or a species of psychology, or some hybrid not yet catalogued, is a question that is unfortunately beyond the scope of this book. The issues are deeply important to the discipline itself, however, shaping how students are taught and how research develops, among other critical effects.

Other specifics that worry the chairmen are not only relevant to the national well-being, but they are easy to understand. They are also, in a sense, Siamese triplets: the life of one depends on the life of them all.

Unlike most academics of the 1970s and 1980s, the

chairmen have no complaints about student enrollments (unless you count a human tidal wave as cause for complaint). From 1975 to 1981, undergraduate majors in computer science doubled; their numbers were conservatively estimated to grow another 60 percent by 1987. If their sole motive is money, they've made a wise decision. In 1980, each B.S. holder could pick from an average of twelve offers and expect starting salaries of $20,000 per year and up (and the salaries keep rising). For Ph.D.'s in computer science the prospects were even more dazzling. A new computer science Ph.D. had, in 1980, thirty-four positions to choose from. Unfortunately, if the new Ph.D. chose to stay in academia, all he or she could expect after those many years of graduate studenthood was the salary equivalent of the fresh bachelor. In a bit of donnish understatement, Peter Denning, president of the Association for Computing Machinery, the computer professional group, said, "There is clearly little incentive for B.S. holders to contemplate graduate school when their current offers are comparable to those paid the newest faculty."

But the tidal wave consists of more than just computer science majors. At any school where students are bright, they recognize that the computer revolution is real, and regardless of the field they eventually end up in, the computer will be there too. The hunger for computer literacy is swelling introductory programming courses, swamping terminals, and even, in some stone-age schools, tying up the keypunch machines. "The result?" asks Denning. "Existing terminal facilities and computing centers cannot handle the load. Class sizes balloon. Lab facilities are insufficient. Faculty consider industrial positions."[21]

Despite this lack of incentive, some people do continue beyond the bachelor's level. They love the work for its own sake; they love research, the high feeling of knowing, proving, discovering, and inventing at the very edge of a discipline. But even these dedicated souls are gobbled up by industrial laboratories. Everybody from Bell Labs to Lucasfilms wants computer science Ph.D.'s. Thus, even though 1,127 persons turned their backs on easy money and earned a computer science Ph.D. between 1974 and 1978, there was a net increase of only 32 academic positions over that period when everything—death, outflow into industry, and so on—is taken into account.

This phenomenon isn't unique to computer science. Doctorates in physical sciences and engineering in the United States declined 25 percent between 1971 and 1979, in part a result of the irresistible seductions of fast-expanding high-tech industries that gladly take bachelors and those with no degrees, and in part a result of the lower numbers of people going into such fields in the first place. The phrase—by now a cliché—is that industry is eating its own seed corn. And lest we think we can borrow from the neighbors, immigration laws have recently been proposed that would send *all* technically trained foreign Ph.D.'s back to their own countries as soon as their education is finished, for at least two years, before they will be allowed to work in the United States. It isn't a high-minded gesture on the part of Congress to return the prodigals to their less developed countries which can't pay them or even, in some cases, use them; it is a piece of human trade barrier erected by some declining technical professions to protect their own oversupply. Bringing democracy to a particularly fine point, they convinced Congress that if they were drowning, so should everyone else.

Cogent arguments have been made that computer science shortages are temporary and will fix themselves in the free market all in good time. Others have argued that it's sweet and fitting, not to mention lucrative, to be a scarce and valuable national resource. They see an instructive example in physicians who have kept their numbers down and incomes up.

A 1980 report from the President's Office of Science and Technology singled out the computing profession as likely to have shortages persisting into the 1990s. Unless faculty erosion is reversed, it declared, the alternative will be to curtail enrollments. The report generally favors free-market mechanisms except in computing, which it considers too important to be allowed to wait for the slow-moving marketplace to correct. It recommended some government intervention. Unfortunately, the report was prepared under an administration sensitive to the role of high technology in the national welfare; the succeeding administration was unpersuaded and has done nothing.[22]

But the purpose of academic computer science is not only to teach the initiates; its research is of a very special nature, unfettered by immediate commercial applications or proprietary secrecy. It is characterized by long-term rather than short-term goals, and any nation that values being in a position of intellectual and technological leadership (something that cannot be attained, though it can be destroyed, overnight) must have a strong and healthy academic research environment.

To risk laboring the point, the initial research in the central technology of the Fifth Generation, artificial intelligence—in particular, expert systems—was done in universities. Not only did industrial laboratories fail to find AI a cost-effective area to invest in, they virtually competed with each other to phrase their scorn. The exception was SRI International, which built a first-rate AI research group, but did so for federal contracts. Only now are IBM and Bell Laboratories possibly ready to mend their ways.

So the problem for the chairmen has two parts. One part is an embarrassment of riches. Everybody wants to *be* a computer scientist, and everybody wants to *hire* them when they're trained. The other part of the chairman's problem is dire poverty: the paucity of people to train these eager students. If a large proportion of Ph.D.'s in the field don't end up in universities, who will teach them?

One solution to the faculty problem, used successfully by medical, law, and even business schools, is to put such faculty on a different pay scale from the rest of the university. This has already happened informally in some universities and formally and publicly in others, not only causing hard feelings in, say, the classics department, but in at least one case leading to litigation.

Another problem is equipment. Students are often forced to learn on equipment that is out of date after three years. In a field that changes as rapidly as computer science, this is a grave problem. But it can be solved by enlightened cooperation with firms that have the capital to invest in the very latest equipment and will allow university researchers to use it during off-hours (as Xerox's Palo Alto Research Center, for example, allows Stanford computer scientists to use its excellent research machines). The sharing of people in the form of joint appointments between universities and corporations can also help solve the faculty problems, though it requires flexibility on everyone's part, university, corporation, and scientist, and it doesn't solve the problem for universities that happen not to be located near accommodating firms.[23]

There are no easy answers to these problems. A fair

number of good-citizen corporations have made substantial contributions to educational needs—among them DEC's External Research Program, which offers equipment grants in exchange for university research, and IBM's sponsorship of research activities at several universities around the country, some of which involve equipment leases. New tax incentives for industrial contributions to university research (including equipment grants), plus the fact that industrial R&D funding increased 6 percent over the inflation rate for 1981—and is expected to continue at this level—bode well for ongoing support of computer education by industries.

But everyone agrees that the level of funding needed for education and academic research simply cannot, and will not, be met by the private sector. Academics also worry that industry's emphasis on the short term, whether profits, product improvement, or proprietary information, is the functional equivalent of a one-night stand, whereas university computer science needs a well-dowered marriage.[24]

17

Anti-Intellectualism as the American Way

It should go down as one of the great ironies in history that in the country that first brought the world machine intelligence—the emulation of human thinking by a machine—nearly half its citizens do not believe in the theory of evolution. A full 44 percent of Americans believe that "God created man pretty much in his present form at one time within the last ten thousand years," says a recent Gallup poll.[25] The implications give one pause. To hold such a belief presupposes a profound ignorance of chemistry, geology, astronomy, biology, anthropology—in short, of science.

Now surely the numbers of high school students who take no science courses helps explain this, and the fact that 23 million of us cannot read at all (60 million if you count the functionally illiterate: of the 158 member nations of the United Nations, we are 49th in literacy) must share the blame. In a world where knowledge is power, we might well tremble for our country. For although this book is about machines called knowledge information processors, which began their careers as computers, it is ultimately about the centrality of knowledge in human life, today and in the future.

The Fifth Generation and what it represents compel us to confront an enduring theme in American life here. It is anti-intellectualism.

We Americans have had an ambivalent attitude toward knowledge since the founding of the republic. We have always respected *intelligence*, or so we've said, but for *intellect* we reserve suspicion, even mockery. This is because intelligence, according to our national prejudice, is useful and to the point: we like the fact that anyone can see intelligence at work and admire it in action. Furthermore, we believe intelligence is something you're born with (the fundamental assumption of the I.Q.). Intellect, on the other hand, has to be acquired with practice in those suspect places called classrooms, especially those of colleges and universities. Thus intellect seems a frill, something practical people can do without, something that, because it is often difficult and requires self-discipline to acquire, is hopelessly inaccessible to those born without sufficient intelligence. Worse, intellect is slippery, probing such tiresome questions as the meaning of meaning and other sorts of impractical, ultimate things that make ordinary people prone to impatience, not to say exasperation.

A perfect example of this is the practice of the senior senator from Wisconsin, William Proxmire, who has made great sport of awarding something he calls the Golden Fleece to federally funded projects he deems comical, but basically wasteful squanderings of tax revenues. Given the variety of places the federal government spends money, a disproportionate number of Golden Fleeces have been awarded to science projects. Why not? Their titles are long and awkward, the antiscientific bias in the United States is strong and at the same time inoffensive to a majority of voters, and surely there, as anyplace else, smoke implies fire. And yet some of the projects he had the most fun with were of quite practical importance, though they need not have been, since the mandate of the National Science Foundation, say, is to support basic research, with no special attention to its applications.

For example, a study to examine the effects of alcohol on fish gave the senator an opportunity for great public mirth as "the drunken fish boondoggle." In fact, the fight-or-flight behavior of fish is highly stylized and well understood, but fish under the influence of alcohol often mistake the ordinary behavior of their fellows as threatening and respond aggressively. Since the largest proportion by far of violence between persons in the United States is alcohol-related, the researcher's preliminary findings might have begun to allow us to understand this a little better. But Senator Proxmire's public derision, all in the name of practicality and common sense, ensured that the researcher, a respected specialist at the University of California's medical school in San Francisco, would receive no more funds to study "drunken fish."

Even the Department of Defense, usually shielded from such nonsense, is not immune. Controversy once erupted over a DOD study entitled "Why Aborigines Don't Sweat." Funding was allowed to continue only when DOD officials explained that it was, in fact, very important to know why aborigines didn't sweat: American soldiers were suffering greatly from dehydration in the heat of Southeast Asia, yet here was one group of our species, the Aborigines, who had somehow managed to adapt to high temperatures without sweating, which is the way the rest of us deal with the heat. How did they do it, and could we learn something to help American soldiers? The DOD official who told this story to a group of Stanford professors ended with a warning: "Load your titles with scientific jargon. Above all, don't aim to be humorous or lighthearted. Congress won't understand."

In the 1960s this country underwent a large-scale revulsion against the intellect, especially as it was supposed to be embodied by rationality and formal education. Though most participants in the movement did not know it (how could they, when the information was in books they despised?), the movement was as traditional as apple pie, embracing as it did a longtime American tenet that reason was and ever must be antithetical to feelings. At that moment, only feelings counted. The federal government was doing nothing to counteract this myth as it pursued a faraway war with unprecedented viciousness and fancy-dressed that primitive violence in the most specious of rationalizations. The intellectual community was mainly appalled, and mainly protested, but in the public view, the war was being waged and daily justified by former professors and professors-to-be.

In the following decade, the 1970s, intellectualism stopped being an instrument of war, but became instead an obstacle to getting along economically in life. Thus, on the one hand, higher education was chided for being impractical, and on the other, tenured educators, pretty much assured of a steady paycheck themselves, spoke out in sanctimonious indignation against "careerism." In any event, the public schools, having fallen into disarray, now fell into disfavor, and entire cities closed their schools for weeks and even months because the funds to run them had been refused by the taxpayers. (Of course this was not only anti-intellectualism; it was part of a much more complicated reaction to what seemed excessive government: costly, top-heavy, and meddlesome. Moreover, having insisted that the public schools act as the social levelers Americans have traditionally expected their schools to be, taxpayers were chagrined to discover that the schools singlehandedly could not bring together amicably a highly diverse group of antagonistic points of view. To ask that of them exceeded the capacity of the schools as institutions, and they cracked.)

This mistrustful attitude toward our schools is connected to the fact that intellect has always seemed an offense to our egalitarian aspirations. As our children have grown measurably more ignorant, we have, after all, responded variously: denied it; said it doesn't matter; declared it a hopeless cause; exulted in it as a legitimate ethnic heritage; and, in the case of those who could afford to, pulled children out of public schools and put them into private ones where discipline, intellectual stimulation, and personal safety are givens.

But we are left with a nagging question of more than theoretical interest. Can a nation that so disdains the life of the mind summon up the will to enter, let alone compete in, a world where knowledge is the overriding economic concern?

The first edition of this book ended this chapter with that question. As we were writing, tens, perhaps scores, of study groups were busy writing too, and in 1983 there was a blizzard of reports from them, each with their own point of view, but each in consternation about the dismal level of American education, from the primary to the graduate schools. Whether any of those reports will be transformed into a nationwide program of educational improvement remains to be seen. As one observer commented tartly, you may not be able to solve the schools' problems only by throwing money at them, but throwing only reports at them doesn't solve any problems either.

18

Intellectuals in the Cherry Orchard

Since the Fifth Generation—the mass production of intelligent machines—is comparable in human intellectual history to the invention of the printing press, with the certainty of making even greater changes in the life of the mind that books did, we might expect that American intellectuals (in particular those who still talk so reverently about the values of a liberal education, the sharing of the common culture, and so on) are eager to mold this new technology to serve the best human ends it possibly can.

Unfortunately, they're not. Most of them haven't the faintest idea what's happening. If they notice at all, they see the computerization of university campuses, say, as the new barbarism.

"Our Fascination with Electronic Technology Is Myopic—and Quintessentially American" is the title of a recent essay in *The Chronicle of Higher Education*, a trade paper for academics. Its author, a professor of English, rushes to establish his bona fides: "I'm no twentieth century Luddite, rioting against machinery because it threatens an older world of handicrafts. Is it Luddism to believe that extreme love of machinery is unhealthy? That a society with an adolescent lust for its own technology is decadent?"[26] Not Luddism, we'd say, just a misapprehension of the revolution, a confusion of means and ends.

To the computing illiterate, computer users' hunger for intellectual power and expansion looks like lust for gadgetry. In part, it is. So what? Who holds against us that we collect beautiful books with fine bindings and carefully chosen typefaces, at the same time that we honor what those books contain? What's wrong with admiring a beautifully designed computer, or a clever piece of code, human artifacts both? But the main eagerness that propels young-sters to the computer is the same eagerness that propelled earlier generations to literacy in the word.

We can further fault our English professor for not even stirring to discover that the "quintessentially American fascination" is taking place all over the world, in many nations in a more orderly and rational fashion; but at least he has let the matter come to his attention. Most self-styled intellectuals don't even recognize what's happening.

The novelist Hortense Calisher, deep in the middle of a long novel about the space shuttle, wrote an essay about the sublime ignorance and complete lack of interest intel-lectuals demonstrate in the face of another great human adventure, space exploration. "Among intellectuals who eagerly suffered talk of post-Einstein physics, space explo-ration as it might touch us humanly was dimestore stuff and bad form. (Ditto among the literati.) As for politics, just try deflecting the Middle East worry with the query 'What do you think of the chances, good or bad, of the U.N. Committee on the Peaceful Uses of Outer Space?' Most I met had never heard of it. Until then, neither had I."[27]

What *are* American intellectuals thinking about, then? A fair question, and not so easy to answer. For one thing, politics, that most evanescent of interests. For another, art, which no one would quarrel with. Perhaps they even pon-der their own irrelevance. But whose fault is that? Like Madame Ranevsky in Chekhov's *The Cherry Orchard*, they live in a dream world, irresponsible and whimsical, served by faithful old retainers (in the form of periodicals that are high in brow, even higher in self-importance, but low in circulation) that shamelessly pander to their illusions. A pity, but not a tragedy.

Why is it a pity? Because intelligent machines open up a world of possibility, speculation, and intellectual enrichment that could be—and for our children will be—the intellectual's instrument par excellence, a means of testing hypotheses, examining theories, playing "what if?" games, and reshaping human thought at a level of complexity that no other intellectual tool—certainly not the written word, not any form of graphics we use now, or mathematics—has ever been able to provide. The extension of human intellect that the Fifth Generation will give us is simply staggering.

KIPS allow, almost insist upon, the fusion of many different technologies and human services, from communications technology to health care delivery. The same principle is equally valid, and probably even more important, in the realm of ideas. Intellectuals and professionals in highly disparate fields often study the same concept to try to understand and use it, but because they have no common language, they cannot help or provide one another with insights they have acquired in their separate ways.

For example, both professors of English and knowledge engineers think very hard—and very practically—about the representation of ideas in language, but virtually no professors of English know anything about the discoveries knowledge engineers have made in their efforts to represent ideas in language, which will then be transformed into representations in a computer.

In short, no plausible claim to intellectuality can possibly be made in the near future without an intimate dependence upon this new instrument. Those intellectuals who persist in their indifference, not to say snobbery, will find themselves stranded in a quaint museum of the intellect, forced to live petulantly, and rather irrelevantly, on the charity of those who understand the real dimensions of the revolution and can deal with the new world it will bring about.

19

In the Service of the People

Regardless of their longevity, certain patterns of behavior become self-destructive in new circumstances. That is a fundamental law of life which tells us why species either change or disappear from the face of the earth.

Such new circumstances are upon us. The Japanese have already recognized this. Their intellectual distant early warning apparatus long ago gave the signal, and they have had time to prepare. It's easier, to be sure, in a culture where scholars are pop heroes and schoolchildren are driven to excel (and do); where illiteracy is virtually absent; and where the government is consciously working to bring about the knowledge society as soon as possible. The central question is not whether the Japanese are correct—they are—but whether the United States, with its long history of distrust for matters of the mind and distrust of rational planning for the future either by the government or by industries, is capable of adapting to the new circumstances.

Historically there are some precedents. The Wisconsin Experiment, begun by Governor Robert M. LaFollette at the turn of the century, put experts—specialists of various kinds at the University of Wisconsin—at work in the service of the people of that state. It was to be a much copied experiment, and Richard Hofstadter summarizes the experience:

"First there was an era of change and discontent which brought a demand for such men; next, the intellectuals and experts became identified with the reforms they formulated and helped to administer; then, an increasing distaste for reforms arose, often in direct response to their effectiveness. This distaste was felt above all by business interests, which arraigned governmental meddling, complained of the costs of reform, and attempted to arouse the public against reformers with a variety of appeals, among them anti-intellectualism. Finally, the reformers were ousted, but not all their reforms were undone."[28]

This pattern would be repeated in the New Deal, and again in the Kennedy administration; the Johnson and Ford follow-ons were mixed; the Nixon administration, save Professor Kissinger, was highly unmixed; the Carter administration made tentative invitations to intellectuals to help run government, but the Reagan administration put a prompt end to that.

Unlike politicians, business has taken the pragmatic view. It's lost on nobody that the great commercial fortunes are being made these days in high technology, which is science getting down to business, to paraphrase one firm's slightly condescending motto. Whatever the uneasiness between business and intellectuals in the past (or even in the future), at the moment they approach each other rapturously. This is offensive to some scientists, especially in artificial intelligence, who worry that the fast buck is nearly irresistible, and yet antithetical to the growth of healthy science. AI specialists who have taken to the marketplace argue to the contrary, that good science (good artificial intelligence, at any rate) is advanced by trying to solve real-world problems that don't allow the luxury of fudging to fit some preconceived idea of elegant science. In honesty, it's an open question whether AI in particular, or science in general, is best done pure or applied. There's ample precedent for both.

Up to now we have prospered as a nation despite our anti-intellectual streak (and, as Richard Hofstadter emphasizes, it is a streak, not a national passion) because we were blessed with vast natural resources, a lot of arable land, and a flexible ideology that picked up and dropped expertise as casual labor, correctly assuming it would always be around when it was needed again. It may very well be that even in the absence of any national policy to cultivate both knowledge and educated human beings to use it wisely, we shall still prosper, or at least survive. Under such circumstances, knowledge will be comfortably distributed where it is wanted and absent (or at least concealed) in places where it is unwelcome.

That seems a pleasant enough prospect. Yet it may harbor a deadly problem. In time it may lead to a ghastly separation between the knowledge haves and have-nots that cannot be mended by any simple redistribution of wealth. The knowledge have-nots will *not* be equal to those who have, and no amount of inspirational (and basically patronizing) rhetoric will make it so.

McCorduck and Feigenbaum diverge here. Feigenbaum thinks that a world of knowledge have-nots is leftover sixties rhetoric, a rhetoric that failed to foresee the hundred-dollar computer, there for anybody who wants it. McCorduck thinks his view is colored by living in Silicon Valley, whereas hers, colored by living in Manhattan, sees that books are free in libraries and there are still 60 million people in this country who can't read effectively and apparently don't find any compelling reason to learn how. She doesn't want to seem unduly reverent toward ordinary literacy, but it does seem to help you deal with the world in ways you otherwise couldn't. People who can't imagine the value of symbolic inference and knowledge derived from it aren't going to spend ten cents on a computer or the knowledge it could give them.

The intelligent machine—the knowledge information processor, the expert system, whatever—demands intelligent users. The very optimistic suggest that it will help create them. What educators, parents, and cultural leaders have been helpless to inspire in an entire underclass of the already disenfranchised, the intelligent machine will magically effect. The army is leading the way, those optimists point out, by exploring the possibilities of expert systems to help the low-tech recruit in the field deal with the high-tech equipment he or she has to deploy, maintain, and sometimes repair. The pessimists look for someplace to wait out the inevitable conflagration.

Optimists take heart from the example of Andrew Carnegie, forced in early adolescence to support his family because his father, replaced at his loom by an automatic weaving machine, was too demoralized ever to work again. Young Andrew caught on: industrialism was the way of the future. Just wait, say the optimists; the next generation will see which way the wind blows. Pessimists doubt it.

Optimists, pessimists, and all other spectators at the human comedy can smile at this: Carnegie had a deep contempt for formal education which, as it happened, paralleled that of his contemporary Leland Stanford. The two—once immensely successful in their respective businesses—set up educational institutions meant to correct the waywardness of existing schools. Those two institutions now house two of the three great American nurseries of artificial intelligence (the other is M.I.T.).

20

AI and the National Defense

As we pointed our earlier, we have never felt very comfortable as a nation undertaking a large project merely for the common good of the people. We have managed, however, to spend a lot of money on useful (and not so useful) things as long as we could persuade ourselves it was in the national defense.

Artificial intelligence is foremost among these. When no corporation or foundation chose to take AI seriously, or could afford to, the Advance Research Projects Agency (ARPA) of the Department of Defense supported it through two decades of absolutely vital but highly risky research. Since the Pentagon is often perceived as the national villain, especially by intellectuals, it's a pleasure to report that in one enlightened corner of it, human beings were betting taxpayers' money on projects that would have major benefits for the whole human race.

In the late 1970s, as some parts of the technology were ready to move beyond research and into development, venture capitalists and industrialists flocked to AI technical meetings and either adapted the technology to their own needs or set up firms especially to do AI. But the early cultivation had been supported by ARPA, which deserves credit for its enlightened scientific leadership.

Artificial intelligence has gone out into the world, for better or for worse, for commerce or for defense. The Japanese plan to rear this infant to full commercial adulthood. *We believe that Americans should mount a large-scale concentrated project of our own; that not only is it in the national interest to do so, but it is essential to the national defense.*

The so-called smart weapons of 1982, for all their sophisticated modern electronics, are really just extremely complex wind-up toys compared to the weapons systems that will be possible in a decade if intelligent information processing systems are applied to the defense problems of the 1990s. In the summer of 1981, Feigenbaum was asked to give scientific testimony on the current state of research and development in AI and expert systems to a panel of the Defense Science Board, the highest-level scientific group that advises the U.S. Department of Defense. The panel's charter was to assess the possible impact of a large number of current technologies (it is rumored that they examined seventy to eighty) on the defense of the United States. In the report of the panel, AI ranked seventh using an opportunity-versus-risk measure, and second using only an opportunity measure!

Accordingly, it is not surprising that the undersecretary of defense for research and engineering, Richard D. DeLauer, the "R&D chief" of the Pentagon, is quoted as saying, "The Defense Department should press this technology because no one else is pursuing it, and the Japanese have strong programs in both artificial intelligence and Fifth Generation computers with a consortium of government, university, and industry development."[29]

We agree with DeLauer's assessment and would like to support it with five points.

The first looks with awe at the peculiar nature of modern electronic warfare that allows a marginal technological edge (a "shade of gray," in military technology) to be converted by the happy (*not* lucky) holders of that edge into a military result of total dominance ("black and white"). In preparation for the confrontation with Syrian MiG jets by their American-made jet fighters in the 1982 Lebanese war, the Israelis had improved the electronic systems of their planes, which otherwise were more or less the equals of the Russian-made fighters. They improved their electronic countermeasures, and most important, they invented and developed a remarkable plan for "reading" Syrian electronic emissions and commanding their electronic air battle on the basis of the "whats" and "wheres" that these signals revealed. One result was that they completely confused the Syrian command-and-control system defending Syrian surface-to-air missile sites and succeeded in destroying most of those missiles. The major result, however, was the final score: 79–0 in airplanes destroyed. This amazing result was achieved largely by intelligent human electronic battle management. In the future, it can and will be done by computer.

Second, there is the question of access by the Department of Defense to the technology of the intelligent computer systems of the future. If the Defense Science Board's study is even approximately correct, we cannot afford to allow the AI technology to slip away to the Japanese or to anyone else. No matter how loyal an ally Japan is, it will be simply unacceptable for the United States to have to depend on Japan for a vital defense technology. And we cannot assume that our Japanese allies will automatically acquiesce to the imposition of export technology controls that we may deem vital to our defense interests. Japan, as a nation, has a longstanding casual attitude toward secrecy when it comes to technological matters. Except in the firms, Japan is regarded by its allies as a virtual sieve for Western technology to flow indiscriminately into others' hands.

The third has to do with the skyrocketing costs of U.S. defense. While Congress debates huge appropriations for conventional weaponry, the issue of "smart bombs" takes on a new interest. In defense applications, the objective for any weaponry utilizing expert systems is *zero probability of error*, which means that individual targets will be sought out by sensing devices informed by intelligence data, eliminating the need for massive blanket bombing to achieve desired objectives. The economic impact of an intelligent armaments system that can strike targets with extreme precision should be apparent to even the most ardent national defense advocates—fewer weapons used selectively for maximum strike capability.

Fourth, it is essential that the newest technological developments be made available to the Defense Department.

Technological leads are usually short-lived. We must retain the capability to accelerate the passage of technology from laboratory to military system under our control using our defense contractors. We cannot afford to be in the position of waiting for the Japanese to push products through their development cycle to the commercial marketplace.

Finally, the Defense Department needs the ability to shape technology to conform to its needs in military systems. A Fujitsu or a Hitachi marches to a different drummer from a Rockwell or a Lockheed. Our defense industry must obtain and retain a strong position in the new advanced computer technologies.

Until recently, the United States has led the information revolution. Our semiconductor technology was recognized as the best. This is no longer so. The outcome of the great chip wars of the early 1980s is not final, but for many important hardware components, Japan is ahead. Japanese supercomputers are comparable to American ones. Japan is moving into other kinds of hardware and even, as we have seen, into software development. If we doubt that diligent nation's ability to do the same for machine intelligence by the end of ten years, we need merely look back ten years to see where Japan was in computing technology then. The simple answer is nowhere.

It has been a very long time since national defense was a matter of mere numbers of bodies and armaments. (If we believe Sun Tzu, there was never such a time.) In any event, for all our thrilling propaganda about America's being the arsenal of democracy during the Second World War, a careful reading of history tells us that brains, not brawn, won there. Most people are already familiar with the code-cracking adventures of the European Theater and the critical role intelligence played in the victory of the Allies. What might not be as familiar is a similar sort of strategy that went on in the Pacific.

A failure of intelligence, as everybody knows, had allowed the attack on Pearl Harbor to take place. Five months later, after nothing but "cataracts of disaster," as Winston Churchill called the news from the Pacific, Colonel James Doolittle made a quixotic but basically harmless air raid on Tokyo. Most military strategists considered it mere propaganda for the folks at home, who needed cheering very badly. In fact, it inadvertently turned out to be a great deal more than that. The Japanese were so shocked by an attack on the homeland, despite the lack of damage Doolittle was able to inflict, that the Imperial Navy overreacted and sent out nearly every warship in the combined fleet.

"This generated a vast amount of radio signal traffic," one historian writes, "which gave the U.S. Navy the chance to win an unexpected yet crucial secret victory. Although they lacked naval strength to match Japan's, they enjoyed an enormous advantage in the clandestine electronic war—the key to tactical supremacy in the vast reaches of the Pacific battleground. This intelligence provided the vital clues that would reveal how the 'victory disease' was impelling the Japanese to disperse their overwhelming superiority in support of too many operations across too great a distance. Forewarned of the weakness in the enemy strategy, Admiral Nimitz would be able to concentrate his limited naval strength against each move in turn, and so disrupt Japan's intended advance south and west into the Pacific."[30]

Simply put, intelligence, in its narrowest and broadest meanings, is essential to our national defense, and its role can only continue to grow. It is crucial that we have the best.

Aside from direct combat—which, if it is nuclear, makes everything in this book irrelevant, we hasten to say—our industrial base is also a vital part of our national defense. If industry continues to be run by old-fashioned methods using old-fashioned technology, it will be nothing but a costly white elephant to us. There has been much talk about the reindustrialization of the United States, and it is no doubt a good idea; but its success will rely on the large-scale integration of intelligence and knowledge technology into industrial processes.

Robert Kahn, of ARPA's Information Processing Techniques Office, sat and mused on this situation one sunny afternoon not long ago. "Yes," he said, "ARPA has acted as the conscience of information processing research in the U.S. We virtually had to thrust the ARPANET down the throats of the computer science community, and now they can't function effectively without it. In the past, things were different. So what if IBM was slow to introduce time sharing and virtual memory? So what if it took AT&T ten years to come around on packet switching? It didn't matter very much because time was on our side, the industry was strong, and we could afford to wait. But it's not as strong now and the competition is much greater. Like General Motors, it's beset by competition it once dreamed would never exist. At the same time, markets are opening up it hadn't anticipated and is slowly learning how to serve. High tech isn't just for breakfast anymore. Yet nobody knows quite what to do or where to go; there's no place providing the necessary leadership or the catalysts to keep us competitive. In the past, the industries or the government could get together and set standards—that happened with the railroads and it happened in highways, it happened in radio and TV. But we can't do that very effectively with electronics and particularly software; changes are happening now, or need to happen next Tuesday, and what's more, those changes are often invisible." Such problems are now well beyond the scope of one small government agency to solve, no matter how visionary it is.

We calculate that in 1982, the aggregate spent in the United States on artificial intelligence research from all sources—governmental and private—was about $50 million. This is just about equal to the amount the Japanese government expects to spend on an average per year over the next ten years for its Fifth Generation (and does not count Japanese internal industrial AI support that may double or triple the amount). If we continue as we have, we two nations will act as guinea pigs for an interesting experiment in planned, as opposed to unplanned, research.

At the moment, we Americans are placing our economic and defense bets on a method that has more or less worked for us in the past (though our current economic situation throws some doubt on its utility in a complex postindustrial world). That method, of course, is wholly decentralized planning, cutthroat competition, and a touching faith that the best will win because economic laws work that way.

The Japanese part of the experiment is different. Although it parallels our notions of economic competition at the end of the process, it separates that part from the beginning of the process, the research and development of goods, in this case, knowledge technology. Research and development, the Japanese believe, require some central planning. Though individual pieces of research are to be contracted out to various laboratories, such research will be coordinated by workers at ICOT in Tokyo. The Japanese believe that human intelligence is a precious resource that must be carefully deployed. Money is also precious and cannot be wasted.

We, on the contrary, are currently betting that uncoordinated development of the information processing industry is a luxury we can still afford. We are behaving as if we have talent to spare and can use it on projects important or frivolous, depending on who has cash to put up. We behave as if there's plenty of such cash. On these assumptions a critical part of our national defense depends.

VII

EPILOG, OR IT IS HARD TO PREDICT, ESPECIALLY THE FUTURE

1

Alternatives for America

The Japanese have announced that in ten years they will produce knowledge information processors. Several options are open to Americans, but few of them offer truly palatable alternatives to undertaking our own version. Let us examine them.

1. We can maintain the status quo. We can continue doing a lot of short-term (shortsighted, in the view of many), research and development, spurred by nothing but immediate market considerations. We can penalize the farsighted by removing them from power, industrial *or* political, every time the bottom line fails to give us instant gratification. We can embrace antitrust as infallible revelation and litigate ourselves into national collapse. Uncoordinated planning, investments in the frivolous, and lack of investment in the serious might still allow us to muddle through. Somehow.

2. We can form industrial consortiums to meet the Japanese challenge and as citizens insist that the Justice Department take a reasonable stance regarding joint industrial R&D. This might take an act of Congress. Americans, however, have little experience with such joint ventures.

3. We could enter a major joint venture with the Japanese. Their Fifth Generation proposal gives a lot of

lip service to international cooperation. They might not have really meant it, but we could give their lip service a test. There is also the possibility that as the end of various phases of the project approach, the Japanese might find themselves falling short of their targets—either technologically or financially—and would welcome American collaboration. The United States and Japan would complement each other, and the joint venture could be powerful internationally.

4. As a variation on the third plan, we know that the economic value of KIPS (the so-called value added) is primarily in their software, or their knowledge, and we have a proven record as specialists in great software ideas. We could forget about producing the machines and produce only the software instead, styling ourselves after the razor blade company that gave away razors because profits were in the blades. Chips are cheap, and we've seen competition drive profits out of many segments of the computer hardware business. Let's make software instead. In software, capital investment can be low and profits huge.

5. We can form a national laboratory for the promotion of knowledge technology. It might be a mega-institute, like Los Alamos, embracing all forms of knowledge technology. Or it might be a smaller multiple-university-run laboratory (such as Brookhaven and Fermilab in physics). Or it might have one university as the prime contractor (like the Stanford Linear Accelerator Center). Whatever form it takes, the national laboratory must be newly created. Institutions have a natural life cycle, being most energetic and creative when new and unbureaucratic. We cannot look to the existing national laboratories for the kind of innovations a knowledge technology laboratory must produce, freighted as they are with tradition, stodginess, and bureaucracy. Those three horsemen of the intellectual apocalypse will eventually come to the new laboratory, but while it is still new, it has at least a fighting chance to achieve brilliance.

6. We can prepare to become the first great agrarian postindustrial society. We are blessed with huge tracts of fertile, arable land. Progress in our agrosciences and in automation applied to agriculture has always been impressive. We absolutely shine in growing things. As General Motors and General Electric decline, we can

organize General Agriculture to maintain our balance of trade.

As Americans, we are not without alternatives, however unpalatable the reality of some of them may be. *Our* own first choice, a center for knowledge technology, follows.

2

The National Center for Knowledge Technology

The United States is not Japan. The U.S. Commerce Department is not the Ministry of International Trade and Industry, and the Pentagon should not be, even by default. Nearly everyone in the information processing industry agrees that some sort of cooperative effort is necessary to ensure well-educated researchers, fruitful research, and an end to the frittering away of resources in short-term get-rich schemes that benefit the very few. We do *not* have unlimited resources of any kind—not unlimited talent, money, or time—and other nations are moving off into a future where we must follow whether we like it or not, but where we could lead if we wanted.

Though there have been several different attempts by industrial groups to pool certain resources, good intentions have been frustrated by a deeply ingrained tradition of commercial competition (legally reinforced by means of strict antitrust laws), by the lack of any suitable framework in which to carry out cooperation, and by the lack of widely shared national goals.

One eminent scientist has quite seriously suggested that all who are concerned about the Japanese Fifth Generation should put all their energy into persuading our own great national resource, IBM, to take on the task of competing with the Japanese project—that IBM is our best hope. Though the idea has its beguiling aspects (not to mention its bizarre ones), it seems a bit fanciful. Moreover, it would give to one firm an exclusive command over a technology that many firms ought to share, as the Japanese themselves have recognized.

Let us make another proposal. The United States should form a national center for knowledge technology. By "knowledge technology" we mean computing certainly, but we also mean other related forms of knowledge distribution, such as libraries, for which there are important technological needs and exciting opportunities. This idea of a national center of knowledge technology isn't original with us; industrialists, educators, and government officials have all suggested variations on such a plan.

An alternate form of the plan would be a national center for information processing technology, conceived recently by a senior government science administrator. It would cut more deeply into the world of technology but less broadly across the world of knowledge systems. This center would not compete with industry. On the contrary, it would play an ARPA-like role, supporting the kind of basic research no single firm or even group of firms can afford to risk. Like ARPA, it would fund and coordinate high-risk projects through their early research stages until industries could take the results into the development stage. Its responsibilities would be long-term results, not short-term profits. Thus its funds might come from all who would stand to gain from such a center, in both the public and the private sectors. To be effective, funding has to be generous; the amount to vary depending on how widely or narrowly knowledge technology is construed.

If it is narrowly construed, a pilot project something like the Japanese Fifth Generation might be undertaken—we certainly believe the United States owes it to itself to continue the research it pioneered, to develop it, and to reap its obvious benefits. But if the center is broadly construed, it would embrace research in an enormous complex of information and knowledge technologies, from telecommunications to publishing, from new computer designs to new curriculum designs for our schools. Eventually it must assign priorities to national research and take the difficult step of setting standards flexible enough for new technology to be accommodated, yet stern enough to avoid the wasteful incompatibilities we have seen, for example, in video discs and computer software.

Though funds must come first from the government, this should not be a government agency. The civil service salary structure cannot cope with the need, and the civil service machinery is too ponderous to allow the center to work with the speed and suppleness it must have. Indeed, it should probably be staffed by people on temporary loan from firms, research laboratories, universities, and other talent pools.

The difficulties are obvious. How are intellectual property rights to be properly assigned and rewarded? Common law has a long tradition of dealing with real property, but its dealings with intellectual property have been uninspired. We have already talked about the dearth of qualified scientists and engineers in AI and the rest of computer science, and such a center would drain talent from universities and other research laboratories. But this is a problem, like the problems of intellectual property rights, that our society will have to face anyway. The establishment of a center might in fact help in the solution. How is technology to be transferred effectively from the laboratory to industry? How is a high level of innovation to be maintained? There are other, equally serious problems. But what real choice do we have?

The center we propose would be an expression and institutional embodiment of national will, much as the Kennedy and Manned Spacecraft Centers of NASA have been. There has never been an organization like it in the United States. Projects of this magnitude (and there are few enough) have been government- or military-controlled, as, for example, the space program was. But then there has never in our history, or in the history of the world, come such a sudden and profoundly exciting opportunity: the convergence of many disparate social functions such as publishing, manufacturing, health care and other professional services, education, entertainment, and newsgathering, to name a few, waiting to be fused into a set of very much more powerful technologies that will allow those functions to thrive with more efficiency, accuracy, and effectiveness for everyone.

We have the opportunity at this moment to do a new version of Diderot's *Encyclopedia*, a gathering up of all knowledge—not just the academic kind, but the informal, experiential, heuristic kind—to be fused, amplified, and distributed, all at orders of magnitude difference in cost, speed, volume, and *usefulness* over what we have now. A book in a library may have important information, but if your library happens not to have that volume, or the volume is crumbling to dust because most books in the last fifty years were printed on acidic papers that self-destruct, the knowledge is lost. If knowledge is buried in a Niagara of information, it is lost to the overburdened human who cannot take the time, or does not have the fortitude, to interpret Niagaras of information.

What faces us, if you like, is the Louisiana Purchase in the manifest destiny of computing. The initial cost seems high, and the skeptics are already having fun. But to the visionaries the investment promises multiple dividends, not the least being a revitalization of the national will, and the pleasures of becoming, once more, the country of "why not?"

Knowledge in our world right now is a cat's cradle of threads which even the most skillful human being cannot grasp in two hands as he or she goes about daily work. The Japanese believe they can weave those confusing, fragile, and all too easily dropped threads into a garment that will shelter, nurture, decorate, and empower the human intellect. They're also convinced that for national survival, they must.

So can Americans. And for national survival, perhaps we must, too. National security is a multidimensional state of affairs that depends on healthy, productive industry, agriculture, education, commerce, and government, all thriving on the rapid creation, diffusion, and utilization of knowledge.

Should our knowledge technology goals continue to be set only by the military, certain compromises must occur. First, such research might become strategic, subject to government regulation, which would mean an end to the rapid and free exchange of ideas that has so enriched the early work in AI, knowledge systems, and computing in general. Second, research might eventually be skewed primarily toward military objectives. Military and civilian goals can be harmonious, but they are different.

If, of course, Americans can only bear the burden of financial support in the name of national defense, we can call it national defense. We built the interstate highway

system in the name of national defense, and with the same
justification we educated a generation of college students
in everything from Asian art to zoology. In a national
center for knowledge technology, we are suggesting no
more than insurance in a world where other nations have
already perceived the centrality of knowledge to their
self-interest, and are acting upon it.

3

The Strategic Computing Program

Well, so we wrote in the first edition of this book, and it
must have caused some smiles around the Pentagon, for
plans had been forming since 1982, first for a major push
in supercomputers, and then for a major push in artificial
intelligence, under the auspices of DARPA. In the opinion
of DARPA insiders we would later speak to, the announcement of the Fifth Generation had simply helped to sharpen
what were a series of good ideas in their formative stages.

One of the first hints that something new might be
emerging from DARPA came during a pleasant summer
lunch with Lynn Conway and her colleague, Mark Stefik,
just after the first edition of this book had been published.
Conway wanted to know why we hadn't taken the idea
embedded in "A Network of Minds" and applied it to our
Center for Knowledge Technology. Why were we so taken
with a bricks-and-mortar center, when the lesson of the
network adventure was that an electronic center (a virtual
center, as computer jargon would put it) was now not only
possible, but really more sensible, at least for as large and
heterogeneous a country as the United States?

Just hadn't thought of it, we frankly confessed.

Such an electronic center for research in knowledge

technology is an important part of a plan called "Strategic Computing: New Generation Computing Technology, A Strategic Plan for Its Development and Application to Critical Problems in Defense" that emerged in October 1983 from the Defense Department's Advanced Research Projects Agency (DARPA).

The plan's major objectives are comprehensive and ambitious: its ultimate aim is to provide a broad base of machine intelligence technology for application to critical defense problems, *and* to create a strong industrial capacity to support national security requirements. (This might be the first time that any official document of the Defense Department has explicitly proposed to create a technology to strengthen the industrial sector, and by extension, to strengthen the national economy.)

The plan itself is a skillful (and characteristically American) blend of the concrete and the abstract. Three specific and ambitious military applications have been chosen because they focus and stimulate the creation of the technology, and then provide a ready laboratory to show whether the technology actually works. They are: first, autonomous vehicles, such as unmanned aircraft, submersibles, and land vehicles; second, expert associates for pilots in the cockpit; and third, large-scale battle management systems. These three particular projects are expected to lead to spinoffs that will benefit both national security and the economy.

As the report points out, computing already plays an essential role in defense, but old-style computers are awkward and inflexible, and limited in their adaptability to unanticipated circumstances. DARPA envisions a new (but pointedly not "fifth") generation of computers that can transcend today's computers by a quantum jump. The new generation will be driven by expert systems, and equipped with sensory and communications devices that allow them to hear, talk, see and act on information and data they receive, or develop themselves.

In this, DARPA is only planning to exploit in a grand and coordinated manner a lot of scattered research that the agency itself has largely underwritten in the past two decades, research that has yielded a number of advances, but all in separate areas of artificial intelligence, computer science, and microelectronics. The agency's planners see the opportunity for the joint development of these advances to produce highly intelligent machines.

The three specific projects provide different, though sometimes overlapping and sometimes complementary opportunities for research. The autonomous vehicle, for example, whether for land, air or sea, would be a true robot that can see and sense, and respond specifically to general instructions or goals. Thus such a land vehicle might be capable of planning a route toward some destination from data it knows about the terrain it will move over, and will then be able to rearrange that route based on information from its sensors as it moves along resolving ambiguities between sensed and pre-stored data: checking on itself as it moves by comparing its route to anticipated landmarks, just as a human traveler might. The computer, of course, can occupy no more than 6 to 15 cubic feet in such a vehicle, can weigh no more than 500 pounds, and should consume less than 1 kw of power. As the DARPA plan points out, these requirements will mean at least one to four orders of magnitude reduction in weight, space, and power over today's computing systems. For other kinds of space, air and sea vehicles, the requirements would be even more stringent, including the ability to operate in high radiation. DARPA's ten-year goal is a robotic reconnaissance tank that can navigate 80 miles from one destination to another at an average of 40 miles per hour, computing all the while. Here, then, are goals of miniaturization, robustness, and intelligent functions, such as reasoning and understanding, on an unprecedented scale.

In combat, a pilot is nearly overwhelmed by the information that floods into the cockpit, and yet he must base life-and-death decisions on his own quick grasp of the situation. Thus the second specific project proposed by the DARPA program is a pilot's associate to help him in the air as well as on the ground, not replacing but complementing him, by taking over lower-level chores and performing special functions so that he can focus on tactical and strategic objectives. In its simplest form, the personal associate does routine tasks, and when so instructed, initiates actions on its own. In its advanced form, the personal associate performs a set of tasks which are difficult or altogether impossible for the pilot, such as the early detection and diagnosis of an impending malfunction. It's an associate he can talk to and receive answers from in natural language or graphics, and it will be personal to a specific pilot, trained by him to respond in certain ways and perform particular functions that he considers important. Here again are miniaturization and robustness in hardware, combined with goals for processing among complex, integrated knowledge-based systems that must be a hundred times faster than current systems; and also unambiguous voice communication in extremely noisy surroundings.

Finally, battle management in modern warfare means decision making under uncertainty. There are open and hidden problems, solutions with various consequences, and conflicting goals. When decisions are made, they must be monitored, and may have to be adjusted as circumstances evolve. Individual intelligent systems address some of these problems, but no single system addresses them all. The battle management system envisioned by DARPA would be the compleat assistant. It would be capable of comprehending uncertain data to produce forecasts of likely events. It could draw on previous human and machine experience to suggest potential courses of action, evaluating them and explaining rationales for them. At this point, it could develop a plan for implementing the option selected by the human commanders, disseminate the plan to those concerned, and report progress to the decision maker during the execution phase. All this would take place in natural language between humans and machine. This project includes the much more subtle goals of natural language communication more so, say, than the pilot's associate (which could function with a small command vocabulary based on recognition rather than understanding). Other goals include new and particularly hardy devices for sensing and signal processing, and of course highly sophisticated decision support systems based on the fusion of data and knowledge from many sources.

In summary, the DARPA plan calls for integrated intelligent functions of vision, speech recognition and production, natural language understanding, and expert systems technology to be realized with newly designed software and hardware. In addition, the development of microelectronics technology to support all these must be fostered in a multitude of locations.

Although the research DARPA supports during this project is intended to meet the goals of the three military applications, the resulting technology will be generic, stretching across the spectrum of computing from hardware and other devices through software design and implementation. Signal processing (which is the interpretation of data from a sensor) and symbolic processing (which deals with non-numeric objects, their relationships, and the ability to infer or deduce new information with the aid of programs that reason) will also be pushed far ahead. The program will put strong emphasis on accelerating and exploiting the miniaturization of microelectronics by dramatically reducing the usual delays between basic research innovations in fabrication and packaging technology and their subsequent exploitation by designers.

Silicon will continue to be the mainstay of the program because of its maturity and accessibility to all researchers. The processors' power consumption will be reduced as computational power is increased. But, to meet the ultimate demands of the plan, a new fabrication technology will be developed to yield devices that are an order of magnitude smaller than those produced today.

The agency expects to manage the activities of a large number of people and groups in universities, research institutes and industry across the United States. To do so, the initial focus (and funds) will concentrate on the "bricks and mortar" of an electronic research center, in other words, the means to coordinate and disseminate technology not only among the participants, but across U.S. industry. Thus, a major part of the budget during the first years will be devoted to upgrading the computing and communications equipment of the participants. (The Strategic Computing Plan's total budget is $50 million in 1984, $95 million in 1985, and $150 million in 1986, leading to costs of approximately $600 million over the first five years of the program.) This high initial investment in computing and communications equipment will also magnify the effect of the most critical resource: trained people. For DARPA, too, notes how few qualified people there are in these fields.

DARPA's Strategic Computing Plan is surely the right plan at the right time. But managers at DARPA expect to undertake a task of management and coordination that is not only staggering in its complexity but unprecedented in its decentralization. Popular futurists assure us that decentralization is the wave of the future, and it is probably true, but DARPA is riding just ahead of the wave. It is a dangerous and heady place to be, as any surfer can attest. The thrills are exceptional, but the wipeouts can be catastrophic.

A key part of the project depends on rapid prototyping and rapid transfer of technology from research laboratories into the firms. But American research laboratories, particularly in the universities, have long enjoyed the luxury of producing experimental devices that need not answer to real-world requirements; they may be astonished to have to try. American firms, on the other hand, are mainly accustomed to evolutionary changes; the revolutionary changes required by the Fifth Generation may be more than cautious American managers are ready to cope with. A habit of looking only at short-term profits as opposed to long-term endurance might be hard for American industrialists to break.

Moreover, the Strategic Computing Program differs from the Japanese Fifth Generation Plan in that although it embraces many of the same goals, in its brash American way it also embraces goals the Japanese have prudently assigned to other national projects, such as the National Superspeed Computing Project and the National Robotics Project. The singular focus of the Fifth Generation Project is therefore somewhat diffused among a number of projects in the Strategic Computing Program.

On the other hand, the concrete objectives of the American plan—the three testbeds—may, after all, focus research just as effectively as the Japanese manage to by organizational means.

Finally, some Americans might be uneasy about depending solely on the Defense Department—however visionary its planners, and however reluctant Americans are to spend money, except in the name of national defense—to provide them with important new knowledge technology. As we have already pointed out, knowledge technology goals, set only by the military, could entail compromises that this democracy might eventually find intolerable. Others were thinking that way too, particularly the group of industrialists who had gathered together in Orlando, Florida, in February of 1983 to form the research consortium called the Microelectronics and Computer Technology Corporation.

4

An American Industrial Response

As soon as the appointment of former Admiral Bobby Ray Inman as president and chief executive officer of the Microelectronics and Computer Technology Corporation (MCC) was announced, changes in that organization began to take place. His appointment not only brought new firms in at once; it continued to attract additional firms. The total number by the end of 1983 was fourteen, and included: Advanced Micro Devices, Allied, Control Data, Digital Equipment, Harris, Honeywell, Martin-Marietta, Mostek, Motorola, National Semiconductor, NCR, RCA, Rockwell and Sperry. The MCC's by-laws make it a for-profit corporation, with a maximum of thirty shareholder companies. It will deliver product-independent technology, the patents of which will belong to MCC, but which the shareholder companies can license and turn into products. Those shareholder companies that support the initial research have a three-year lead in licensing; after that, anybody, including foreign firms, can be licensed. The corporation eventually expects to employ between 400 and 600 people, with a budget that will climb from $50 million a year to $100 million a year.

MCC requires a relatively modest initiation fee of $250,000 for a firm to become a member (and there is a further requirement, that member firms be at least 51% U.S.-owned), but the real expenses for shareholder firms come in the programs they elect to support, expenses that could run as high as ten million dollars a year if a firm decides to participate in all major programs. The three-year advantage shareholder firms have in licensing gives them an incentive to support as many programs as they can afford. As in the Japanese Fifth Generation project, each participant in a program is expected to supply one individual as a technical liaison, who will be resident at MCC, but who will return regularly to his or her sponsoring firm to report information.

Before Inman's arrival, a research agenda had already been put together by preliminary task forces, which included the four major areas mentioned earlier, namely: microelectronics packaging, CAD/CAM, software productivity, and advanced computer architectures (this last is an eight- to ten-year program, originally called Alpha-Omega, meant to focus on architectures for human interfaces with machines, knowledge-based systems, data base systems, and parallel processing; in other words, an American Fifth Generation).

Once he became its president, Inman had the task of finding a site for MCC; hiring the scientists and managers who would guide the projects; managing a collaboration among the shareholder firms; persuading them that the results would not come soon, but would be worth waiting for; and maintaining a friendly relationship with the federal government, especially the Justice Department. None of these would be easy; several were daunting.

The site selection consumed some six months, with a newly-sensitized set of American states and cities eager to take advantage of the benefits that were perceived to flow from a high-tech industrial presence. Fifty-seven cities in 27 states vied to be chosen, including such obvious sites as Minneapolis, the home of Control Data and Honeywell; Atlanta; the Research Triangle in North Carolina; San Diego; Silicon Valley; the Boston-Cambridge area; and Pittsburgh.

The winner was Austin, Texas. This was due not to the fact that it was Bobby Inman's home town, but instead due to exemplary cooperation—"on a scale not seen since World War II in the United States," Inman would say later—among three segments of the community, namely, state and local government, academics, and the private sector.

In MCC's assessment, each segment in Austin wanted to attract the new corporation for its own purposes, yet could cooperate with the others to make sure that the goal was accomplished. This was extremely important, because Inman and MCC detected only hopes and promises at some of the other sites they considered, with a locality making promises that its state government might not honor, or vice versa. Inman himself feared that, in some cases, the enthusiasm for MCC would disappear with the election of a new governor or mayor. Since MCC would produce no research results in the short term, it needed a long-term commitment on the part of its host.

In Texas, however, legislators had already been asking what would happen to their state when the oil ran out, exhibiting a foresight rare among elected representatives. By the mid-1970s, the Texas legislature was enacting laws that would make Texas a more hospitable place for high-technology corporations. It was almost as if Texas were preparing itself for something like the MCC: the state's commitment preceded its opportunities, and once the opportunity came, it was ready. A fair amount of trading took place between the state and the city of Austin. The University of Texas pledged itself ready to pour more resources into its already respected computer science department and pledged to cooperate with Texas A & M, where the latter school had specialized expertise the University did not—a crucial point for MCC, because it needed to be somewhere where young talent would be coming out to join the consortium five years down the road.[1] The private sector, in the form of the public-spirited wealthy, simply got out checkbooks to make sure that MCC was supplied with important extras, such as mortgage money for MCC employees that was slightly below the market rates, and a job-placement bureau for their spouses. It was all a form of enlightened self-interest, because everybody expects that MCC will create a ripple effect, which is to say it will help create the broad base of high technology that Austin and the state of Texas seek.

"Austin is a good place to work for many reasons," Inman would say in the temporary offices that housed MCC in late 1983. "But maybe the most important reason is that Austin still has a can-do attitude, and that's infectious. It's also essential for an effort like ours." He is a slender, soft-spoken man, articulate and quick, who retains just a touch of the sailor's walk. And though he laughs readily, almost impishly at times, there is ever present the sense of will and discipline that one would cross at one's peril.

Inman's next task was hiring. MCC's planning documents show a deep concern with quality appointments, not only for purposes of good research, but also for attracting researchers from outside the participating firms. Inman sought people who were capable of conducting both long-term, quality scientific research, and of managing that research. "Those two qualities don't often come in the same person," he explained, "and so the obvious answer—and the strategy I've used in the past—is to assemble teams of people who had one or the other and could work together."

He discovered, perhaps not surprisingly, that although there was a good supply of management talent, there was a somewhat scarcer supply of scientific talent, and the timetable he had originally hoped for, that research would be underway at MCC by late 1983, had to be adjusted. Research for most of the programs began in February 1984, and the remainder was underway by late April 1984. Talent already aboard has been preparing detailed roadmaps for the research to be undertaken. Almost Japanese-style, bonuses of up to 50% of a researcher's salary will eventually be rewarded for scientific achievements (not profits). "I'm choosing people for the long-term, and I'm being very choosy," he said.

Among the first persons he chose was MCC's chief scientist, John Pinkston. Inman sees his own great strength as a manager of collaborative efforts, where he has had much experience, whether the collaborations were among various government agencies, or the different armed services. But he readily admitted his own lack of technical expertise. "So my job was to find a technical person I could treat as an alter ego, somebody I could trust absolutely, to be my chief scientist. For that, I went back to my own past, and I expect that raised a lot of eyebrows."

It had not raised eyebrows so much as it puzzled the computer science community; having done all his work on secret projects, Pinkston was an unknown. But Pinkston had been in the government for seventeen years, where he was in charge of the production of "some very high-level, complex machines for government classified purposes, which the public will not know about for many, many years to come. He has deep technical knowledge, a great intellectual curiosity, and is greatly excited to be doing this."

One of Inman's first challenges, in managing a rather obstreperous collaboration of independent firms that had no experience of cooperation with each other, centered on the Alpha-Omega program, the part of MCC's research most closely resembling the Japanese Fifth Generation. Since it accounts for about half of MCC's commitment to research, trouble there was big trouble. A number of the shareholder firms expressed great uneasiness about a single leader for Alpha-Omega, as called for in the original plan put together by Gordon Bell and his task force. The firms were concerned that a single leader for such a crucial project might bias the research, push the project in one particular aspect—for example, knowledge-based systems, or parallel processing—at the expense of the other parts of the program. This, in turn, might benefit the products of one supporting firm but not the products of another. Inman decided that these fears were reasonable, and committed to manage the Alpha-Omega effort as four independent programs, each to be headed by a separate but equal chief. At the end of 1983, chiefs for three of the positions, data base management, human interface, and parallel processing, had been found, but the knowledge-based systems slot remained open.

Also by the end of 1983, the detailed scientific plans were still being worked out. When complete, these would not be disclosed in any detail. "I used to guard the nation's secrets, and now I guard proprietary secrets. However, we're trying to plan in such a way that we won't build up a bureaucracy." Again, Japanese-style, MCC hopes to identify intermediate technology spinoffs and deliver them to the participating firms. In spite of this, the planning documents acknowledge the problems of efficient technology transfer, including doing it in such a way that no participant has a special advantage over another. This problem will be solved in part by the technical liaison officers each firm appoints.

Is there a chance that some cooperation can be worked out between MCC and the Strategic Computing Program, inasmuch as some of its goals are similar? MCC made an early policy decision to avoid becoming a government contractor, especially in its early years. But Inman notes that if the Strategic Computing Program demonstrates that certain of its goals are exactly congruent with the goals already set by the MCC, then he has been empowered to pursue such a contract sometime in the future.

One of the persistent problems MCC faces is scrutiny by

the Justice Department for violating antitrust laws. MCC reportedly spent half a million dollars in its first year-and-a-half on legal fees alone, but at the end of 1983, Inman was confident that the Justice Department would raise no objections to the work MCC proposed. However, he expected that lack of objection to be very specific to MCC, not the clear signal that other parts of American industry were hoping for in their own efforts to collaborate on research and development.

And the baby consortium is already subject to criticism. Outside computer scientists are disturbed (perhaps correctly) by the breakup of Alpha-Omega, because they worry that its goals cannot be reached without the most intimate cooperation among the four segments, each drawing from and helping, not rivaling, the other. Moreover, if Inman waits for just the right people to fill his top positions, he draws criticism for not moving the MCC forward quickly enough, thus delaying even further the American response to the Japanese challenge. (Of course, if he settled for second-rate people, he would be severely criticized for that.) Finally, scientists who are used to working in an open environment, with the free and easy exchange of ideas, predict that the MCC's intentions to make its walls impermeable for proprietary reasons will act as a two-way barrier, preventing the cross-fertilization from the outside that makes basic research flower.

Yet MCC is an optimistic organization with an optimistic and accomplished leader, and it has found a home in an American boom town. Austin is an appealing blend of the Old South and the Old West (though decidedly not the Old Southwest). If its chalky Hill Country brought generations of early farmers to grief, and if it now struggles with all the late-twentieth-century difficulties, such as preservation vs. development, the best way to cope with the homeless, or with fierce complaints from minority groups, the town's natural beauty and its energetic atmosphere ("its can-do attitude," in Inman's phrase) are still apparent to any visitor.

There are more ways an organization as fragile and unprecedented as MCC can go wrong than there are paths to its success. The shortage of first-rate trained scientists and engineers is an international problem, but MCC must also coordinate among fractious firms who have spent corporate lifetimes in savage competition with each other, and convince their technologists and managers alike that long-range research goals are worth pursuing with patience, even for firms that must show profits every relentless quarter. MCC could somehow succeed at all that, and still find itself under attack from well-meaning but legalistic adversaries, who believe antitrust laws are a secular equivalent of the Decalogue.

Nearly everybody agrees that if MCC can succeed at all, it has its best chance because of the unique combination of intelligence, tact, persuasive powers, varied experience, and will, possessed by the remarkable Bobby Inman.

5

It Is Hard to Predict, Especially the Future

The title above is taken from a wise aphorism attributed to the physicist Niels Bohr, and a little examination of matters adds to its obvious persuasiveness.

If, just after it got under way in Jericho in about 6500 B.C., we had asked a prophet of the agricultural revolution what she expected its effects to be, she might have been able to reply confidently that human beings would no longer need to depend on chance for their food—the chance of gathering, the chance of the hunt. With truly astonishing insight, she might also have predicted that surplus food would allow the formation of specialties in labor. But that this, in turn, would lead to the rise of the cities, international trade, or the peanut as an ingredient in shampoo, ink, and linoleum is unlikely to have occurred to her.

With deep insight into the human spirit, she might have been able to predict that a folklore would grow up surrounding cultivation, but she could not have specifically named Persephone, Johnny Appleseed, the death of the Fisher King, or even laetrile.

She would probably have found the idea hilarious that some human beings, with access to unlimited calories, would develop body fat that was socially repugnant, unhealthy, and in some cases even life-threatening, because nature had genetically selected us for survival in a feast-or-famine world.[2]

In other words, if we humans are luckily endowed with the imagination to create revolutions, we nevertheless can hardly anticipate their long-term effects.

This book is concerned with an aspect of the so-called information revolution, the mass production of machine intelligence soon to come. In some sense *revolution* hardly seems the apt term at all: perhaps *evolution* is a better word to describe the history of knowledge in the human race. As we now theorize that the evolution of organisms takes place—slow change, punctuated by quick and radical change, followed by slow or even no change for a long time again—so it is with the evolution of knowledge and its various technologies.

Spoken language between humans was a major step in the transfer of knowledge (and some anthropologists link it with the establishment of the nuclear family), but that, once established, prevailed for a very long time, perhaps 50 million years. Then humans began to draw pictures that stood for the objects that surrounded and concerned them. This kind of pictorial communication was a magnificent achievement, for it meant that information could be preserved beyond mortal human lifetimes and fallible human memory, although the awkwardness of pictographs ensured that writing would remain the specialty of an honored and valuable few.

A modern-day speaker of, say, English, can in time-machine style taste the awkwardness and ambiguities of that stage of the evolution of Indo-European languages by trying to find her way around central Tokyo when she neither speaks nor reads Japanese. Of course she is supplied with a map. But the streets, when they are named at all, are spelled on her map in Roman letters. They appear in Kanji on the street signs. Unless she is very clever about making that conversion (and most casual tourists are not), she must rely on little pictographs scattered about her map that represent well-known buildings. Finding oneself, then, is a matter of matching the building one is standing before with a picture on a small map. But the scales are greatly different. The pictures are somewhat stylized. A great deal of guessing and hoping goes on. Mistakes ensue. Misunderstandings occur with regularity. Subtlety of thought is out of the question.[3]

Around 1000 B.C., the Phoenicians, in their brisk, no-nonsense way, cut through the difficulties of pictographs and produced one of the most influential versions of that abstraction called the alphabet. What inspired them was trade—pictographs slowed down the business of business intolerably. They surely had no conscious intention of fomenting revolution; they simply wanted to make profits. Aside from the fact that they were Mediterraneans, it seems lost to us now precisely who first got the bright idea to have one mark or letter correspond to one sound, therefore streamlining writing most wonderfully and, not incidentally, allowing written words to appear for concepts that didn't lend themselves to being pictured. It was a potent device and was eventually to accelerate the record-ing and diffusion of knowledge dramatically. Moreover, it also changed the way we think.

Then came another lull in the evolution of knowledge technology. There were small changes, of course. Both Greeks and Romans added letters to the Phoenician alphabet, and paper and vellum caught on as scribes real-ized those could, for all practical purposes, be made as permanent as stone, with the advantages of portability. Books replaced scrolls. So it went: nothing spectacular, but a slow and steady change by small accretions of differences.

Then came Gutenberg and what we now call the Guten-berg Revolution. In fact, first the Koreans and then the Chinese had developed movable type by the thirteenth century, but they hadn't been much interested in export-ing the idea. Traders who traveled the Silk Route were quick to appreciate the advantages of movable type and the printing press, but the idea seems not to have got beyond the Middle East, where it was squelched for theo-logical reasons.

In any event, Gutenberg's invention was a great success (though not for the poor man himself, who died in debt), and in the space of fifty years nearly ten million books were distributed in a Europe that, until then, had boasted only scores of thousands of manuscripts. It was an astonishing proliferation under any circumstances, but given the crude means of transport, it was nearly a miracle. We do not know whether Johannes Gutenberg had any idea of the revolution he began; surely his wildest dreams couldn't have pictured products as diverse as the *Physician's Desk Reference Manual,* James Joyce's *Ulysses,* and the *National Enquirer* in the hands of anyone with money to pay for them (and not much money at that). Or perhaps he might have. Arcane information, poetry, and gossip have been staples for the human mind as long as we have records. What Gutenberg surely would have missed—putting him now in the position of prophet—would have been the effects of our old friend, order of magnitude. It bears repeating that from fewer than 100,000 volumes, Europe went in fifty years to acquire nearly ten million volumes, thanks to Gutenberg's new technology. With that acquisition would come the rapid spread of literacy, then knowledge, and then the profound social effects of both (we know that thousands learned to read solely to get at Tom Paine's radical politics), leading to new governments called democratic republics, which replaced divine right with majority rule by vote, and similar unanticipated changes.

Nearly everybody understands that the development of the computer has begun another spurt of fast revolutionary change in the processing of information, but most of the prophecies have been gadget-centered. These are all quite wonderful, from electronic mail to hand-held expert systems that a barefoot doctor can take into the remotest village in Henan province and thereby supply the most advanced medicine the world has to offer to one of the poorest provinces in one of the poorest countries on earth.

We read predictions that our newspapers and magazines, which up to now we have had to buy in full editions, either delivered to us by human carriers or at a newsstand, will arrive on our home terminals, and, more important, we can pick and choose what we read out of them; we needn't be burdened with the whole thing. The same will be true of books, which will not be bound objects on a shelf, but unbound (in the largest sense: open to update, comment, revision, and change as necessary) pieces of knowledge called on only when needed, stored cheaply, and accessible to anybody, anywhere, any time. (And, yes, our home terminal will allow us to have hard copy to read in the bathtub if that's our heart's desire.)

All these are wonderful indeed and can't come soon enough. They promise enormous savings in energy, in paper, in time. They promise enormous intellectual leverage: fingertip access not to tons of information, but to well-selected, well-designed knowledge. They also promise—or threaten—severe, if temporary, dislocations in certain industries and many jobs. We can prepare for those changes in a sensible and compassionate way, or we can construct patchwork defenses that in the end will leave us worse off to certain historical inevitabilities than we need be. This book, of course, is an unambiguous plea for rational planning and preparation, but we are well aware that others hold different views.

We stand, however, before a singularity, an event so unprecedented that predictions are almost silly, since predictions, by their very nature, are extrapolations from things as we know them, and the singularity called reasoning machines will change things from how we know them in vastly unpredictable ways. "The appearance on earth of a nonhuman entity with intelligence approaching or exceeding mankind's would rank with the most significant events in human history," *Fortune* magazine declared in a recent series of articles on thinking machines. "While human beings can't possibly imagine the full consequences, the effects on technology, science, economics, warfare— indeed, on the whole intellectual and sociological development of mankind—would undoubtedly be momentous."[4]

We are no different from our fellow human beings. We can't possibly imagine the full consequences of the widespread use of KIPS either. If hundreds of thousands learned to read so that Tom Paine's pamphlets might persuade them that they had justification for revolting against monarchies as a form of government, who can say how universal access to machine intelligence—faster, deeper, better than human intelligence—will change science, economics, and warfare, and the whole intellectual and sociological development of mankind?

6

Shadows and Light

No profound change in human fortunes has ever been completely benign. Even the agricultural revolution had some unintended side effects, though few people would wish to return to hunting and gathering, with all that those imply. Much more recently, the widespread distribution of medicine has overtaken our abilities or our will to control world population, but both ethics and compassion tell us that rather than withdrawing medicine, we should prevent overpopulating the globe instead. The great increase in knowledge—by orders of magnitude, as we have tiresomely pointed out in this book—is unlikely to be different. Surely some people will believe they were better off in the good old days.

Automatic creation of knowledge has unpredictable effects. When a machine can use up all the knowledge we have given it, and use it systematically in ways that we cannot, and can make inferences more deeply than we can (because it is not limited, as we are, by our evolutionary legacy of about four items that we can attend to simultaneously), what will happen? We do not know. We may forget how to do things. Though it was drilled mercilessly into us in secondary schools, very few adults today remember how to take square roots. Hand-held calculators do the job beautifully; why burden ourselves and our minds?

We do not know whether, even given the same heuristics that humans use, a system that can think faster and deeper will necessarily think down the same avenues that humans do. If it should go elsewhere, we do not know what lies at the end of such different avenues.

We do not know whether new knowledge can be discovered by a machine (though we suspect it can and have early intimations of it). If so, we do not know what the implications of such new knowledge might be.

We do not know whether such a knowledge network, worldwide as the Japanese envisage or only nationwide, will offer unprecedented opportunities for mischief on the part of governments or of outlaws. In transitional times, such as these now are, we are all accustomed to our fellow humans abrogating their personal responsibilities by blaming it on the computer. Will those possibilities grow more menacing? Will legal systems be devised that can cope with them, even as such systems must cope with intellectual property rights, problems of privacy, and other unpredictable problems? Will fail-safe systems be devised to protect us from the immense amounts of power that are about to be placed in our hands?

We do not know how to imbue humans with the critical intelligence to evaluate the knowledge they are exposed to. The problem is already a difficult one for readers of the written word. We do not know whether the ability to interrogate a reasoning machine, to make it explain itself, will help with this problem or exacerbate it.

For humans who do not value knowledge, we do not know what a world, deeply steeped in knowledge, will seem like. There have been suggestions that the enormously rich recreational possibilities of KIPS will either sedate or stimulate that disenfranchised group that now scorns knowledge. Knowledge as narcotic isn't especially attractive to us, but the other possibility, KIPS as a stimulant toward knowing more, is a hopeful one. Since KIPS are planned to be as easy to use as a telephone or TV, it might be heartening to remember that in the United States the number of television sets grew from 6,000 to 15.5 million in a matter of five years. We might wish KIPS such success.

Not long ago, Feigenbaum was at the San Jose airport, ready to board a plane. An antique craft came wheeling by, a beautiful biplane that had been one of Trans World Airlines' first passenger planes. It struck him that this was where knowledge engineering and expert systems were right now; that they were struggling to transform themselves from a potentially powerful technological novelty into an integrated part of human life. Airplanes are still not perfect. Sometimes they're late; sometimes they crash catastrophically. But they are ours, and we could hardly imagine life without them. Symbolic inference machines are at the same stage as the Trans World plane that Feigenbaum watched: an elegant promise of things to come.

But we must return to a somber present. In this book we have described a technology that promises to change our lives the way few have: reasoning machines are, as we have said, not just the second computer revolution, but the important one. If the details of the technology itself are complicated, the issues that surround it can be understood by nearly everyone. A superiority in knowledge technology provides whoever holds it with the power to resolve shades of gray into black and white—provides in brief, an unequivocal advantage—whether we are speaking of personal power, national economics, or warfare.

The Japanese understand this perfectly. They have already begun to translate that understanding into the new technology that will give them unequivocal advantage over the rest of the world, perhaps by the middle of the next decade. Other nations recognize the soundness of the Japanese strategy—and, of course, its inevitability. In response to the farsighted Japanese, ambitious national plans are being drawn up in many places. But the United States, which ought to lead in such plans, has, until very recently, trailed along in disarrayed and diffuse indecision.

We have resisted calling this a crisis for the United States. We could pursue a dark thought, imagining artificial intelligence technology to slip away out of our control, which would ultimately have severe effects on our general industry, our standard of living, and our national defense.

We prefer instead to regard this Japanese challenge as an opportunity for the United States to revitalize itself, to join the Japanese and other nations in the world in the exhilarating adventure of moving the Empire of Reason, as historian Henry Steele Commager could once, with justification, call the United States, decisively into the Age of Reasoning Machines.

In the end, we have no choice. We can decide *when* we shall participate, not *if*. The question of when begets how.

The first question of when, we urge that it be at once. To the second question of how, we urge only that whatever plan is chosen, it embody what the American revolutionary generation possessed in abundance and ought to

be ours once more: optimism, energy, authority, pragmatism, candor, audacity, and a taste for succeeding.

At the beginning of this book, we asserted that knowledge is power. We meant it not only in the vulgar sense,
that one sleek, smart missile can clobber tons of dumb
battleship, though that is demonstrably true; or even that
a scientific instrument with built-in intelligence can outperform its dumb cousin that costs much more money,
though that too is true. Most applications we've described,
or we anticipate, have been material ones. For one thing,
they're easiest to describe. For another, those are what
Westerners are most comfortable with.

But there's a further dimension to a society dominated
by knowledge that we should like to address, a nonmaterial dimension. The Japanese, having a very long history
of putting material things in their place, which is an important place but clearly subordinate to and often in the
service of nonmaterial concerns, are better at sensing the
spiritual change the knowledge society might bring. A
book by Yoneji Masuda, *The Information Society as Post-
Industrial Society*, has some provocative things to say about
the future.[5]

Masuda makes a dense, detailed, and finally plausible
case that our knowledge-rich future will coax us away
from a preoccupation with material concerns and toward
a preoccupation with the nonmaterial. He sees this taking
the form of the freedom for each of us to set individual
goals of self-realization and then perhaps a worldwide
religious renaissance, characterized not by a belief in a
supernatural god, but rather by awe and humility in the
presence of the collective human spirit and its wisdom,
humanity living in a symbiotic tranquillity with the planet
we have found ourselves upon, regulated by a new set of
global ethics.

It is decidedly *not* an otherworldly religious spirit, which
makes it different from religious passions of the past. On
the contrary, it is sharply focused on this world, with
humans having a serious, direct, and continuous say in all
matters that affect their lives. But those exercises will be
characterized less by the "me first" attitude that has often
prevailed in human affairs, and more by a spirit of mutual
assistance toward shared goals.

It sounds utopian. And "utopian" often means hopelessly idealistic, beyond human reach. Surely, we can argue,

Masuda's prophecies are unduly shaped by living as he does in a prosperous, homogeneous society where the seeds of such a way of life are already planted and sprouting. But "utopian" also means something we have said many times and in many ways that we deeply desire as a human good. Indeed, Masuda reminds us that all this corresponds to Adam Smith's vision in *The Wealth of Nations* of a universal opulent society, a condition of plenty that frees the people from dependence and subordination to exercise true independence of spirit in autonomous actions. What Masuda is saying is that soon the technology will be in place to permit such a society to exist all over the globe.

The reasoning animal has, perhaps inevitably, fashioned the reasoning machine. With all the risks apparent in such an audacious, some say reckless, embarkation onto sacred ground, we have gone ahead anyway, holding tenaciously to what the wise in every culture at every time have taught: the shadows, however dark and menacing, must not deter us from reaching the light.

APPENDICES

A

Generic Categories of Knowledge Engineering Applications

CATEGORY	PROBLEM ADDRESSED
Interpretation	Inferring situation descriptions from sensor data
Prediction	Inferring likely consequences of given situations
Diagnosis	Inferring system malfunctions from observables
Design	Configuring objects under constraints
Planning	Designing actions
Monitoring	Comparing observations to plan vulnerabilities
Debugging	Prescribing remedies for malfunctions
Repair	Executing a plan to administer a prescribed remedy
Instruction	Diagnosing, debugging, and repairing student behavior
Control	Interpreting, predicting, repairing, and monitoring system behaviors

From Frederick Hayes-Roth, Donald A. Waterman, and Douglas B. Lenat, eds., *Building Expert Systems* (Reading, MA: Addison-Wesley, 1983).

B

Selected Experimental and Operational Expert Systems

DOMAIN	SYSTEM/DESCRIPTION	RESEARCH AND DEVELOPMENT ORGANIZATION
Bioengineering	MOLGEN: Aids in planning experiments involving structural analysis and synthesis of DNA	Heuristic Programming Project, Stanford University
Chemical industry	DENDRAL: Interprets data produced by mass spectrometers and determines not only a molecule's structure, but also its atomic constituents	Heuristic Programming Project, Stanford University
	SECS: Operational expert system to assist chemists in organic synthesis planning	University of California, Santa Cruz
Computer systems	DART: An experimental expert system for diagnosing computer system faults; used in field engineering	Heuristic Programming Project, Stanford University, and IBM

	R1 and XCON: Operational expert systems that configure VAX computer systems	Carnegie-Mellon University and Digital Equipment Corporation
	SPEAR: An expert system under development for analysis of computer error logs; used in field engineering	Digital Equipment Corporation
	XSEL: An extension of XCON that assists salespeople in selecting appropriate computer systems	Digital Equipment Corporation
	——: An experimental expert system for diagnosing VAX computer failures	M.I.T.
Computing	PROGRAMMER'S APPRENTICE: An expert system for assisting software construction and debugging	M.I.T.
	PSI: Composes simple computer programs based on English descriptions of the task to be performed	Kestrel Institute, Systems Control Technology
Education	GUIDON: An experimental intelligent computer-aided instruction (CAI) system that teaches the student by eliciting and correcting answers to a series of technical questions	Heuristic Programming Project, Stanford University

	——: An expert system under development that will teach computer languages to programmers	Computer Thought, Inc.
Engineering	EURISKO: An experimental expert system that learns by discovery; applied to designing new kinds of three-dimensional micro-electronic circuits	Heuristic Programming Project, Stanford University
	KBVLSI: An experimental system to aid in the development of VLSI designs	Xerox Palo Alto Research Center and Stanford University
	SACON: An operational expert system that assists structural engineers in identifying the best analysis strategy for each problem	Heuristic Programming Project, Stanford University
	——: An expert system under development for nuclear power reactor management	Hitachi Energy Lab
	——: An expert system under development for diagnosing fabrication problems in integrated circuit manufacturing	Hitachi System Development Lab
General-purpose tools	AGE: A system that guides the development of expert systems involving hypothesis formation and information fusion	Heuristic Programming Project, Stanford University

AL/X: A commercial expert system that assists diagnostic experts in encoding their knowledge of a scientific domain, thus generating a system able to exercise knowledge on their behalf; based on PROSPECTOR design — Intelligent Terminals, Ltd.

EMYCIN: A basic inference system derived from MYCIN that is applicable to many fields; used in building PUFF, SACON, and many other systems — Heuristic Programming Project, Stanford University

EXPERT: A basic inference system used in oil exploration and medical applications — Rutgers University

KAS: An experimental knowledge acquisition system that creates, modifies, or deletes various kinds of rule networks to be represented in the PROSPECTOR system — SRI International

KEPE: A commercially available knowledge representation system — IntelliCorp, Inc.

KS-300: A commercial basic inference system for industrial diagnostic and advising applications — Teknowledge, Inc.

	LOOPS: An experimental knowledge representation system used in KBVLSI	Xerox Palo Alto Research Center
	MRS: "Metalevel Representation System" for knowledge representation and problem-solving control	Heuristic Programming Project, Stanford University
	OPS: A basic inference system applicable to many fields; used for R1 and AIRPLAN	Carnegie-Mellon University
	ROSIE: a basic inference system applicable to many fields	RAND Corporation
	SAGE: A basic inference system applicable to many problems	SPL International
	TEIRESIAS: Transfers knowledge from a human expert to a system and guides the acquisition of new inference rules	Heuristic Programming Project, Stanford University
	UNITS: A knowledge representation system used in building MOLGEN and in conjunction with AGE	Heuristic Programming Project, Stanford University.
Law	LDS: An experimental expert system that models the decision-making processes of lawyers and claims adjusters involved in product liability legislation	RAND Corporation

	TAXMAN: An experimental expert system that deals with rules implicit in tax laws and suggests a sequence of contractual arrangements that a company can use to attain its financial objectives	Rutgers University
Management science	KM-I: An experimental knowledge management system that attempts to integrate the capabilities of the data management system and knowledge base system	System Development Corporation
	RABBIT: An experimental system that helps the user formulate queries to a data base	Xerox Palo Alto Research Center
	———: An expert system under development for project risk assessment for large construction projects	Hitachi System Development Lab
	———: An expert system under development for cost estimation of steam boilers	Hitachi System Development Lab
Manufacturing	CALLISTO: An experimental system that models, monitors, schedules, and manages large projects	Robotics Institute, Carnegie-Mellon University
	ISIS: An experimental system used for job shop scheduling	Robotics Institute, Carnegie-Mellon University

Medicine	ABEL: An expert system for diagnosing acid/base electrolyte disorders	M.I.T.
	CADUCEUS: An expert system that does differential diagnosis in internal medicine	University of Pittsburgh
	CASNET: A causal network that associates treatments with various diagnostic hypotheses (such as the severity or progression of a disease); applied to glaucoma	Rutgers University
	MYCIN: An operation expert system that diagnoses meningitis and blood infections	Heuristic Programming Project, Stanford University
	ONCOCIN: An oncology protocol management system for cancer chemotherapy treatment	Heuristic Programming Project, Stanford University
	PUFF: An operational expert system that analyzes patient data to identify possible lung disorders	Heuristic Programming Project, Stanford University
	VM: An expert system for monitoring patients in intensive care and advising about respiratory therapy	Heuristic Programming Project, Stanford University
Military	AIRPLAN: An expert system under development for air traffic movement planning around an aircraft carrier	Carnegie-Mellon University and U.S.S. *Carl Vinson*

	HASP/SIAP: An expert system for identification and tracking of ships using ocean sonar signals	Systems Control Technology, Inc., and Heuristic Programming Project, Stanford University
	TATR: An expert system for tactical air targeteering; uses ROSIE	RAND Corporation and U.S. Air Force
	——: Prototype expert system for analysis of strategic indicators and warnings	ESL, Inc., and Teknowledge, Inc.
	——: Prototype expert system for tactical battlefield communications analysis	ESL, Inc., and Teknowledge, Inc.
Resource exploration	DIPMETER ADVISOR: An expert system that analyzes information from oil well logs	Schlumberger
	DRILLING ADVISOR: An operational expert system for diagnosing oil well drilling problems and recommending corrective and preventive measures; uses KS-300	Teknowledge, Inc., for Elf-Aquitaine
	HYDRO: A computer consultation system for solving water resource problems	SRI International
	PROSPECTOR: An expert system that evaluates sites for potential mineral deposits	SRI International

| | WAVES: An expert system that advises engineers on the use of seismic data analysis programs; for oil industry; uses KS-300 | Teknowledge, Inc. |
| Science | GENESIS: A commercially available knowledge-based system that helps scientists plan and simulate gene-splicing experiments | IntelliCorp, Inc. |

——: system not yet named
From SRI International, Business Intelligence Program

C

Worldwide Artificial Intelligence Activity

ORGANIZATION	LOCATION	APPLICATION AREA
AIDS	Mountain View, CA	Expert systems
Applied Expert Systems	Cambridge, MA	Financial expert systems
Artificial Intelligence Corp.	Waltham, MA	Natural language systems
Automatix, Inc.	Billerica, MA	Robotics and vision systems

Bell Laboratories	Murray Hill, NJ	Natural language and expert systems, data base interface
Boeing Co.	Seattle, WA	Robotics and process planning systems
Bolt Beranek & Newman, Inc.	Cambridge, MA	Natural language and instructional systems
Brattle Research Corp.	Boston, MA	Financial expert systems, market survey
Carnegie-Mellon University	Pittsburgh, PA	Robotics, vision and process planning systems
Cognitive Systems, Inc.	New Haven, CT	Natural language systems
Columbia University	New York, NY	General AI
Computer Thought Corp.	Richardson, TX	Instructional systems
Daisy	Sunnyvale, CA	Expert systems and professional work station
Digital Equipment Corp.	Maynard, MA	Expert systems
Electrotechnical Laboratory	Tsukuba, Japan	Robotics and general AI
Fairchild Camera & Instrument Corp.	Mountain View, CA	VLSI design and expert systems
Fujitsu-Fanuc Ltd.	Kawasaki, Japan	Fifth Generation computer
General Electric Co.	Schenectady, NY	Robotics, process planning and expert systems
General Motors Corp.	Detroit, MI	Robotics and vision systems

Hewlett-Packard Co.	Palo Alto, CA	Expert systems
Hitachi Ltd.	Tokyo, Japan	Fifth Generation computer
Honeywell, Inc.	Minneapolis, MN	Robotics systems
Hughes Aircraft Co.	Torrance, CA	—
Imperial College, London	London, England	General AI
IntelliCorp	Palo Alto, CA	Expert systems
Intelligent Software, Inc.	Van Nuys, CA	General AI
International Business Machines	Armonk, NY	Robotics and fault diagnosis systems, data base interface
Jaycor	Alexandria, VA	Expert systems
Kestrel Institute	Palo Alto, CA	Automated programming
Lisp Machines, Inc.	Cambridge, MA	Professional work station
Lockheed Electronics	Plainfield, NJ	Intelligent interface
Arthur D. Little	Cambridge, MA	Consulting
Machine Intelligence Corp.	Sunnyvale, CA	Robotics, vision and natural language systems
Martin Marietta Aerospace Co.	Denver, CO	Robotics systems
Massachusetts Institute of Technology	Cambridge, MA	Robotics and sensor systems, general AI
Mitre Corp.	Bedford, MA	Command control and decision support systems

Mitsubishi Electric Corp.	Tokyo, Japan	Fifth Generation computer
Nippon Electric Co. Ltd.	Tokyo, Japan	Fifth Generation computer
Nippon Telephone & Telegraph Corp.	Tokyo, Japan	Fifth Generation computer
Ohio State University	Columbus, OH	Robotics and general AI
RAND Corp.	Santa Monica, CA	General AI
Rutgers University	New Brunswick, NJ	General AI
Schlumberger-Doll Research	Ridgefield, CT	Expert systems
Smart Systems Technology	Alexandria, VA	Instructional systems, AI tools
SRI International	Menlo Park, CA	Robotics and sensor systems, general AI
Stanford University	Stanford, Ca	Robotics, vision and expert systems, VLSI design
Symantec	Palo Alto, CA	Natural language systems
Symbolics	Cambridge, MA	Professional work stations
Systems Control, Inc.	Palo Alto, CA	Expert systems
Teknowledge, Inc.	Palo Alto, CA	Expert systems
Texas Instruments	Dallas, TX	Instructional and robotics systems
Three Rivers Computer Corp.	Pittsburgh, PA	Professional work stations
TRW, Inc.	Cleveland, OH	Expert systems

United Technologies Corp.	Hartford, CT	General AI
University of Edinburgh	Edinburgh, Scotland	General AI
University of Illinois	Urbana, IL	Robotics and general AI
University of Marseilles	Marseilles, France	General AI
University of Massachusetts	Amherst, MA	Robotics and vision systems, general AI
University of Michigan	Ann Arbor, MI	Robotics and vision systems, general AI
University of Sussex	Sussex, England	General AI
Westinghouse Electric Corp.	Pittsburgh, PA	Robotics and expert systems
Xerox Corp.	Palo Alto, CA	Professional work stations, data base interface, VLSI design
Yale University	New Haven, CT	General AI

From *American Metal Market/Metalworking News*, January 10, 1983

D

Fifth Generation Computer R&D Themes

RESEARCH AND DEVELOPMENT SUBJECTS		SCHEDULE/COMMENTS
Problem-solving and inference systems	Problem-solving and inference mechanisms: • Fifth-generation kernel language (PROLOG) • Cooperative problem-solving mechanisms • Parallel inference mechanisms Problem-solving and inference machines: • Data flow machines • Hardware to support abstract data • Hardware for parallel inference	To be developed over initial, middle, and final stages
Knowledge-based systems	Knowledge-based mechanisms: • Knowledge representation systems • Large-scale knowledge-based systems	To be developed over initial, middle, and final stages

	• Distributed knowledge-based management systems Knowledge-based machines: • Relational data base machines • Hardware to support parallel relational operations and knowledge operations • Hardware for basic knowledge-based management systems	
Intelligent human-machine interface systems	Intelligent human-machine interface systems: • Natural language processing • Speech processing • Graphics and image processing	To be developed over initial, middle, and final stages Initial stage includes development of fundamental techniques for basic applications systems
	High-level human-machine interface for dedicated special purpose processors (speech and others)	Existing products will be used in the initial stage. To be developed in the middle stage and later
Development support systems	Pilot models for software development: • Hardware system for a sequential inference machine • Software system for a sequential inference machine	To be developed in the initial stage, and to serve as tools for research and development in the middle stage and later

	Techniques for integration in VLSIs and systems architecture: • Intelligent VLSI-CAD system • Software and hardware development support system	VLSI-CAD to start from the second year. Systems architecture will be studied by extending development support systems, which will include many experimental software and hardware systems
Basic applications systems	Machine translation systems	Researched as part of intelligent human-machine interface systems and a model system developed for evaluation in the initial stage. Concentrated development in the middle stage and later
	Consultation systems	Researched as part of knowledge-based mechanisms and a model system developed for evaluation in the initial stage. Concentrated development in the middle stage and later
	Intelligent programming systems: • Modular programming system • Meta/specification description and verification system • Program synthesis and algorithm banks	To be developed over initial, middle, and final stages

From SRI International, Business Intelligence Program

E

Glossary

Artificial intelligence (AI). A subfield of computer science concerned with the concepts and methods of symbolic inference by a computer and the symbolic representation of the knowledge to be used in making inferences. A computer can be made to behave in ways that humans recognize as "intelligent" behavior in each other.

Data base. A collection of data about objects and events on which the knowledge base will work to achieve desired results. A **relational data base** is one in which the relationships between various objects and events are stored explicitly for flexibility of storage and retrieval.

Expert system. A computer program that performs a specialized, usually difficult professional task at the level of (or sometimes beyond the level of) a human expert. Because their functioning relies so heavily on large bodies of knowledge, expert systems are sometimes known as **knowledge-based systems.** Since they are often used to assist the human expert, they are also known as **intelligent assistants.**

Heuristics. Experiential, judgmental knowledge; the knowledge underlying "expertise"; rules of thumb, rules of good guessing, that usually achieve desired results but do not guarantee them.

Human interface. One subsystem of an expert system (or any computing system) with which the human user deals routinely. It aims to be as "natural" as possible, employing language as close as possible to ordinary language (or the stylized language of a given field) and understanding and displaying images, all at speeds that are comfortable and natural for humans. The other two subsystems in an expert system are the knowledge base management subsystem and the inference subsystem.

Inference system. See **Symbolic inference.**

Knowledge base. Facts, assumptions, beliefs, and heuristics; "expertise"; methods of dealing with the data base to achieve desired results such as a diagnosis, or an interpretation, or a solution to a problem.

Knowledge base management system. One of three subsystems in an expert system. This subsystem "manages" the knowledge base by automatically organizing, controlling, propagating, and updating stored knowledge. It initiates searches for knowledge relevant to the line of reasoning upon which the inference subsystem is working. The inference subsystem is one of the other two subsystems in an expert system; the third is the human interface subsystem with which the end-user communicates.

Knowledge engineering. The art of designing and building expert systems and other knowledge-based programs.

Knowledge Information Processing Systems (KIPS). The new, "fifth" generation of computers that the Japanese propose to build which will have symbolic inference capabilities, coupled with very large knowledge bases, and superb human interfaces, all combined with high processing speeds, so that the machines will greatly amplify human intellectual capabilities.

Network. Computers and communication links that allow computers to communicate with each other and to share programs, facilities, and data and knowledge bases. A network can be local (one room, one office, one institution), national, or even international.

Representation. Formalization and structuring of knowledge in a computer so that it can be manipulated by the knowledge base management system.

Symbolic inference. The process by which lines of reasoning are formed; for example, syllogisms and other common ways of reasoning step by step from premises. In the real world, knowledge and data—premises—are often inexact. Thus, some inference procedures can use degrees of uncertainty in their inference making. In an expert system, the inference subsystem works with the knowledge in the knowledge base. The inference subsystem in an expert system is one of three subsystems necessary to achieve expert performance; the other two subsystems are the knowledge base management subsystem and the human interface subsystem.

VLSI. Very Large Scale Integration of transistors and other electronic components on microelectronic chips. Chips in current production carry half a million transistors at most. American and Japanese firms are aiming for chips with ten million transistors on them.

F

Notes

Part One

1. *Tao and War, Lao Tzu and Sun Tzu*, trans. Charles Scamahorn (Berkeley, CA: private printing, 1977).

2. "People and Productivity: A Challenge to Corporate America." Study from the New York Stock Exchange Office of Economic Research, November 1982.

3. Calling the next generation "fifth" is controversial among some in the American computer industry who claim that by the time it reaches the market it will be the sixth. We'll skirt the terminological controversy by using "fifth" because the Japanese do so, without claiming that they are correct in so doing.

4. All quotations in this section, unless otherwise noted, are from *Proceedings of the International Conference on Fifth*

Generation Computer Systems (New York: Elsevier–North Holland, 1982).

5. These working papers can be found in the *Proceedings* mentioned in note 4.

6. "People and Productivity: A Challenge to Corporate America." Study from the New York Stock Exchange Office of Economic Research, November 1982.

7. R. Ewald et al., "Foreign Travel Trip Report: Visits with Japanese Computer Manufacturers." February 1–10, 1982, CDO/82–6782A, Computing Division, Los Alamos National Laboratory, Los Alamos, NM, April 5, 1982. Indeed, as a direct consequence of their visit, an American supercomputer research consortium was formed in 1983. It is called Project SPREAD, for Supercomputer Project for Research, Experimentation, Access and Development, and its founding members include SRI International, Lawrence Livermore National Laboratories, and Los Alamos National Laboratories. SPREAD is planned as a network that will allow researchers in universities, laboratories, and private industry all across the country access to certain ultra-fast experimental computers located at Los Alamos and Livermore. However, funding must be secured, and broadband communications equipment must be designed and put in place before research can begin.

8. "Outline of Research and Development Plans for Fifth Generation Computer Systems" (Tokyo: Institute for New Generation Computer Technology [ICOT], May 1982).

9. As an instructive example, American computing might look at the Swiss timepiece industry, which in less than a decade plunged from overwhelming world predominance to the status of an industrial curiosity. Its only ambitions now are to hold on to some tiny fraction of the electronic watch market, to provide mechanical watches to sheiks who want the prestige and, in the resigned words of one Swiss watch industry spokesman, to "hikers, people in developing countries who are afraid they might not get the batteries, or just for the people who want a good backup watch in the drawer."

10. Daniel Bell, *The Coming of Post-Industrial Society* (New York: Basic Books, 1976).

11. Ibid.

12. Ezra Vogel, *Japan as Number One* (New York: Harper Colophon Books, 1980), p. 9.

13. Ibid., p. 27.

14. Bell, *Post-Industrial Society*, p. 127.

15. Jahangir Amuzegar, "Oil Wealth," *Foreign Affairs*, Spring 1982.

Part Two

1. Pamela McCorduck, *Machines Who Think* (San Francisco: W. H. Freeman Co., 1979).

2. Even as we write, all this is changing. Millions are being seduced into playing with computers in a way they never were before the past two years, and the personal computer is rapidly becoming a status symbol. In the form of video games alone, computing in the United States matched the movies and the record industry together in gross revenues for 1982.

3. Early computers were usually stand-alone service machines not linked to other computers or to users. It soon became clear that there needed to be routine communication between computers at speeds faster than that of mailing a magnetic tape or a deck of cards, and also between each computer and the teletypewriters (later video terminals) of its users. The national telephone system went everywhere and was capable of carrying the signals, and so it was a natural starting place for computer communication links. But the telephone system was designed for voice communications with direct linkage between people, not for high-speed digital data exchange between machines. Some changes were necessary that could adapt the existing telephone system to the new requirements.
Two communities felt the need pressing. The Department of Defense saw computers entering its service at an increasing rate, performing military tasks for which high-speed transfer of digital information was essential. (Security of the information was also essential; that is relatively easy to achieve when the information is sent as discrete symbols but difficult in the traditional voice-signal technology.) The community of computer scientists doing advanced

research in the field felt the technological imperative. Its leaders saw the enormous advantages of having separate machines in geographically dispersed locations linked together. A fast, easy-to-use digital intercommunication network would allow the sharing of software, ready access to each other's facilities for resource sharing and backup in case of down time, and the sharing and rapid dissemination of research materials that exist in electronic text files (for example, brand-new research results, memos about new ideas, or prepublication versions of technical reports). The impact of electronic mail in welding a national research community, an electronically facilitated "invisible college," was something the leaders had not planned for, but it later became the most important side effect of the network.

To bring this network dream to reality, and to do it in a way that would realize the goals of both communities, required planning and coordination of a high order, much money, and the dedicated talents of some of the best computer scientists and engineers in the United States. The Defense Department's Advanced Research Projects Agency, the funder of so much of the nation's innovative computer and communications research, took the initiative in planning, coordination, and provision of the necessary funds. The network that came into being is called the ARPANET. The hardware and software of the ARPANET took several years to build and test and went into operation in the early 1970s. It was a worldwide sensation and has served as a model for the digital communications networks of other nations and for the commercial digital networks in the United States.

The ARPANET links computers at major university computer science research labs, not-for-profit research institutes, government laboratories, some defense contracting companies, and certain military laboratories and sites using high-speed lines rented from commercial vendors. A few hundred computers are connected through about eighty nodes. Most users access the ARPANET via the connected computer at their own place. Some users do not have a computer at their place but access the ARPANET through special nodes that allow direct interactions with computer terminals. Such users have accounts on some remote ARPANET machine at which they receive their electronic mail, store their files, and do their computer processing. There are about twenty of these nodes scattered throughout the country. The ARPANET also extends overseas to Hawaii, Norway, and Great Britain. Its user community in 1982 was at least ten thousand people and growing.

4. C. Mead and L. Conway, *Introduction to VLSI Systems* (Reading, MA: Addison-Wesley, 1980).

5. The adventure continues. The capability is still being made available to the research community supported by ARPA, with help from Xerox, by the information Science Institute of the University of Southern California.

6. L. Conway, "The MPC Adventures: Experiences with the Generation of VLSI Design and Implementation Methodologies," Xerox Palo Alto Research Center, VLSI-81-2.

7. M. Stefik and L. Conway, "Towards the Principled Engineering of Knowledge," *AI Magazine*, Summer 1982.

8. K. Fuchi, "Aiming for Knowledge Information Processing Systems," *Proceedings of the International Conference on Fifth Generation Computer Systems* (New York: Elsevier–North Holland, 1982).

Part Three

1. H. Penny Nii, "An Introduction to Knowledge Engineering, Blackboard Model and AGE," preliminary draft.

2. Randall Davis, "Expert Systems: Where Are We? and Where Do We Go from Here?" *AI Magazine*, Spring 1982.

Part Four

1. Vogel, *Japan as Number One*, p. 71.

2. Ehud Y. Shapiro, "Japan's Fifth Generation Computers Project—a Trip Report," Department of Applied Mathematics, Weizmann Institute of Science, Rehovot 76100, Israel, January 11, 1983.

3. Bro Uttal, "Here Comes Computer Inc.," *Fortune*, October 4, 1982.

4. *Business Week*, August 30, 1982, p. 59.

5. *Proceedings*, p. 12.

6. Bell, *Post-Industrial Society*, p. 274.

7. E. Reischauer, *The Japanese* (Cambridge: Harvard University Press, 1977), p. 226.

8. Richard Lynn, "IQ in Japan and the United States Shows a Growing Disparity," *Nature* 297 (May 20, 1982).

9. Richard Dolen, "Japan's Fifth Generation Computer Project," *The ONR Far East Scientific Bulletin* 7, no. 3 (July–September 1982).

10. Reischauer, *The Japanese*, p. 202.

11. Ibid., p. 226.

12. Ibid., p. 227.

13. Ibid., p. 386.

14. Ulric Weil, "Fifth Generation Brouhaha," *Morgan Stanley EDP Research Note*, September 30, 1983.

15. Okakura Kuzuko, *The Book of Tea* (Rutland, VT, and Tokyo: Charles E. Tuttle, 1956), p. 8.

16. Vogel, *Japan as Number One*, pp. 163–164.

17. Thomas P. Rohlen, "Japan's High Schools," ms. quoted in "People and Productivity: A Challenge to Corporate America," Study from the New York Stock Exchange, November 1982.

Part Five

1. George Ball, *The Past Has Another Pattern* (New York: Norton, 1982), pp. 17–18.

2. In *Machines Who Think*, McCorduck reported that five years after the Lighthill report, funding had resumed at a satisfactory, if not generous, level for British AI research. As Rick the barkeep in *Casablanca* put it, "I was misinformed."

3. Hayes's assessment of British higher education is not brutally unfair. University budgets were cut an average of 15 percent (in real terms) for FY 1983–1984, though this average disguises the fact that some universities took only a 1.5 percent cut, while some were cut 44 percent. Allocations are provided by the University Grants Committee in block grants to individual universities and must be distri-

buted between teaching and research as the individual university sees fit. However, research commitments are less painful to reduce than teaching staff, and as static funding is the best a university can hope for, new research can be undertaken only at the expense of already established research. The government expressed its unhappiness with decisions made by local universities that preserved teaching (or teachers' jobs) at the expense of research and threatened to step into the decision process itself if the universities didn't change. The situation was made all the more vexing by the government's perceived favoritism toward Oxbridge over more technologically oriented universities, although science and technology were what the government claimed to want and need. The entire sum the University Grants Committee disbursed in the 1982–83 academic year ($1.92 billion) can be compared to official estimates of what the government had spent in the Falklands adventure ($1.19 billion plus matériel losses amounting to $1.4 billion, or about $2.6 billion altogether, with anticipated expenses of $678 million per year, according to the *New York Times*, January 23, 1983, to maintain the Falklands garrison). David Dickson, "British Universities in Turmoil," *Science* 217 (August 27, 1982).

4. A dispassionate and detailed account of the history of artificial intelligence in the U.K. by James Fleck, a sociologist of science, "Development and Establishment in Artificial Intelligence," appears in Elias, Martins, and Whitely, eds., *Scientific Establishments and Hierarchies. Sociology of the Sciences*, vol. 6 (Boston: D. Riedel, 1982).

5. *Computing*, February 4, 1982.

6. "A Programme for Advanced Information Technology: The Report of the Alvey Committee" (London: Her Majesty's Stationery Office, 1982).

7. Philip Gummett, *Scientists in Whitehall* (Manchester: Manchester University Press, 1980).

8. Vogel, *Japan as Number One*, p. 136.

9. Donald Michie, letter to the editor, *Computing*, March 18, 1982.

10. Gummett, *Scientists in Whitehall*, p. 233.

11. *Business Week*, May 30, 1983.

12. David Brand, "Soviet Science Serves Industry Badly as Lines of Authority Cross," *Wall Street Journal*, September 3, 1982.

Part Six

1. George E. Lindamood, "Japanese Computer Project," letter to the editor of *Science*, 9 September 1983.

2. . . . though Bell prefers to think of it as generation six.

3. A longer description of Inman's role at the NSA appears in James Bamford, *The Puzzle Palace* (Boston: Houghton Mifflin, 1982).

4. Each field of research has a group of problems that it regards as central to its concerns. The Japanese efforts reflect a mainstream artificial intelligence point of view, a point of view that predominates not only in Japan but in the United States and Europe. Central to all these efforts are problem-solving methods and inference systems and languages; knowledge representation; and knowledge-base management software. IBM has done some research on English-language understanding and on speech understanding. The Japanese relegate these research topics to the part of their system diagram labeled "intelligent interface" hardware and software (see part 4, section 4). While these are important topics, they are peripheral (pun intended). A senior researcher at Yorktown Heights summed it up, although not for attribution: "IBM hasn't been systematically anti-AI, but working on AI was equivalent to wearing sneakers to work."

5. *Scientific American*, January 1982.

6. *Wall Street Journal*, July 23, 1982.

7. James A. White, "IBM Is Aggressively Claiming a Widening Lead in Technology," *Wall Street Journal*, July 30, 1982.

8. Jordan Lewis, "Technology, Enterprise and American Economic Growth," *Science* 215 (March 5, 1982).

9. Vogel, *Japan as Number One*, p. 135.

10. Robert B. Reich, "Making Industrial Policy," *Foreign Affairs*, Spring 1982.

11. Ibid.

12. William G. Ouchi, *Theory Z* (Reading, MA: Addison-Wesley, 1981; New York: Avon, 1982), pp. 49–53.

13. Senator Paul E. Tsongas, speech before members of the International Business Center of New England, Copley Plaza Hotel, Boston, May 21, 1982.

14. Ibid.

15. *New York Times*, May 17, 1982.

16. The proposed legislation has been withdrawn, at least for now. The Bell Labs director of research, Dr. Arno Penzias, argued in public hearings that while the breakup of Bell Labs might make all the players equal in the United States, it would leave us decidedly less than equal against Japan.

17. A recent study prepared by Pat Choate for the U.S. Congress, "Retooling the American Workforce," says that a lack of national strategy for retraining displaced workers is a major barrier to America's economic renewal. It predicts an imminent loss of 10 to 15 million manufacturing jobs and a similar loss in service jobs.

18. Lewis, "Technology, Enterprise. . . ."

19. MITI officials have told the Berkeley scholar Chalmers Johnson that they do not consider their ministry comparable to the U.S. Department of Commerce, but rather to the U.S. Defense Department, and the comparison is well-taken: MITI officials represent the entire country, not just big business, and they do so over the long term. In an address to the Japan Society of New York, Johnson observed wickedly: "For Americans, it's one thing to be challenged by a communist. That they can understand. But to be challenged by a better capitalist! Why, that's cheating!"

20. John R. Opel, "Education, Science, and National Economic Competitiveness," *Science*, September 17, 1982.

21. Peter J. Denning, "A Discipline in Crisis," *Communications of the ACM*, June 1981, 24, 6.

22. See J. F. Traub, "Quo Vadimus: Computer Science in a Decade," *Communications of the ACM*, June 1981.

23. Ibid.

24. Robert L. Jacobson, "Industry's Emphasis on Profits Cited as Bar to Business-University Ties," *The Chronicle of Higher Education*, July 21, 1982.

25. "Nearly Half in U.S. Reject Evolution," *San Francisco Chronicle*, August 13, 1982.

26. Paul Connolly, "Our Fascination with Electronic Technology Is Myopic—and Quintessentially American," *Chronicle of Higher Education*, September 22, 1982.

27. Hortense Calisher, "Warm Bodies," unpublished.

28. Richard Hofstadter, *Anti-Intellectualism in American Life* (New York: Alfred A. Knopf, 1963).

29. Clarence A. Robinson, Jr., "DeLauer Urges Technology Spending," *Aviation Week & Space Technology*, September 6, 1982.

30. John Costello, *The Pacific War* (New York: Rawson, Wade, 1981).

Part Seven

1. For other universities wishing to play the game, the numbers are instructive. The University of Texas pledged six prestigious and well-paying chairs for professors in computer science and electrical engineering, thirty further faculty positions, $750,000 a year for ten years for graduate assistantships, and $1 million per year for operating expenses, plus odds and ends of endowments in the hundreds of thousands to assist junior faculty in their research. At least one losing finalist, the Atlanta/Athens, Georgia area, was determined not to make that mistake again, and the Georgia state legislature allocated $80 million toward sweetening the acquisition of the next high-tech opportunity, which soon came along: a research spinoff from Control Data Corporation called Project Eta, eta being the seventh letter of the Greek alphabet, and the project standing for the seventh generation of computers.

2. Losing body fat is now a $10-billion-per-year business in the United States. Talk about technology creating unpredictable new markets!

3. A different reaction to the same experience is found

in Roland Barthes, *Empire of Signs*, trans. Richard Howard (New York: Hill and Wang, 1982).

4. Tom Alexander, "Teaching Computers the Art of Reason," *Fortune*, May 17, 1982.

5. Yoneji Masuda, *The Information Society as Post-Industrial Society* (Tokyo: Institute for the Information Society, 1980).

G

Books for Further Reading

Barr, Avron; Feigenbaum, Edward A.; and Cohen, Paul R. *The Handbook of Artificial Intelligence*, 3 vols. Los Altos, CA: William Kaufmann, Inc., 1981.

Boden, Margaret, *Artificial Intelligence and Natural Man*. New York: Basic Books, 1977.

Evans, C. *The Micro Millennium*. New York: Viking Press, 1979.

Hayes-Roth, Frederick; Waterman, Donald A.; and Lenat, Douglas B., eds. *Building Expert Systems*. Reading, MA: Addison-Wesley, 1983.

Hofstadter, Douglas R. *Gödel, Escher, Bach: Eternal Golden Braid*. New York: Vintage Books, 1980.

Johnson, Chalmers. *MITI and the Japanese Miracle: The Growth of Industrial Policy, 1925–1975*. Stanford: Stanford University Press, 1982.

McCorduck, Pamela. *Machines Who Think*. San Francisco: W. H. Freeman Co., 1979.

Ouchi, William G. *Theory Z*. New York: Avon Books, 1982.

Reischauer, Edwin O. *The Japanese*. Cambridge: Harvard University Press, 1977.

Simon, Herbert A. *The Sciences of the Artificial*, 2nd ed. Cambridge, MA: M.I.T. Press, 1981.

Vogel, Ezra F. *Japan as Number One*. New York: Harper & Row, 1980.

Index